The Military Intelligence Community

Westview Special Studies

The concept of Westview Special Studies is a response to the continuing crisis in academic and informational publishing. Library budgets are being diverted from the purchase of books and used for data banks, computers, micromedia, and other methods of information retrieval. Interlibrary loan structures further reduce the edition sizes required to satisfy the needs of the scholarly community. Economic pressures on university presses and the few private scholarly publishing companies have greatly limited the capacity of the industry to properly serve the academic and research communities. As a result, many manuscripts dealing with important subjects, often representing the highest level of scholarship, are no longer economically viable publishing projects--or, if accepted for publication, are typically subject to lead times ranging from one to three years.

Westview Special Studies are our practical solution to the problem. As always, the selection criteria include the importance of the subject, the work's contribution to scholarship, and its insight, originality of thought, and excellence of exposition. We accept manuscripts in camera-ready form, typed, set, or word processed according to specifications laid out in our comprehensive manual, which contains straightforward instructions and sample pages. The responsibility for editing and proofreading lies with the author or sponsoring institution, but our editorial staff is always available to answer questions and provide guidance.

The result is a book printed on acid-free paper and bound in sturdy, library-quality soft covers. We manufacture these books ourselves using equipment that does not require a lengthy make-ready process and that allows us to publish first editions of 300 to 1000 copies and to reprint even smaller quantities as needed. Thus, we can produce Special Studies quickly and can keep even very specialized books in print as long as there is a demand for them.

About the Book and Editors

An exhaustive study of all facets of the intelligence profession, this book treats military intelligence as the process of collecting, analyzing, and disseminating information for use by commanders and policymakers. Contributors to this volume, writing for intelligence officers and analysts at all levels, examine the structure of the intelligence community, the role of the Department of Defense, intelligence information, and counterintelligence. In a final section, the areas of convergence and tension between the military intelligence community and Congress, the media, and research and development institutions are explored.

<u>Gerald W. Hopple</u> was formerly a senior analyst at Defense Systems, Inc. <u>Naval Commander Bruce W. Watson</u> is a faculty member at the Defense Intelligence College and an adjunct professor in the Russian Area Studies Program at Georgetown University.

To Danny Hopple

The Military Intelligence Community

edited by Gerald W. Hopple
and Bruce W. Watson

Westview Press / Boulder and London

UB
251
.U5
M55
1986

Westview Special Studies in Military Affairs

The views expressed in this book are solely those of the authors and do not represent the positions or policies of any agency or department of the United States Government. The following chapters were derived from unclassified publications and sources and are intended to neither confirm nor deny, officially or unofficially, the views of the United States Government.

All rights reserved. No part of this publication may be reproduced or transmitted in any form or by any means, electronic or mechanical, including photocopy, recording, or any information storage and retrieval system without permission in writing from the publisher.

Copyright © 1986 by Westview Press, Inc.

Published in 1986 in the United States of America by Westview Press, Inc.; Frederick A. Praeger, Publisher; 5500 Central Avenue, Boulder, Colorado 80301

Library of Congress Cataloging in Publication Data
The military intelligence community
　　(Westview special studies in military affairs)
　　Bibliography: p.
　　Includes index.
　　1. Military intelligence--United States--Addresses, essays, lectures. I. Hopple, Gerald W. II. Watson, Bruce W.
UB251.U5M55　　　1984　　　355.3'432'0973　　　84-15218
ISBN 0-8133-7009-4

Printed and bound in the United States of America

　　The paper used in this publication meets the minimum requirements of the American National Standard for Permanence of Paper for Printed Library Materials Z39.48-1984.

10　9　8　7　6　5　4　3　2

Contents

List of Tables and Figures ix
Preface xi
Acknowledgments xiii

PART 1 - THE ORGANIZATION

1. THE INTELLIGENCE COMMUNITY by Jack E. Thomas 3
2. THE DEFENSE INTELLIGENCE COMMUNITY by J. Thompson Strong . . 15

PART 2 - COLLECTION

3. SIGNALS INTELLIGENCE by David L. Christianson 39
4. HUMAN SOURCE INTELLIGENCE by Jack E. Thomas 55
5. IMAGERY INTELLIGENCE by Stephen S. Beitler 71

PART 3 - ANALYSIS

6. THE CRUCIAL MANAGER by Alan R. Goldman 89
7. BASIC INTELLIGENCE by Stephen J. Andriole 99
8. CURRENT INTELLIGENCE by E. Luther Johnson 117
9. ESTIMATIVE INTELLIGENCE by G. Paul Holman, Jr. 129
10. SCIENTIFIC AND TECHNICAL INTELLIGENCE by Bernard J. Grundy . 145
11. PRINCIPLES OF WARNING INTELLIGENCE by Timothy M. Laur . . . 149
12. COUNTERINTELLIGENCE AND COMBATTING TERRORISM
    by Stephen S. Beitler 169
13. BASIC COMMUNICATIONS SKILLS FOR THE INTELLIGENCE ANALYST
    by Gerald W. Hopple 197

PART 4 - THE ISSUES

14. ETHICS AND INTELLIGENCE by Malcolm Wallop 211

15. LAW AND INTELLIGENCE by Morton H. Halperin 225

16. THE INTELLIGENCE COMMUNITY AND THE NEWS MEDIA
    by George H. Quester 245

17. CONGRESSIONAL OVERSIGHT: FORM AND SUBSTANCE
    by Gary J. Schmitt 265

PART 5 - SUMMARY

18. THE FUTURE OF THE INTELLIGENCE COMMUNITY
    by Bruce W. Watson 289

About the Editors and Contributors 295

Tables and Figures

Tables

11.1   Warning Response Matrix 164

Figures

2.1   The Organization of the Defense Intelligence Agency 19
2.2   The Organization of Army Intelligence 23
2.3   The Organization of Naval Intelligence 27
2.4   The Organization of Air Force Intelligence 30
2.5   The Organization of Marine Corps Intelligence 32
7.1   A Strategic Intelligence Matrix 104
7.2   Flow-Chart of NATO Mobilization Process 111
11.1 National Operations and Watch Officers Network 157
11.2 Warning Cycle 162

Preface

The military intelligence community is one of the most misunderstood and maligned facets of the U.S. government. To much of the American public, intelligence means an organization of James Bonds, sophisticated, super-individualists, John Waynes who live slightly beyond the law. To others, military intelligence is considered as a constant threat to American democracy, a danger that must be contained and minimized.

It is not enough to say that such impressions are fantasies. Rather, what is needed is a firm understanding of the military intelligence community, so that the public can deal with it more responsibly. In recent years, many books have been written on the community, and many U.S. universities have included courses on intelligence in their curricula. These efforts have done much to dispel the public's misconceptions concerning the subject. However, to date, no one has provided a book which fully discusses the organization and processes of intelligence, and the major issues concerning the intelligence community. This book attempts to fill that gap by presenting the views of several experts.

We begin by examining the organization of the national intelligence community, and then, in chapter two, direct our attention to the military intelligence community's composition. We then determine what the community does. We begin logically by examining how the community collects its information. Then the means by which the community processes or analyzes this information to produce intelligence are discussed. (The community's third major function, disseminating intelligence, while important, is discussed adequately in the first two sections of the book.) Then the major issues of intelligence, specifically how it relates to both American ideals and other U.S. institutions, are addressed. An institution as provocative as the U.S. military intelligence community certainly creates controversy, and it is our intention to shed greater clarity on the major issues. Finally, the book concludes with a chapter that looks to the future and attempts to determine whether any progress can be made toward resolving the existing problems and controversies.

To conclude, this book has attempted to further define the nature, composition, and inherent problems of military intelligence and to examine the community's major controversies. If it generates additional thought and discussion, then we feel that it will have served its purpose.

Gerald W. Hopple
Bruce W. Watson

Acknowledgments

We wish to thank all of the contributors for participating in this study.

We are also indebted to Fred Praeger, Barbara Ellington, Dean Birkenkamp, and the staff of Westview Press for their advice, assistance, and encouragement.

We would also like to express our gratitude to Colonel John D. Macartney, U.S. Air Force, Commandant, and Dr. Robert De Gross, Provost of the Defense Intelligence College, for their support of this book.

Without the competent and patient support of the individuals who typed all of the drafts and final versions of the chapters of the book, this work would never have been possible. We are thus indebted to O. C. Moreland, Jr., Deborah J. Phillips, Mary H. King, Gloria D. Porche, Norma J. Dorey, and Jacquline D. Cooper.

We also wish to thank Sue Watson, who proofread and reviewed the manuscripts and Susan M. O. Watson, who assisted in the artwork.

G.W.H.
B.W.W.

Part 1
The Organization

1
The Intelligence Community
Jack E. Thomas

WHAT IS THE INTELLIGENCE COMMUNITY?

What in recent years has come to be formally designated the "intelligence community" embraces most of the military intelligence activities conducted by components of the Department of Defense. This means that the intelligence function, to the extent that it involves "national intelligence," is treated differently within the Defense Department than are other functions related to national security.[1]

The Director of Central Intelligence (DCI)--not the Secretary of Defense--approves the programs and budgets of Defense Department components that are part of the intelligence community and thereby come within the National Foreign Intelligence Program. The Director tasks and sets the priorities for those components that collect national intelligence; if they are intelligence producers whose analysis contributes to national intelligence, the Director can task them and insure that any judgments contained in the resulting estimates are those with which he agrees.

In terms of both personnel and resources, Defense Department components represent the bulk of the intelligence community, which is defined in President Reagan's Executive Order 12333[2] as including:

Defense Department Components

The National Security Agency (NSA)
The Defense Intelligence Agency (DIA)
The offices within the Department of Defense for the collection of specialized national foreign intelligence through reconnaissance programs
The intelligence elements of the Army, Navy, Air Force, and Marine Corps

Non-Defense Components

The Central Intelligence Agency (CIA)
The Bureau of Intelligence and Research of the Department of State
The intelligence elements of:
  The Federal Bureau of Investigation (FBI)
  The Department of the Treasury
  The Department of Energy
  The staff elements of the Director of Central Intelligence

3

All Defense Department intelligence components, except for the Marine Corps intelligence elements, utilize sizeable numbers of personnel and major funding. Aside from the CIA, none of the non-Defense components is large in numbers of personnel or funding. The FBI component is only that relatively small part of the bureau that is concerned with foreign intelligence and counterintelligence; the law enforcement elements of the FBI are not part of the intelligence community.

Various national intelligence activities are conducted on a community-wide basis in that they are handled jointly, or are fully coordinated, or are executed by one organization as a "service of common concern" on behalf of the entire community.[3] Among the functions dealt with on a community basis are indications and warning, review of research and development needs, security standards, intelligence aspects of technology transfer, use of computers for information handling, and so on. The flavor of matters that come under intelligence community cognizance can be illustrated by a brief consideration of three major aspects of community interaction: intelligence collection; national intelligence production; and development of the National Foreign Intelligence Program and its budget.

THE COMMUNITY ROLE IN COLLECTION

In the years following World War II, components of the Defense Department and the CIA developed collection capabilities that could support the intelligence needs of the entire government--not merely the requirements of a single department or organization. Signals intelligence and overhead reconnaissance systems are the prime examples. This led to intelligence community actions to define and prioritize requirements for the information that was needed, to levy tasks on collectors, and to coordinate activities where appropriate. In each case, the actual collection operations remained under the control of the relevant collection organization.

Over the years, the community role has been handled in considerable part by Director of Central Intelligence committees, composed of representatives of the various organizations of the community.[4] In collection, these committees have played an important role in reviewing and validating requirements, coordinating collection activities where an overlap or conflict could occur, and working directly with collectors to facilitate the effectiveness of operations. Of the committees directly associated with collection, the Signals Intelligence (SIGINT) Committee has been functioning since 1946, a committee to coordinate the handling of defectors since 1948, the Committee on Imagery Requirements and Exploitation (COMIREX) and its predecessors since 1955, and the Human Resources Committee since 1974.

Recognition of a common need spurred the activities of the committees, but it was not until 1978 that the Director was formally assigned a collection tasking mission. In Executive

Order 12036, President Carter directed him to establish a National Intelligence Tasking Center (NITC) under his "direction, control and management" for coordinating and tasking national foreign intelligence collection activities.[5] Then-Director Stansfield Turner divided his intelligence community staff into a Collection Tasking Staff (CTS) and a Resource Management Staff (RMS).[6] A major portion of the CTS manning came from the full-time staff of the COMIREX, the Human Resources Committee, and the SIGINT Committee, which had been assigned to the intelligence community staff. There were two other interesting aspects of the Executive Order's provision concerning collection tasking. The first was that the NITC was to be the means by which the Director provided "advisory tasking" for collecting national foreign intelligence by departments and agencies that had information collection capabilities or intelligence assets but were not part of the National Foreign Intelligence Program for which the DCI was responsible.[7] The second was the charge to the Director to "maintain readiness" for transferring control of the NITC and the Director's tasking authorities to the Secretary of Defense "upon the express direction of the President" (presumably during a major crisis or wartime).[8]

President Reagan's Executive Order 12333 made no mention of a NITC--and the Director melded his collection tasking and resource management staffs into a single intelligence community staff--but the order reaffirmed the Director's tasking authority. He was specifically made responsible for establishing mechanisms which translate national foreign intelligence objectives and priorities approved by the National Security Council into specific guidance for the intelligence community; resolving conflicts in tasking priority; providing departments and agencies having information collection capabilities that are not part of the National Foreign Intelligence Program advisory tasking concerning the collection of national foreign intelligence; and providing for the development of plans and arrangements for transferring required collection tasking authority to the Secretary of Defense when directed by the President.[9]

Executive Order 12333 charges the Secretary of Defense to "collect national foreign intelligence and be responsive to collection tasking by the Director of Central Intelligence,"[10] but the Secretary of Defense is also given responsibility to "collect, produce and disseminate military and military-related foreign intelligence and counterintelligence as required for execution of the Secretary's responsibilities."[11] The potentiality for conflict between the responsibilities of the Secretary of Defense and the Director in time of crisis, contingency action, or wartime is obvious, which is why Executive Order 12333 makes provision for transferring the Director's tasking role to the Secretary when the President considers that appropriate.

A substantial part of the National Foreign Intelligence Program budget is devoted to collecting and processing intelligence data acquired by technical systems. The Director's role in collection, therefore, goes far beyond his authority to task existing assets. He has the major additional functions of providing program guidance to the collection organizations, including those within the Defense Department, and he is responsible for approving the NFIP budget submitted to the President. This budget reflects what new or improved collection capabilities are to be made available in the future through investment included in the current budget.

THE COMMUNITY ROLE IN PRODUCTION

One of the basic pressures leading to today's intelligence community was a desire at policy levels of the government that intelligence "speak with one voice." Senior national intelligence users did not want to deal with estimates on the same subject from different production organizations.

World War II had barely ended when the Intelligence Advisory Board (IAB) was formed in 1946 and the heads of the then-existing U.S. intelligence organizations began meeting with the Director (then head of the Central Intelligence Group, predecessor to the CIA) to review and coordinate on substantive estimates. In 1947 the IAB became the Intelligence Advisory Committee (IAC), which in 1958 became the United States Intelligence Board (USIB) and in 1976 the National Foreign Intelligence Board (NFIB). The heads of all components of the intelligence community attend the NFIB, although since 1963 (shortly after establishment of the Defense Intelligence Agency), the senior intelligence officers of the Military Services have participated as observers rather than members. The primary function of the NFIB is to advise with and make recommendations to the Director concerning producing, reviewing, and coordinating national foreign intelligence--and particularly the National Intelligence Estimates (NIEs) and Special NIEs. Thus, the senior role of the Director in the community's national intelligence production was established early.

In 1951 the Director, General Walter Bedell Smith, who was disturbed at the production organizations' failure to provide warning of the Korean War, established the Board of National Estimates (BNE) to take the lead in the production of national estimates. Smith made it clear that the judgments expressed in such estimates would be those with which he agreed. Other members of what was then the IAC could disagree and take footnote positions, but the judgments were the Director's and would not be determined by majority vote. To this day, directors have held to this position.

The BNE functioned as the community focal point for national estimate production until William Colby abolished the Board in 1973 and replaced it with a dozen National Intelligence Officers (NIOs), each of whom was directly responsible to the Director for production relating to his assigned region or topic, such as conventional military forces (for which the NIO always has been an active duty flag or general officer). The extent to which each

NIO worked in a community milieu or dealt essentially with CIA varied markedly.

In 1980, Admiral Stansfield Turner organized the NIOs into a National Intelligence Council, established positions for several "general" NIOs, and in effect recreated an organization comparable to the former Board of National Estimates.

National Security Council Intelligence Directive No. 1, "Basic Duties and Responsibilities," effective February 17, 1972, listed "producing national intelligence required by the President and other national consumers" as one of the Director's four major responsibilities.[12]

President Ford, in his 1976 Executive Order 11905, charged the DCI to "supervise production and dissemination of national intelligence" and to provide the President and other Executive Branch officials with foreign intelligence "including national intelligence estimates."[13]

In Executive Order 12036 (1978), President Carter gave the Director "full responsibility for production and dissemination of national foreign intelligence" and additionally gave him authority to "levy analytic tasks on departmental intelligence production organizations, in consultation with those organizations." The President further charged the Director to "ensure that diverse points of view are considered fully and that differences in judgment within the Intelligence Community are brought to the attention of national policymakers."[14]

When he promulgated Executive Order 12333, President Reagan repeated the production and task-levying responsibilities and authorities assigned to the Director in Executive Order 12036, and reaffirmed that he was to ensure that "appropriate mechanisms for competitive analysis are developed" so that diverse points of view would be made apparent.[15]

Overall, intelligence production is a manpower intensive operation and only a small portion of the personnel and funding of the intelligence community is devoted to the analysis and production effort. Yet, understandably, since finished intelligence is what users see, the analytic quality, timeliness, and accuracy of intelligence products provide the primary basis upon which the effectiveness of the entire intelligence effort is judged.

The record since World War II has been mixed. Basic intelligence on problems of important interest has usually been good. Some estimative forecasts have been good; others have been wide of the mark. Production devoted to indications and warning has been marked by both successes and failures. For the past twenty years, with the improvement of technical collection capabilities, production on orders of battle and foreign weapons development has been quite good.

The Community's analytic personnel declined in both numbers and experience level during the 1970s, but a rebuilding process is underway. Increased attention is being given to strengthening and improving the analytical capabilities of the individual production organizations within the Community. Procedures and mechanisms for community coordination and review are already well established.

Most of the foreign intelligence required and used by the Department of Defense, except for that needed at tactical levels of the operational forces, is broadly viewed as national intelligence. Because of this, Defense Department production resources, such as those of the Defense Intelligence Agency and the scientific and technical intelligence components of the Military Services, are part of the National Foreign Intelligence Program and budget, for which the Director is responsible.

THE NATIONAL FOREIGN INTELLIGENCE PROGRAM (NFIP) BUDGET

The NFIP budget, developed and recommended to the President by the Director, is classified and is unique in that it is the only government-wide single-function budget. Contained in it are resources for the Central Intelligence Agency and the intelligence community entities of five Executive departments--State, Defense, Treasury, Justice, and Energy. The concept of a multi-department intelligence budget, for which the Director would issue program guidance and be responsible for budget review and approval, came into being because an awareness of the size and scope of the U.S. peacetime intelligence effort caused serious concern in the White House and in the Congress as to whether there was unnecessary duplication and overlap in the activities of the separate, and often competing, intelligence organizations. Four successive Presidents have decided that the Director is the proper person to develop the annual national intelligence budget that is approved by the President and submitted to the Congress.

President Nixon[16] in 1971 charged the Director to prepare a consolidated intelligence program budget. However, he did not give him the authority to overcome the Secretary of Defense's unwillingness to permit the Director's representatives on the intelligence community staff[17] access to data needed in the early stages of the budget review process. Essentially, the Defense concept was that, after it had developed budgets for its intelligence components, the Director should consolidate the Defense inputs with budgets prepared by other entities of the intelligence community.

President Ford sought to eliminate what was a virtual impasse in 1976 by creating, through Executive Order 11905, a National Security Council Committee on Foreign Intelligence (CFI), of which the Director was chairman, and charging the CFI to develop the NFIP Budget for the President.[18] The Department of Defense obtained legislative authorization for a second Deputy Secretary of Defense, with a primary mission of serving on the CFI and negotiating with the Director on intelligence community budget matters.

The CFI did its job quite well, with the Director's staff providing support, but the CFI ceased to function when President Carter took office and soon directed that the Director be solely responsible for the intelligence community's budget. This direction was contained in Executive Order 12036 of January 1978, which assigned to the Director "full and exclusive authority" for approving the budget submitted to the President and for the reprogramming of NFIP funds.[19] The order also directed him to "provide guidance for program and budget development to program managers and heads of component activities, and to department and agency heads;" to "review and evaluate the national program and budget submissions;" to develop the consolidated budget, and to present it to the President.[20] The heads of departments and agencies involved in the NFIP were charged to "ensure timely development and submission" to the Director of proposed national programs and budgets (in the format designated by the Director) and to ensure that he was provided "in a timely and responsive manner" all information necessary to perform his program and budget responsibilities.[21] For the first time, the Director's budgeting authorities matched his assigned responsibilities.

The stage was thus set for a truly active and responsible role in determining what resources each element of the intelligence community could request and have funded. To facilitate implementation of his budget role and his new responsibility for the National Intelligence Tasking Center (NITC), the Director divided and expanded what had been his intelligence community staff into a Resource Management Staff (RMS) and a Collection Tasking Staff (CTS).

By the time President Reagan took office in 1981, there was general agreement in the intelligence community that the Director's role in the program and budget process was serving the interests of the community quite well. In the drafting of what became President Reagan's Executive Order 12333, no effort was made to diminish the Director's program and budget responsibilities or authority, although the wording was changed. The pattern had been established, and provisions in the new order were quite brief. The Director was to:

> Develop, with the advice of the program managers and departments and agencies concerned, the consolidated National Foreign Intelligence Program budget and present it to the President and the Congress;
>
> Review and approve all requests for reprogramming National Foreign Intelligence Program funds, in accordance with guidelines established by the Office of Management and Budget;
>
> Monitor National Foreign Intelligence Program implementation and, as necessary, conduct program and performance audits and evaluations.[22]

The responsibilities of department and agency heads involved in the NFIP were to provide the Director with the information he needed, when he wanted it, and in the format he prescribed for execution of his program and budget responsibilities.[23]

As already indicated, the Director consolidated his Resource Management Staff and Collection Tasking Staff in 1981 into an Intelligence Community Staff that includes more than 200 personnel and is responsible to him for conducting the program and budget review process.

It is more than ten years since the Director first was charged by the President to prepare a National Foreign Intelligence Program budget, and the arrangements that have evolved have been accepted in the intelligence community. Early Defense Department concerns have faded as experience indicated that the Director's involvement in the program and budget approval system did not result in a diminishing of military intelligence activities. Resource ceilings and personnel reductions posed major problems for the intelligence community during the 1970s, but in the past few years the situation has improved and military intelligence activities are sharing in this upturn.

IS THE INTELLIGENCE COMMUNITY A TRUE COMMUNITY?

Even though most of the Department of Defense intelligence assets, along with intelligence elements of other parts of the Executive Branch, are part of what is titled "the intelligence community," and although there are numerous collection, production, program and budget, and other activities properly described as being "community" in nature, it is fair to examine whether the overall result reflects a "true community." This can be briefly explored by identifying the characteristics of a "community" and determining whether the intelligence community has these characteristics. First, a community has a recognized leader, and there is little question that the Director fills that role. He is clearly the spokesman for the intelligence community with the President, in the National Security Council, and at the Congress. His command-line writ runs only to the CIA, but his role in program and budget approval, in collection tasking, and in the production of national intelligence stamps him as a recognized leader. Second, a community has a recognized senior council or other means of advising the leader and developing community positions and viewpoints. The intelligence community has such bodies in the National Foreign Intelligence Board (NFIB), the National Foreign Intelligence Council (NFIC), the Intelligence Community Staff, and the various Director's committees, on which each interested element of the community has membership. From above the intelligence community, guidance and direction are provided by the President and the National Security Council and its supporting structure. Third, a community has an accepted body of rules, beliefs, and doctrine that are unique. The intelligence community has specialized rules embodied in the Presidential Executive Order, National Security Council Intelligence Directives, and Director of Central Intelligence Directives. Formally agreed upon "doctrine" is fragmentary, but various Directors have promulgated "objectives" on which there is general community agreement. Fourth, a community embraces members who have a sense of belonging and of loyalty to the community. It is here that the intelligence community is still somewhat deficient. A military intelligence officer tends to put loyalty to his Service and his organization above support to the intelligence community as a whole; a CIA officer tends to think first of what is good for CIA. Such loyalties are commendable. What is yet to be developed in the intelligence community is greater recognition that an intelligence officer should not only sustain a sense of loyalty to his own organization, but also give loyalty and support to the intelligence community and to the furtherance of what may be best for the community as a whole. Until there is greater recognition of the need to view the intelligence community as an entity deserving such support, it will lack one of the essential elements of a true community.

The fact remains that the intelligence community of the 1980s is far more of a community than it was in the 1950s, or the 1960s, or the 1970s.

NOTES

1. Definitions of intelligence have posed problems in the intelligence community since the same information can be used for a variety of purposes. It is use, not who collected it or how, that determines which definition a particular variant of intelligence falls within. National intelligence is "that intelligence required for the formulation of national security policy, concerning more than one department or agency, and transcending the exclusive competence of a single department or agency" (NSC Intelligence Directive No. 1). Departmental intelligence is "that intelligence any department or agency requires to execute its own mission" (NSCID No. 1). Tactical intelligence is "intelligence which is required for the planning and conduct of tactical operations. Tactical intelligence and strategic intelligence differ primarily in level of application, but may also vary in terms of scope and detail" (JCS Dictionary of Military and Associated Terms, June 1, 1979). (Tactical intelligence is not defined in an NSCID or Executive Order.) Strategic intelligence is "intelligence which is required for the formulation of policy and military plans at national and international levels. Strategic intelligence and tactical intelligence differ primarily in level of application, but may also vary in terms of scope and detail" (JCS, Dictionary of Military and Associated Terms). (This term is not defined in an NSCID or Executive Order.) Foreign intelligence is "information relating to the capabilities, intentions and activities of foreign powers, organizations or persons, but not including counterintelligence except for information on international terrorist activities" (Executive Order 12333).

2. "United States Intelligence Activities," promulgated December 4, 1981.

3. An example is the Foreign Broadcast Information Service (FBIS), which monitors public broadcasts on a worldwide basis for the intelligence community and, in fact, for the entire government.

4. These committees are organized by function or topic, and are often categorized as collection, production, or support committees. In recent years, the committees and their subcommittees and task groups have involved at least the part-time services of several hundred persons as members and staffs. Four committees were established in 1946-50, another six by 1960, one more in 1968, and two in 1973-74. During 1980-82, six new committees were formed. Two absorbed roles of earlier committees; the Critical Intelligence Problems Committee replaced the Critical Collection Problems Committee, and the Technology Transfer Intelligence Committee incorporated the role of the former Committee on Exchanges. The Watch Committee, originally formed in 1954 and abolished in 1974, was reestablished in 1982.

5. "United States Intelligence Activities," signed January 24, 1978.

6. The intelligence community staff had been established in 1972 to respond to a newly-assigned Director's responsibility to prepare a consolidated intelligence community budget.

7. Executive Order 12036, section 1-502(d).

8. Ibid., section 1-504.

9. Executive Order 12333, section 1.5(m).

10. Ibid., section 1.11(a).

11. Ibid., section 1.11(b).

12. The other three were: planning, reviewing, and evaluating all intelligence activities and the allocation of intelligence resources; chairing and staffing all intelligence community advisory boards and committees; and establishing and reconciling intelligence requirements and priorities within budgetary constraints (Section 3.a).

13. "United States Foreign Intelligence Activities," signed February 18, 1976, section 3 (d) (1) (iv).

14. Executive Order 12036, section 1-603.

15. Executive Order 12333, section 1.5 (k).

16. An unclassified summary of the President's classified memorandum is in Weekly Compilation of Presidential Documents,

November 9, 1971: "Reorganization of the U.S. Intelligence Community; Announcement Outlining Management Steps for Improving the Effectiveness of the Intelligence Community. November 5, 1971," p. 1482.

17. Director John Alex McCone had formed a small National Intelligence Program Evaluation (NIPE) staff within CIA in 1963 to aid him in his community role. Director Richard M. Helms expanded and reorganized the NIPE staff in early 1972 to form an Intelligence Community Staff (ICS), manned by CIA personnel, the primary focus of which was the community budget. When James R. Schlesinger became Director in February 1973, he completely reorganized the ICS, released most of the CIA personnel, and brought in active duty military officers and civilian detailees from Defense and State.

18. Executive Order 11905, section 3(b).

19. Executive Order 12036, section 1-602 and 1-602(f).

20. Ibid., section 1-602(a) and (c).

21. Ibid., section 1-602(b).

22. Executive Order 12333, section 1.5(n), (o) and (p).

23. Ibid., section 1.6(a) and (b).

2
The Defense Intelligence Community

J. Thompson Strong

While the lineage of the U.S. intelligence community, most specifically military intelligence, can be traced to the Revolutionary War, it was not until recently that the term "community" could be applied to the family of U.S. intelligence agencies. Even the National Security Act of 1947, the instrument that gave impetus to the concept, did little more than suggest what some then envisioned.

It was not until 1971 that the President levied on the Director of Central Intelligence (DCI) the task of developing a sort of de facto "community" among the intelligence agencies by charging him to consolidate the budgets of the agencies. However, it quickly became apparent that this was a responsibility with only the potential for, not the reality of, effective authority over the infant community. Each of the departments with intelligence agencies, most particularly the Department of Defense (DoD), simply provided the DCI with a non-negotiable budget. The message was clear: departmental prerogatives in intelligence would continue to be absolute.

In the case of DoD, this should come as no surprise: Then, as now, it owned by far the largest part of the intelligence community. The DoD and each of the Military Services had developed large and vigorous intelligence organizations to support their perceived needs and predilections. Furthermore, they viewed any attempt to centralize intelligence organizations as a usurpation of the department's or service's power.

Finally, in 1977, President Carter gave the DCI the authority with which to back his responsibility when he made the DCI solely responsible for the entire national foreign intelligence budget. The result was a world of more centralized direction into which the agencies could grow toward communal maturity.

Today, like the rest of the National Foreign Intelligence Community (NFIC), the DoD Intelligence Community may be viewed as both centralized and decentralized. Under the leadership of the Secretary of Defense, who has delegated the Department's intelligence portfolio to his Deputy Secretary,[1] all members of this community respond to the requirements of the Secretary and other executive branch officials, including the DCI and the President. Guidance and direction is provided to the military intelligence agencies by the Secretary of Defense in accordance with his intelligence responsibilites.[2]

Moreover, the service intelligence agencies respond, in an autonomous manner, to the requirements of their intelligence chiefs, the Unified and Specified (U&S) Commanders, and to field or operating commanders. Each of the military agencies also undertakes a host of delegated collection, production and dissemination assignments in support of sister Services, DoD, and other NFIC-member needs.

Accomplishing the myriad missions necessary to meet the demands placed on the military intelligence community by its consumers obviously demands a sizeable investment in organization, manpower and money. The DoD intelligence apparatus leads the NFIC in all of these areas: of the thirteen official NFIC members, seven (the National Security Agency (NSA), the Defense Intelligence Agency (DIA), the intelligence units of the Army, Navy, Air Force and Marine Corps, and elements within the Office of the Secretary of Defense) belong to DoD. Also, resources drawn from "... the Department Intelligence Budget ... compromise 80% of the direct national United States intelligence budget."[3]

THE NATIONAL SECURITY AGENCY (NSA)

In a 1952 Presidential Directive, NSA was created by President Harry S. Truman.[4] Its purpose was to collate all U.S. signals intelligence (SIGINT) operations under the Secretary of Defense who would act as the government's executive agent for all SIGINT activities. No other element of the NFIC has this distinction. The result is that NSA has the major responsibility for collecting strategic and tactical SIGINT, the product of which is shared by all branches of the government.

As electronic technology became more sophisticated, NSA grew from its somewhat humble 1952 beginnings as inheritor of the comparatively meager assets of the Armed Forces Security Agency (AFSA). Today, NSA is a global organization headquartered at Ft. George Meade, Maryland, and is assisted by the Service Cryptological Elements (SCEs) of the Army, Navy, and Air Force.

The relationship of these SCEs to NSA is as unique as are NSA's responsibilities. With the exception of the Marine Corps, whose immediate SIGINT interests are tactical rather than strategic, each of the services provides NSA the needed resources for collecting SIGINT. The services relinquish control of these elements to the Director of NSA who also heads the Central Security Service (CSS) through which the SCEs are provided their policies, orders, and priorities governing strategic SIGINT operations.[5] The services retain control of their service personnel with respect to assignments, promotions, etc., but do not directly task the elements to collect service required strategic intelligence. Even in the tactical SIGINT collection arena the Director of NSA, as the agent of the Secretary of Defense, delegates authority to the services to conduct these activities. Legally, this includes the delegation of the service's own resources to accomplish its tactical SIGINT mission.[6]

At both the tactical and strategic levels, SIGINT consists of communications intelligence (COMINT) and electronics intelligence (ELINT). COMINT can be defined as intelligence derived from intercepting electronic communications signals from such sources as radios, wires, and data links. ELINT results from intercepting non-communications electronic emanations such as radars and beacons. For both it is NSA that is solely responsible for collecting, processing, and disseminating all signals intelligence data and information for national foreign intelligence and counterintelligence purposes.[7]

NSA also provides a variety of other services for the government. For example, it conducts the government's communications security (COMSEC) program, which includes designing and testing all government codes and cyphers, as well as the equipment that produces and sends encrypted messages around the world.[8]

These undertakings are intended to insure that the U.S. government's signals are secure from collection and exploitation by hostile intelligence SIGINT efforts. History is replete with examples of the prices paid for failures to adequately protect communications: lost battles during the Civil War due to wire tapping; the Japanese loss of advantage in negotiations with the United States following World War I when their diplomatic codes were broken by the American Black Chamber; and the death of Admiral Yamamato in World War II, when his plane was shot down by American P-38s after his air travel route was compromised by intercepted communications. It is the National Security Agency's mission to see that such disasters are not suffered by the United States through weaknesses in signals intelligence, counterintelligence, and security.

THE DEFENSE INTELLIGENCE AGENCY (DIA)[9]

DIA was formed not by legislation or Executive Order, but by the direction of the Secretary of Defense.[10] The need for such a capstone agency to coordinate the national foreign intelligence efforts of the services had been identified in a number of studies which date as far back as the first Hoover Commission in 1948. That study, four other studies in subsequent years and Secretary of Defense MacNamara's frustration caused by his inability to receive consistent, non-parochial intelligence estimates from the services led to DIA's creation in 1961.

While the years since its foundation have often been stormy ones for DIA, prompting a number of reorganizations to meet the demands of the services, the Joint Chiefs of Staff (JCS) and the Secretary of Defense, DIA today has relatively harmonious relationships with these organizations. This results from both the Director's personal relationship with the four heads of the service intelligence agencies and from the Director's position as the manager of the General Defense Intelligence Program (GDIP).[11]

As a part of the National Foreign Intelligence Program (NFIP) budget, the GDIP competes in the federal budget process not with the DoD budget, but only with the budgets of the other members of the NFIC. This has turned out to be a tremendous advantage to all of the departmental intelligence organizations, including DIA.

As the ultimate arbiter and decisionmaker on service and other departmental intelligence budgets, the Director of DIA has a great deal of influence over the intelligence processes and products of these organizations. Further, the Director of DIA's role as the JCS's J-2 (intelligence officer) and his position as intelligence advisor to the Secretary of Defense and the Chairman of the Joint Chiefs of Staff (CJCS) places DIA in a very strong position.

However, as absolute as this power base appears, it is somewhat diminished by DoD intelligence relationships. For example, the GDIP includes all military units and activities in the NFIP <u>except</u> satellite, cryptologic, and counterintelligence programs. Since these areas are not funded within the GDIP, and therefore are not under the Director's purview, his power over the defense intelligence community is diluted. Another specific example of this is the Tactical Intelligence and Related Activities (TIARA) budget.

Created by Congress in the late 1970s, this aggregation of programs ostensibly makes Congressional budget review easier because it separates those programs and monies funded for the strategic arena by the NFIP/GDIP budgets from those funded for tactical intelligence operations by the DoD budget. This arrangement eases Congress' job to some extent, but the intermingling of strategic and tactical programs, platforms and missions results in a very complex management problem. For example, the Air Force's many reconnaissance aircraft, carrying a wide variety of sensors, may in one flight support a number of strategic and tactical requirements.[12] This tends to complicate the budget process to a considerable degree, and if nothing else makes tracking programs difficult.

These issues aside, the missions of DIA include: collection, production, or, through tasking and coordination, provision of military and military-related intelligence for the Secretary of Defense, the Joint Chiefs of Staff, other Defense components, and, as appropriate, non-Defense agencies; collection and provision of military intelligence and counterintelligence products; coordination of all Department of Defense intelligence requirements; management of the Defense Attache system; and provision of foreign intelligence and counter intelligence staff support as directed by the Joint Chiefs of Staff.[13]

To accomplish these missions the agency, headed by a vice admiral or a lieutenant general, is organized into five major directorates (See Table 2.1). Generally, the position of Director rotates between the Army, Navy and Air Force but the order of this rotation has not remained constant. Furthermore, the Directorates have been reorganized over the years reflecting the internal responses of any large, corporate-like body shifting to meet new

Figure 2.1

THE ORGANIZATION OF THE DEFENSE INTELLIGENCE AGENCY

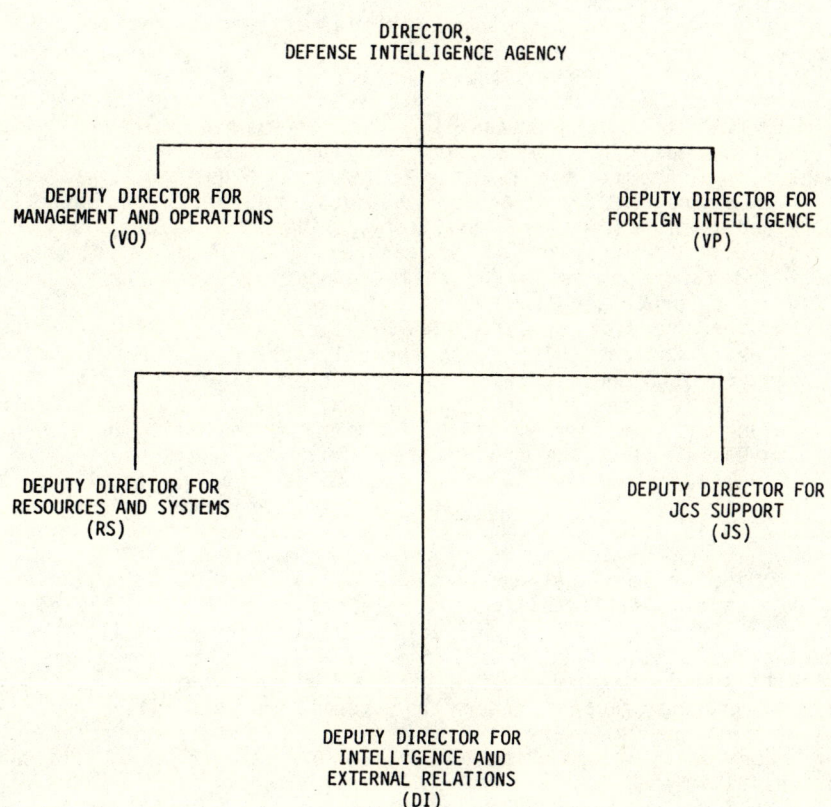

demands. Today, the "product-managers" are organized into the Directorates for Management and Operations (VO), External Relations (DI), Foreign Intelligence (VP), JCS Support (JS) and Resources and Systems (RS) (see Table 2. 1).

Within the first directorate, Management and Operations (VO), lies DIA's only resource for fulfilling its mission of direct collection: the Defense Attache System. The "DATTs," as they are known throughout the community, are military officers accredited as diplomats to U.S. embassies around the world. They provide military advice to the Ambassador, maintain liaison with the host country's military, conduct the affairs of the DoD's Security Assistance Program in selected countries, and report on overtly collected information of military interest. Support and coordination for this effort is managed by VO from selection of the DATTs (upon nomination by their respective services), through training, to processing the reports of the attaches.

Another service provided by VO is sponsoring the Defense Intelligence College (DIC). As the only accredited post-graduate institution of higher learning in the nation offering a Masters of Science in Strategic Intelligence degree, DIC provides both education and training to all elements of the NFIC on a non-tuition basis and is the home of the Defense Attache School.

Finally, since the majority of DoD's foreign intelligence collection is actually conducted by the separate services and other agencies, it is VO that manages and coordinates this effort through its Directorate for Collection Management (DC). The Directorate accomplishes these tasks by validating, prioritizing, and registering all intelligence collection requirements levied on DoD and by operating a Collection Coordination Facility for tasking collection systems and operations. Due to the scope of activities and the number of entities involved, this is a highly refined process managed under the overall responsibility of the DCI through the Intelligence Community Staff. However, Management and Operations is not the only DIA Directorate with liaison responsibilities.

The Directorate for External Relations (DI), while obviously responsible for public affairs for the agency, also fulfills a series of responsibilities assigned to the NFIC by Executive Order and to DIA by DoD Directive. Specifically, these include arrangements with foreign governments on intelligence matters and interagency exchanges of foreign intelligence information.[14] The second duty is shared between DI, VO, and the Directorate for Foreign Intelligence (VP), DIA's analysis arm.

An element of production is analysis and VP has two offices of analysis: the Assistant Vice Director for Estimates (DE) and the Assistant Vice Director for Research (DB). DE contributes to the production of national foreign intelligence by developing and producing DIA contributions to National Foreign Intelligence Board (NFIB) tasked National and Special National Intelligence Estimates (NIEs and SNIEs). Additionally, DE conducts analysis to: support DoD research, design and acquisition processes; support Office of Secretary of Defense (OSD) and JCS planning activities; and satisfy the intelligence requirements that the National Security Council (NSC) levies on DoD through the NFIB. Lastly, the Estimates Directorate provides or coordinates DoD intelligence contributions to international military organizations such as NATO, of which the United States is a member.

The second analytical division of DIA/VP is DB, which produces all-source, finished military intelligence. Such intelligence runs the gamut from counting weapons and equipment, to studies on military doctrine and tactics, to providing biographic and economic intelligence. DB also accounts for DIA's participation in the National Photographic Interpretation Center (NPIC) and in the development of imagery-exploitation equipment.

The final office in VP is a production management element, the Assistant Vice Directorate for Scientific and Technical (S&T) Intelligence (DT). DT manages the S&T intelligence efforts of the services through a process known as delegated production which permits DIA to levy analytical requirements on the military S&T intelligence units. In terms of maximizing the taxpayers return on the intelligence dollar, this is a real bargain--DIA eliminates redundancy by assigning an individual service the responsibility of conducting a particular type of intelligence analysis.

For example, the Foreign Technology Division of the Air Force Systems Command (AFSC) has sole responsibility for S&T analysis of aircraft and land-based strategic ballistic missiles, while the Army's Missile and Space Intelligence Center undertakes analysis of surface-to-air missiles and tactical surface-to-surface missiles. An example of total delegated production of all responsibility for a given type of intelligence is the Armed Forces Medical Intelligence Center (AFMIC) through which the Department of the Army conducts virtually all analysis on medicines, chemicals and associated equipment for the entire NFIC.

The final two elements of DIA are the Directorate for JCS Support (JS) and the Directorate for Resources and Systems (RS). The JS organization serves as the DIA focal point for the Joint Staff by providing the Joint Chiefs of Staff (JCS) administrative intelligence support, current intelligence, an indications and warning capability and an alert center. In essence, DIA has served as the intelligence staff element of the JCS, its J-2, since the establishment of the Agency in 1961.

The Directorate for Resources and Systems (RS) has two primary functions, one internal and one external to the agency. The internal responsibility is largely composed of housekeeping functions including a comptroller and the operation of communications facilities, a graphics center and a photographics laboratory. Externally, RS manages the DoD Intelligence Information System (DoDIIS) and is the focal point for structuring the worldwide intelligence information systems architecture.

In sum, DIA is the flagship of DoD's military intelligence fleet. While each of the military services maintains an autonomous intelligence apparatus, DIA serves to organize the process of collection, production and dissemination of intelligence material throughout DoD, between itself and the other members of the NFIC and for the consumers of DoD intelligence.

ARMY INTELLIGENCE

From a historical perspective the term "Army Intelligence" is almost synonymous with "U.S. Intelligence." It was George Washington, as the Commander-in-chief of the Continental Army, who was literally the father of the current National Foreign Intelligence Community. This grand beginning continued, albeit on a smaller scale, in the years between the Revolutionary and Civil wars with such efforts as the western explorations of Lewis and Clark, and Zebulon Pike. However, by the time of the Civil War Army intelligence had atrophied to the point that the North had to rely on the Pinkerton Detective Agency for its intelligence.

It took two world wars to establish the field of national military intelligence as a legitimate, enduring and indispensable peacetime profession. Today, Army Intelligence is divided into the staff support and operational areas (See Table 2.2). The senior Army intelligence officer is a lieutenant general who holds the position of Assistant Chief of Staff, Intelligence (ACSI, pronounced "ack-see"), to the Chief of Staff of the Army. The ACSI is a staff support element and, as such, commands no combat units. This reflects the military philosophy that field commanders report to higher echelon commanders, not to staff officers.

Directly under the ACSI are six major directorates: the Plans, Programs, and Budget Office; the Directorates of Foreign Liaison, Counterintelligence, Intelligence Systems, Foreign Intelligence, and the Intelligence Automations Office.

The Army's macroscopic intelligence and counterintelligence activities, financial plans and budgets are prepared by the Plans, Programs, and Budget (PPB) Office which also conducts quarterly budget executive reviews. The PPB Office also develops the Army Intelligence Management Plan, a formulation of practically all of the Army's intelligence activities.

All overt intelligence coordination with foreign governments, army agencies, military attaches and officials is done by the Foreign Liaison division, much as the U.S.-foreign interface is done by the External Relations Directorate of the Defense Intelligence Agency. This directorate coordinates visits, tours and the like, and represents the Army at foreign diplomatic functions.

The Directorate of Counterintelligence provides policy on counterintelligence (CI) investigations, CI operations, security support to the Army and the contemporary terrorist threat. Signals and automation security is another growing responsibility of the Counterintelligence Directorate which also monitors the troublesome area of technology transfer to other nations. This directorate also conducts reviews of information provided to foreign governments, the Congress and the public, and is directly involved in processing Privacy Act and Freedom of Information Act requests.

Figure 2.2

THE ORGANIZATION OF ARMY INTELLIGENCE

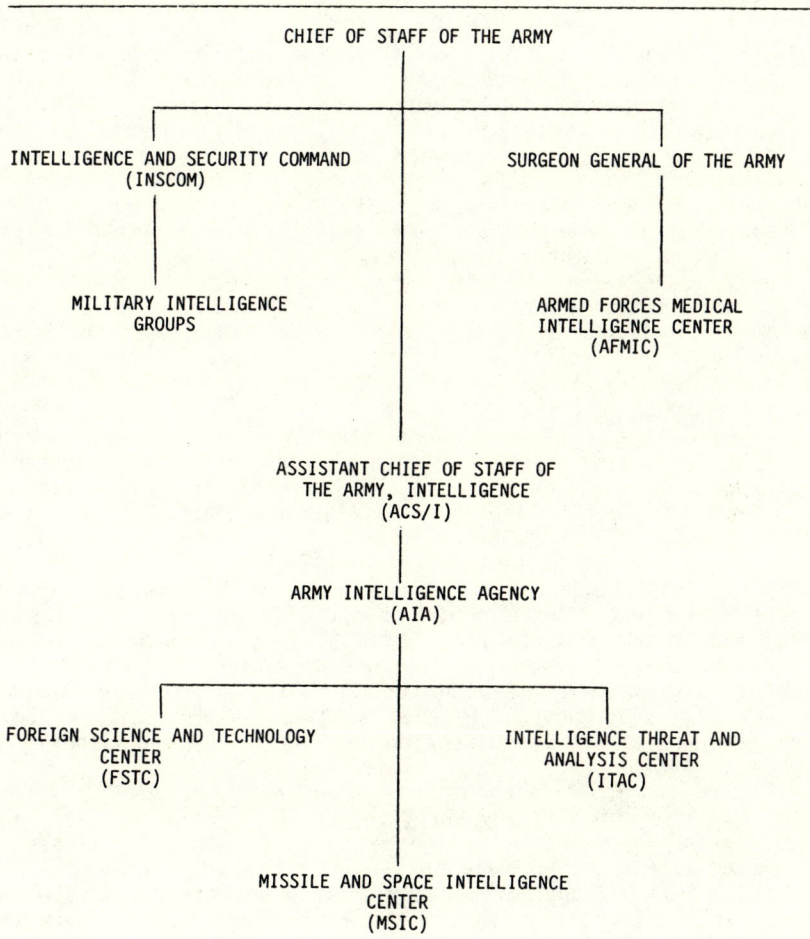

Responsibilities for the three major intelligence disciplines--imagery intelligence (IMINT), signals intelligence (SIGINT), and human intelligence (HUMINT)--rest primarily with the Directorates of Intelligence Systems (IS) and Foreign Intelligence (FI). The management of training and modernization of tactical intelligence units is done by IS, as is the formulation of the Army's unique SIGINT policy and collection requirements, and oversight of the Army's cryptologic, electro-optics, and electronic warfare operations. FI handles the country desk officers, threat integration, the scientific and technological threat, and current intelligence.

Away from the staff side, Army Intelligence is broken into two elements: the Intelligence and Security Command (INSCOM) and the Army Intelligence Agency (AIA). As noted earlier, army commanders do not report to staff officers and in keeping with this tradition the commander of INSCOM reports not to the ACSI, but to the Chief of Staff of the Army.

INSCOM, then, is the Army's operational intelligence arm. Formed in January 1977, it is concerned primarily with strategic intelligence. To perform its mission it drew from the assets of the U.S. Army Security Agency, the ACSI organization, U.S. Army Forces Command (FORSCOM) and the old U.S. Army Intelligence Agency. As INSCOM states, its mission "is to provide multi-discipline intelligence, security and electronic warfare operations for the Army at Echelons Above Corps (EAC) in war and peace, and be prepared to respond to tasking as needed and/or as directed by the Department of the Army in order to contribute to deterring war, warning of impending war, and winning the war."[15] Since it satisfies such high-level taskings (from echelons above corps level), it receives direction from both national authorities and the Army ACSI.

INSCOM has both single and multidiscipline groups. The former comprise the Military Intelligence (MI) groups specializing in particular areas of intelligence such as counterintelligence, electronic warfare or operations security support. Examples of single discipline groups are INSCOM's field units that compose the army's Service Cryptological Element under NSA's Central Security Service (CSS). The multidiscipline groups contain some of all the specialties. Both kinds of groups are to be found around the globe from the Far East through the Western Hemisphere to Europe.

By comparison to INSCOM as the operational arm of Army Intelligence, its research arm is the Army Intelligence Agency (AIA). In structure AIA is so new (it was founded on October 1, 1984) that it is, as of this writing, still going through the birth pains of determining exact internal relationships. As of August 1985, a general officer was assigned as the Commanding General of AIA, a Field Operating Agency of the ASCI. Since AIA is not a "Command" this is in keeping with the tradition mentioned earlier.

AIA is composed of three elements, all of which were transferred on paper from other commands as of October 1, 1984: the Foreign Science and Technology Center (FSTC); the Missile and

Space Intelligence Center (MSIC); and the Intelligence Threat Analysis Center (ITAC). FSTC and MSIC (until recently the Missile Intelligence Agency (MIA)) had been assigned to the Army Material Command (AMC), the commander of which reported directly to the Chief of Staff of the Army; ITAC belonged to INSCOM and had the same command relationship.

No changes were made in the physical location of any of these organizations: FSTC remains at Charlottesville, Virginia; MSIC is still at Redstone Arsenal, Huntsville, Alabama; and ITAC remains at Arlington Hall Station, Arlington, VA. However, it is quite apparent that the change in command lines has brought to the ACSI a significant increase in his influence over the activities of FSTC, MSIC and ITAC. That this would be the desire of the ACSI is not surprising since all three entities perform intelligence activities (as suggested by their titles) at echelons above corps and therefore support the strategic-and Army-wide policies, plans and programs of the ACSI and the Chief of Staff.

Army Intelligence operations below corps level are mainly tactical. The specialists for these missions are schooled principally at Fort Huachuca, Arizona, and Fort Devons, Massachusetts, for worldwide service in smaller intelligence units which support the Army's corps, divisions, brigades and battalions.

NAVY INTELLIGENCE

The U.S. Navy also has a long tradition beginning with the Revolutionary War. After the war America turned inward to develop and expand, and Naval Intelligence, like Army Intelligence, became of secondary importance to the service. However, there were brief instances of importance between the two World Wars. For example, while it was Army intelligence which assumed responsibility for decyphering foreign codes after the American Black Chamber was closed down by Secretary of State Henry L. Stimson, in 1929, it was Naval Intelligence that, about a year later, took the discipline to heart. The experience gained in these activities eventually led to the navy's breaking of the Japanese PURPLE and MAGIC codes prior to and during World War II.

Like Army Intelligence, Naval Intelligence has undergone many internal changes since World War II. Today, the naval intelligence community is headed by the Director of Naval Intelligence (DNI) who heads the Office of Naval Intelligence (ONI) and who is normally a rear admiral. Under the DNI there are: the DDNI for Operational Intelligence--Commander, Naval Intelligence Command (NIC); and the DDNI for Cryptology--Commander, Naval Security Group (NSG). The DDNI for Security--Commander, Naval Investigative Service Command (NISCOM) serves as the Assistant to the DNI for Counterintelligence and Security (See Table 2.3).

When working in their ONI staff positions, each of the DDNIs and their ONI staffs handle policy-level planning and programming for their specific areas: intelligence requirements and plans; cryptologic plans and programs; security policy; and the normal headquarters staff functions for each area, such as resources management and acquisition policy. These staff elements also provide support to the DNI in his role as principal intelligence advisor to the Secretary of the Navy and the Chief of Naval Operations (CNO). They also support DNI participation in a variety of national-level boards and panels such as the National Foreign Intelligence Board (NFIB) and Council (NFIC), and DIA's preparatory board to the NFIB and NFIC, the Military Intelligence Board (MIB). However, as active as this staff is, the classic naval intelligence work is done by the three subordinate commands, the first of which is NIC.

The Naval Intelligence Command is headed by a commodore (one-star rank) and has four component commands: the Naval Intelligence Processing System Support Activity (NIPSSA); the Naval Operations Intelligence Center (NOIC); the Naval Intelligence Support Center (NISC); and the Commander, Task Force 168 (CTF-168). Each is headed by a captain. These sub-commands are concerned with intelligence relating to science and technology, operational intelligence (foreign naval capabilities), ocean surveillance (to include the increasingly important task of tracking potential enemy ballistic missile firing submarines), data automation, telecommunications, and the like. Much of NIC's effort supports the internal navy demand for naval intelligence analysis, but much of its work also goes into the national intelligence data base in the form of intelligence production for the Defense Intelligence Agency.

Like NIC, the Naval Security Group Command also serves both national-level and naval consumers in its relationship with the National Security Agency as the Navy's Service Cryptologic Element. As the largest of the naval intelligence support commands, the Naval Security Group is concerned with cryptology, security and various forms of electromagnetic support to the fleet.

The Naval Investigative Service Command (NIS) is similar to the Army's Criminal Investigation Division (CID) and the Air Force's Office of Special Investigations (OSI). The NIS investigates criminal activity and conducts counterintelligence and counterterrorist activities relating to the Navy.

Beyond these centrally commanded units the major commanders and fleets have their own intelligence centers which support the worldwide operational requirements of the U.S. Navy. As with the other services these theater centers support their own regional naval forces and the national data base in Washington. For example, the naval intelligence analysts at the Fleet Intelligence Center, Pacific (FICPAC), produce naval orders of battle and other pertinent data bases for the Pacific fleet commanders and communicate this type of information to the national level consumers in Washington through the Ocean Surveillance Information System (OSIS).

Naval intelligence officers serve from the national level agencies down to the larger individual ships, such as cruisers. An aircraft carrier, for example, will have a small intelligence

Figure 2.3

THE ORGANIZATION OF NAVAL INTELLIGENCE

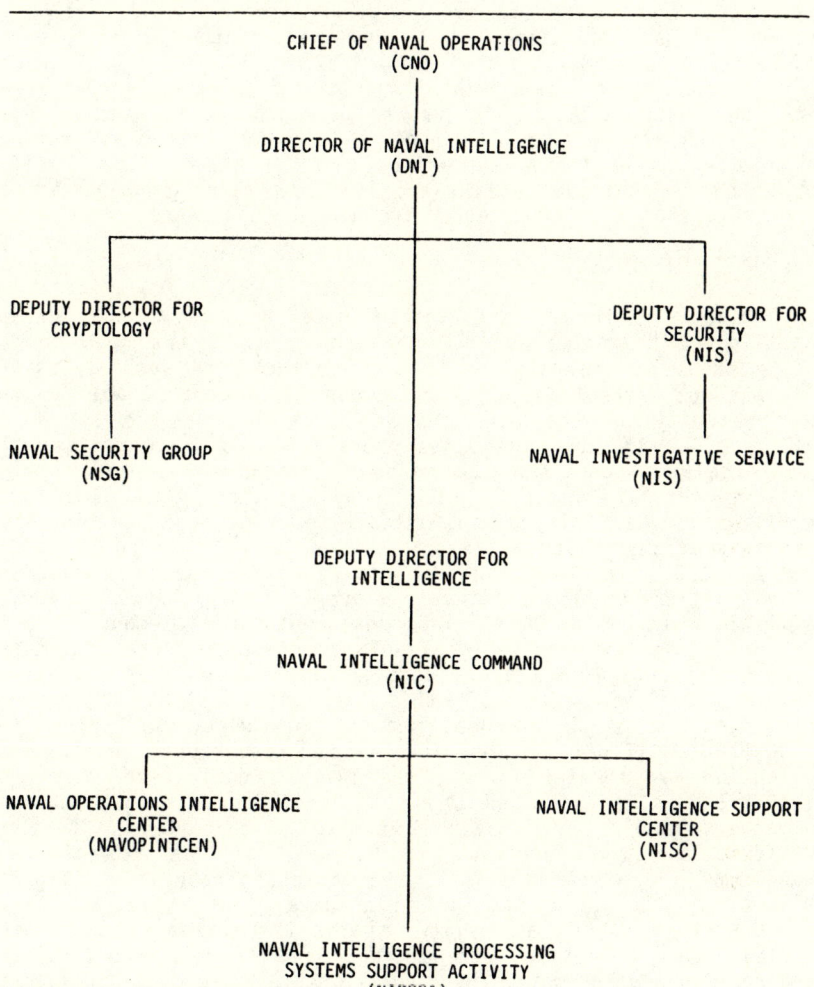

section headed by a commander, while on smaller ships, such as destroyers and frigates, the intelligence functions will be assumed as an additional duty by one of the ship's junior officers.

At all levels Naval Intelligence faces greater challenges today than ever before. The growth in capabilities of the Soviet Navy, particularly the permanent stationing of Soviet nuclear ballistic missile firing submarines off the Atlantic and Pacific coasts of the United States since 1971, is warning enough of the importance that must be attached to Naval Intelligence.

AIR FORCE INTELLIGENCE

While Air Force Intelligence does not have the lengthy intelligence tradition of the Army and Navy, it has been by far the quickest of the services to grow in technical sophistication. This was not without cause: World War II brought to warfare the full maturity of the aircraft as a weapon and the sky as a battlefield. In the comparatively brief period since the war the Air Force has gone from the subsonic to the hypersonic, from "tail-draggers" to space flight. In all of these venues Air Force Intelligence has played an integral part in protecting the interests of the nation.

In 1962, it was an Air Force intelligence collection activity, U-2 overflights, that discovered the presence of Soviet ballistic missiles in Cuba. The subsequent events demonstrated to the world just how fragile the line was between deterrence and the insanity of nuclear warfare. Today, Air Force collection systems are at the forefront of this nation's effort to gather intelligence through technical means. In the tactical arena the RF-4C Phantom II remains the backbone of photographic intelligence collection for theater forces; the TR-1, a derivative of the U-2R,[16] provides tactical and strategic intelligence to both theater commanders and to the National Command Authorities (NCA), the President and the Secretary of Defense; and at the farthest reaches of the atmosphere lurks the fastest airborne intelligence collector in the world, the SR-71 Blackbird.

Operating such a highly sophisticated and complicated intelligence collection, production, and dissemination system requires involving more than just the Air Force intelligence organization. In fact, the process demands considerable investment by several of the Air Force's Major Air Commands: the RF-4Cs are owned and operated by the theater tactical Air Forces; and the TR-1 and the SR-71 are flown not by Air Force Intelligence, but by the Strategic Air Command.

Meanwhile, the intelligence mission at Headquarters U.S. Air Force is more narrowly focused than are the staffs at Army (with AIA attached) or Navy (with NIC, NSA and NIS attached through DDNI commanders). It is primarily devoted to intelligence planning, policymaking, programming, acquisition, tasking, analysis and dissemination. To accomplish these functions Air Force Intelligence is divided into two elements: Air Force Intelligence

(AF/IN), which is the staff of the ACS/I (a major general); and the Air Force Intelligence Service (AFIS), an Air Force Separate Operating Agency (SOA) which is also commanded by the ACS/I (see Table 2.4). This arrangement between AF/IN and AFIS was established in 1972 to meet legislative requirements to reduce the size of the staff of the Chief of Staff of the Air Force, the Air Staff. In reality this same arrangement is extant in the relationships between the Army ACSI Staff and INSCOM, and the DNI and his subordinate commands NIC, NSG, and NIS.

In this relationship the ACS/I has direct control over both his immediate staff, AF/IN, and AFIS. The ACS/I exercises "functional management" over these intelligence staffs and, through AF/IN, develops the Air Force position on foreign military capabilities and potential actions for input to consolidated reports, and provides headquarters review of all Air Force Intelligence functions.

AFIS is concerned largely with operational intelligence, security and communications management, intelligence data management, air attache affairs, Soviet affairs (the Soviet Awareness Program), evasion and escape, intelligence reserve forces management, and direction of the ACS/I's only "in-house" collection activity, HUMINT. This last operation is conducted on a worldwide basis by a subunit of AFIS, the Air Force Special Activities Center (AFSAC).

As suggested above, Air Force Intelligence activities beyond those described as being under the direct control of the ACS/I are both scattered and numerous. For example, unlike Naval Intelligence, Air Force Intelligence does not have its own Service Cryptological Element (SCE). Rather, those responsibilities are undertaken by a separate Major Air Command, the Electronic Security Command, which is the Air Force SCE element of NSA's Central Security Service. Likewise, worldwide regional technical groups--the reconnaissance technical organizations and the Air Force System Command's Foreign Technology Division in the United States--provide special technical assessments of the capabilities and intentions of target nations. As well, the Air Force Office of Special Investigations (OSI), a part of the Air Force Inspector General and not Air Force Intelligence, is responsible for Air Force counterintelligence and antiterrorist activities in addition to the conduct of investigations into criminal activities.

The Air Force major commands have their own intelligence offices which produce specialized intelligence. For example, the Strategic Air Command (SAC) intelligence organizations are concerned largely with all aspects of strategic bomber and missile operations, while the Military Airlift Command (MAC) intelligence personnel are more concerned with intelligence related to worldwide airlift operations (third world airfield security, possible terrorist threats to MAC aircraft, etc.). The U.S. Air Force in Europe (USAFE) focuses on Soviet and other Warsaw Pact threats.

Many of these major command intelligence organizations also produce intelligence for the national data base. For example, SAC

Figure 2.4

THE ORGANIZATION OF AIR FORCE INTELLIGENCE

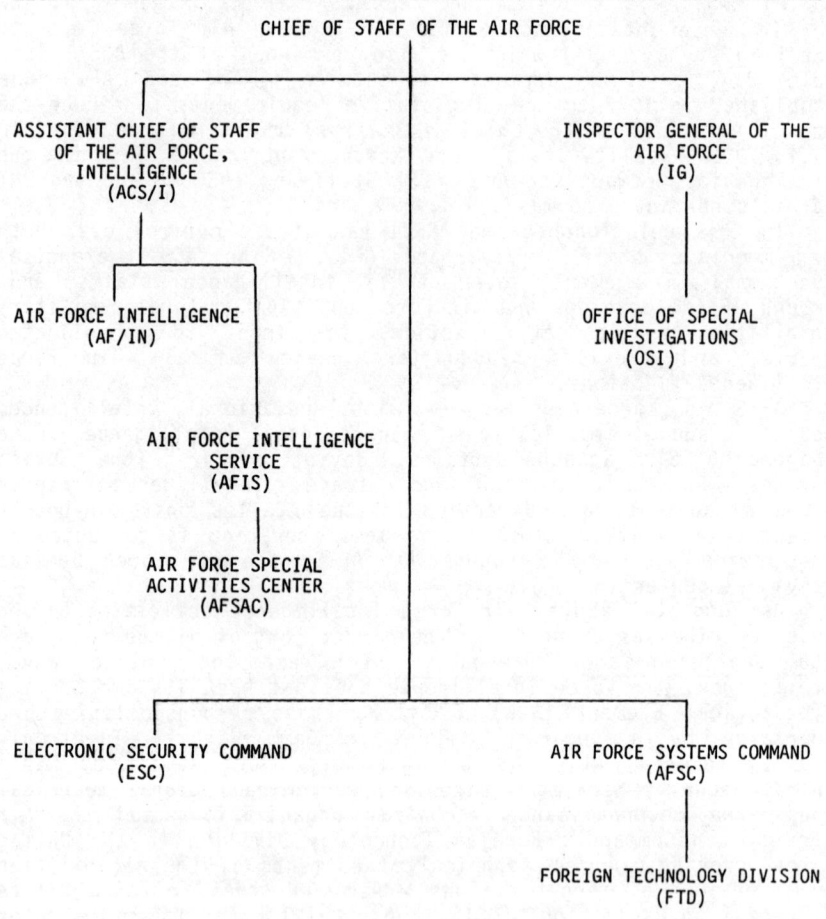

produces the foreign missile orders of battle (MOB), and USAFE produces Warsaw Pact and other air orders of battle (AOB). The national, jointly-manned strategic targeting center is located at Offutt Air Force Base, Nebraska, which is also the headquarters of the Strategic Air Command.

Finally, Air Force Intelligence has a role in the Air Force down through the wing to the squadron level. At squadron level, subjects such as foreign equipment recognition training (ships, planes, etc.), escape and evasion, and specific target information are briefed to aircrews. In return, the aircrews provide major intelligence input to the squadrons and wings during combat.

MARINE CORPS INTELLIGENCE

Since the Marine Corps only become a service with co-equal status in the JCS in 1978, its intelligence tradition has largely been one of the naval intelligence tradition. Almost as a reflection of this newness the Director of Marine Intelligence is the most junior in rank of the service intelligence chiefs, a brigadier general.

The size of the Marine Corps and its doctrine and missions appropriately dictate an emphasis on tactical intelligence (see Table 2.5). And, although individual intelligence officers serve worldwide in unified command headquarters staffs, intelligence in the Corps is directed primarily toward supporting the field commanders and the Air Ground Task Forces. This unique perspective results in the Corps relying on the other services, particularly the Navy, to provide the bulk of its strategic operational intelligence support and, in the realm of equipment, on the Army's intelligence research and development process.

The bulk of Marine intelligence activity is in Fleet Marine Force support where intelligence is gathered by such differing collection methods as electronic and photo-reconnaissance aircraft, division reconnaissance battalions and force reconnaissance companies. Marine imagery analysts are found at all levels while the interrogator-translator effort is an important element of Marine intelligence gathering.

The Marines also perform counterintelligence missions at the tactical, battlefield level. Sensor Control and Management, and Surveillance and Target Acquisition platoons are located at the division and battalion levels. Like the other services, the Marines are participants in the Tactical Exploitation of National Capabilities (TENCAP) program through which intelligence collected by national technical means is made available to the tactical military forces.

Marine Corps intelligence efforts have had to expand over the last few years as the Corps' potential operational areas have increased. It has had little historic involvement with the Persian Gulf or the Central Front in Europe, yet these areas are now high on the list of Marine contingency planning. Additionally, the Corps' experience in Lebanon in 1982 and 1983

Figure 2.5

THE ORGANIZATION OF MARINE CORPS INTELLIGENCE

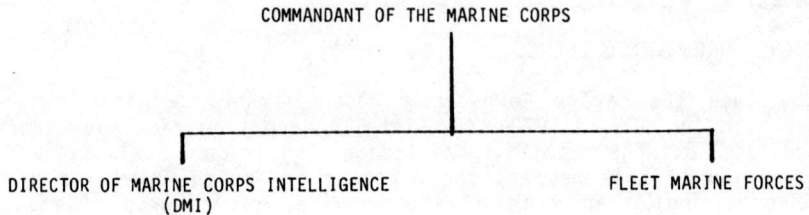

point to the need for a highly refined intelligence capability.

OFFICE OF SECRETARY OF DEFENSE (OSD)

At the beginning of this chapter it was noted that the Department of Defense intelligence community operated under the leadership of the Secretary of Defense (SECDEF), but that much of this community responds to the guidance and direction of the Director of Central Intelligence (DCI). What, then, is the role of the SECDEF in heading this community? The answer to this question lies in the position of the SECDEF as: a Cabinet member (a member, with the President, of the National Command Authorities (NCA)): and the government's executive agent for SIGINT, COMINT, and communications security (COMSEC).

In the first instance it is the SECDEF's position as a Cabinet member that permits him to appeal to the President any program or budget decision of the DCI with which he disagrees. This, combined with his presidential charge to "direct, operate, control and provide fiscal management for the National Security Agency and for defense and military intelligence and national reconnaissance entities,"[17] is largely a reflection of the SECDEF's primary mission as a National Command Authorities member whose responsibilities are the defense of the nation and the guaranteeing of national survival. The significance of these two circumstances is that, in the final analysis, the National Foreign Intelligence Community is a support element, not a command or policy element. As such, DoD intelligence entities must meet the demands of their customers who are the decision and policymakers.

This is reflected in the role of the SECDEF as executive agent for the types of intelligence and security concerns listed above. In each of these instances the agency responsible, NSA, operates under the guidance of the DCI, but its command line runs through the SECDEF to the President.[18]

To accomplish this mission as leader of the Defense intelligence community, then, the SECDEF has established within the Office of the Secretary of Defense a variety of offices that have direct or tangential interest in, or oversight of, the community on behalf of the SECDEF. The first of these elements is the Assistant Secretary of Defense for Command, Control, Communications and Intelligence (ASD/C^3I), a new office established on January 29, 1985.

The function of this office is to review and identify intelligence issues for the Secretary of Defense. This is a broad charter that serves to describe the placement of all C^3I functions "under one head in order to insure consistency of DoD policy development, resource management and program evaluation...," and covers all DoD areas of C^3I-related space systems, security of communications and computers, and staff supervision over DIA and NSA/CSS.[19]

At the national level, the ASD (C^3I) represents the SECDEF "... as the principal DoD member on the National Foreign

Intelligence Council, as the alternate DoD member for issues involving foreign intelligence on the Senior Interagency Group-Intelligence (SIG-I), and as the DoD member of the SIG-I Interagency Group on Intelligence and the SIG-I Committee on Intelligence Priorities ...." However, counterintelligence and security policy, and chairmanship of the Interagency Group-Countermeasures (adjunct of the Senior Interagency Group-Intelligence) has been retained by the Under Secretary of Defense (Policy) (USD/P).[20]

As coherent as this organization appears, there still remains a large amount of divided power in the new arrangement. The Assistant Secretary of Defense for Force Management and Personnel, the Under Secretary of Defense for Research and Engineering, and the Assistant Secretary of Defense for Acquisition and Logistics all have considerable influence in their respective title areas over intelligence affairs and concerns.

The final responsibility of OSD is legal oversight of intelligence activities. As a result of investigations of the NFIC in the early and mid-1970s, elaborate oversight mechanisms have been established by Congress and the President to ensure the fourth amendment rights of U.S. citizens. All members of the NFIC have offices to administer and to oversee these processes. Within OSD the responsible office is the Assistant to the Secretary of Defense for Intelligence Oversight (ATSD/IO). This office oversees subordinate mechanisms present in all DoD intelligence units and agencies and serves to protect all citizens, resident aliens, and U.S. corporations from inappropriate surveillance by the DoD intelligence community.[21]

SUMMARY

In retrospect the defense intelligence community may seem to be a group of organizations which are too numerous, active, spread out and ill-defined to be called a "community." In truth "community" may be too strong a word; perhaps "confederacy" is more appropriate. However, as circumstances would have it, community as a concept which unites the U.S. intelligence effort is a necessity for success, if not for national survival. And the concept of community goes beyond shared purpose to include an even more critical element: shared assets. In today's highly technical and therefore staggeringly expensive world of intelligence, neither the members of the U.S. National Foreign Intelligence Community nor their host departments can afford to maintain a self-sufficient, comprehensive, or wholly independent intelligence capability.

The only reasonable way to address the modern-day international information needs of the government is what exists today: a community of foreign intelligence agencies both inside and outside the Department of Defense. This is not to suggest that refinements to the system are not needed, advisable, or required--rarely in the history of government, if ever, has there existed a perfect bureaucracy. However, whatever tinkering needs to be done, on whatever scale, should be undertaken with the greatest of care so as not to damage the basic concept upon which the current effort is founded. The recent reorganization within OSD, the delegated production system managed by DIA, and the shared "hi-tech" assets of the Defense Department intelligence community are all signs of a basically healthy and vitally important institution.

NOTES

1. This is now (1985), and usually has been, the practice. However, there have been exceptions. Most recently, Secretary Weinberger, after the resignation of DEPSECDEF Thayer, stated that he (Weinberger) would maintain the portfolio. He later relented.

2. The President, "United States Intelligence Activities," Executive Order 12333, Federal Register 46, No. 235, 5 December 1981, Section 1.11.

3. Ibid., Section 3.4 (f). See also: U.S. Congress, Senate, 94th Cong., 2nd Sess., Foreign and Military Intelligence, Book I - Final Report 94-755, April 26, 1976, p. 462.

4. CIA was established by legislation, the National Security Act of 1947; with the exception of NSA all other agencies exist by virtue of departmental order, e.g., Department of State directives established the intelligence arm of that Department, INR. Additionally, neither of the other intelligence disciplines, human intelligence (HUMINT) nor imagery intelligence (IMINT), has a single individual, an executive agent, assigned as its government-wide "tsar."

5. Executive Order 12333, Section 1.12 (b) (7) (8).

6. Ibid., Sec. 1.12 (b) (2).

7. Ibid., Sec. 1.12 (b) (3) (4) (5) (6).

8. Ibid., Sec. 1.12 (b) (8), (9).

9. All descriptions of the Directorates within DIA are taken from DRS-2600-926-85, _DIA Organization, Mission and Key Personnel_ (Washington, D.C.: Defense Intelligence Agency, April 1985).

10. DoD Directive 5105.21, August 1, 1961.

11. DRS-2600-926A-84.

12. _Air Force Magazine_ (May 1985): 154.

13. Executive Order 12333, Sec. 1.12 (a) (1) (2) (3) (4) (5).

14. Ibid., Secs. 1.3 (a) (3) (4), 1.11 (i), and DoD Directive 5105.21.

15. INSCOM, Public Affairs Office, Flier (no date).

16. *Air Force Magazine*, p. 154.

17. Executive Order 12333, Sec. 1.11 (j).

18. Ibid., Sec. 1.11 (e) and 1.12 (b) (1) (3) (4) (5) (7) (8) (12).

19. Secretary of Defense Statement, 29 January 1985.

20. DoD Memorandum for Director, Central Intelligence, "Centralization of OSD Intelligence Functions," March 20, 1985. For a complete description of the responsibilities of the SIG-I, see: *National Security Council*, Statement on the Issuance of a Presidential Directive, January 12, 1982. By way of synopsis of this document, the SIG-I functions as the senior-level review panel on intelligence matters for the National Security Council.

21. DoD Directive 5240.1, and DoD Directive 5148.11.

Part 2

Collection

3
Signals Intelligence
David L. Christianson

Twenty-three hundred years ago, the Chinese military scholar Sun Tzu wrote in his <u>The Art of War</u>, "Now the reason the enlightened prince and the wise general conquer the enemy whenever they move and their achievements surpass those of ordinary men is foreknowledge."[1] Providing foreknowledge of both potential and realized enemy goals, strategies, doctrine, tactics, capabilities, and intentions has been and remains the driving force behind the creation and operations of intelligence organizations regardless of the country or cause they support. Intelligence organizations provide foreknowledge to the national leadership (the "princes") and military commanders (the "generals") by gathering intelligence information from a myriad of sources, evaluating this information to determine its accuracy, analyzing the information from all available sources, and finally producing and disseminating an intelligence product or report to the consumer. There is no ultimate source of intelligence information which is always correct or totally comprehensive. Good intelligence <u>always</u> requires multiple sources as inputs to the analytical equation to broaden the scope of the intelligence product as well as to limit the possibility of enemy deception through the manipulation of a single source of intelligence information. With this caveat about the reliability of information from all single sources clearly in mind, this chapter will provide a general description of Signals Intelligence collection and the role it plays in the intelligence production cycle.

DEFINITION OF TERMS

Signals Intelligence, hereafter referred to by its acronym SIGINT, is intelligence information derived from the following three specific collection disciplines. First and perhaps best known is communications intelligence or COMINT. COMINT is technical and intelligence information derived from the "intercept" (listening to) of foreign communications by <u>other than the intended recipients</u>; it does not include the monitoring of foreign public media or the intercept of communications obtained during the course of counterintelligence investigations within the United States.

The second intelligence collection discipline covered by SIGINT is electronic intelligence or ELINT. ELINT consists of technical and intelligence information derived from <u>foreign</u>

noncommunications electromagnetic radiations emanating from <u>other than atomic detonation or radioactive sources</u>. It does not include information derived from friendly radars (which would be radar intelligence or RADINT) or nuclear radiation (which is nuclear intelligence or NUCINT).

The third and final discipline within SIGINT is foreign instrumentation signals intelligence, FISINT (pronounced fizz-int). Although FISINT appears to fall under the definition of ELINT, FISINT is specifically concerned with electromagnetic emissions associated with the testing and operational deployment on non-U.S. aerospace, surface, and subsurface systems which may have either military or civilian application; it includes but is not limited to the collection of signals from telemetry beaconry, electronic interrogators, tracking/fusing/arming/command systems, and video data links. If we were to put this definition into English, we would say, "FISINT is that collection discipline within SIGINT which is <u>primarily</u> concerned with foreign weapons development such as missile testing."

By now you have discovered, perhaps to your own dismay, that the intelligence profession has, as do other professions, a highly refined professional language or "jargon." As in other professions, the language of intelligence with its specific definitions helps intelligence professionals communicate with one another in a concise, efficient manner. Knowledge of intelligence jargon is required of anyone who intends to work in the intelligence field. Also, by reading the definitions of SIGINT and its components, you have become aware of another aspect of intelligence: there are many more sources of intelligence information than SIGINT and the two collection disciplines of human intelligence and imagery intelligence. There are at least a score more other collection disciplines (such as, NUCINT, RADINT, etc.) which will be discussed. It is the constant evaluation and merging of information from multiple sources which produce the finished intelligence product.

COLLECTION

How is SIGINT collected? Basically, all SIGINT collection (regardless of whether it is COMINT, ELINT, or FISINT) is the same. First, the collector must have a radio receiver capable of collecting or receiving the signal. In other words, the collector must have a radio which will operate on the specific frequency and be able to receive the type of signal desired. In addition to having the correct kind of equipment, the radio receiver and antennae must be within range of the enemy transmitter. In many cases, such as very high frequency (VHF) communications, the collector's radio receiver must be within a line-of-sight of the enemy transmitter. The propagation of electromagnetic energy, regardless of whether it is radar energy or a communications transmitter, is dependent on many factors, including the frequency used, the power of the source, the antennae size and shape, and directivity as well as a host of other factors. It is the factor of electromagnetic propagation that required the USS Liberty and USS Pueblo to sail near hostile waters to conduct their intelligence collection missions in the late 1960s. To use a commercial analogy, it is now possible for individuals to purchase television programs relayed or transmitted by satellites. This is possible because the satellite transmits a clear or unencrypted signal to a specific area on the earth (this area is called a "footprint"), which includes the continental United States. If one moves to Australia, his satellite receiver will not pick up U.S. commercial television because it will be outside the proper "footprint." In summary, to collect SIGINT, one must have a receiver capable of operating on the current frequency, capable of receiving the correct type of signal, and within the range of the enemy transmitter.

Now let us discuss the various types of communications intelligence collection. Perhaps the most common form of communications is voice signals. Voice communications are a rapid means of passing orders, reports, and other information. Voice communications, often used by tactical military units, are frequently the only means of communications aboard aircraft. Although voice communications are often found at the lowest levels of an enemy's organization, they are also used by the highest levels of government for speed and simplicity. We can assume that the telephone communications between President Reagan and Secretary of State Haig reported in the press during the Falkland Islands War were probably intercepted by foreign, potentially hostile COMINT collectors as well as the domestic press. Voice communications are often of low power and short range, which require that the intercept receiver be very close to the transmitter to collect the signal. Additionally, in a military operation, the voice messages intercepted will invariably be in a foreign language, which require a translator.

A major type of communications still used throughout the world today is morse code because it is simple, reliable, and has a high degree of resistance to interference and jamming. The major drawback is its slow speed; however, morse code communications systems usually have a greater propagation range than voice and can therefore be intercepted at greater distances from the transmitter.

The radioteletype, or RATT as it is commonly called, is another form of communications. RATT is used by the AP and UPI news services as well as by a host of other government and commercial users. RATT, like morse code, can usually be received by the proper type of receiving equipment at greater distances than voice communications.

Modern technology has brought us many benefits, including facsimile communications and mutichannel communications. Facsimile communications are commercially available and allow individuals to send copies of letters or drawings electronically across great distances. Like RATT, facsimile communications interception requires compatible receiving equipment. Multichannel communications are actually a combination of all the methods of communications mentioned above. Multichannel communications carry several channels of communications simultaneously and can be mixed (such as combining voice and RATT communications). The major problem with multichannel communications intelligence collection is separating the individual components of the host of signals transmitted simultaneously.

The most difficult forms of communications transmission to intercept are those sent by landline (such as, on some commercial telephones). Unless the system has a radio link, listening to landlines requires the interceptor to be close to some point in the transmission line. Because of this limitation, landline communications offer a high degree of security and resistance to disruptions (such as jamming) to the users. Listening to foreign landline communications is COMINT. If the FBI monitors a telephone as part of a counterintelligence effort, it is performing electronic surveillance, not COMINT.

SIGNALS PROCESSING

Collecting the communications signals is only the first step in the collection process. The signal must be processed or evaluated to discern its meaning. If the communications are in a foreign language, a translator must be used. Unfortunately, the collected information may be of poor quality or may deal with a specific subject area with a distinctive professional jargon. These two possibilities--as well as many others--can make the task of the translator considerably more difficult than simply translating text or clear voice, a service performed by a translator at the United Nations, for example.

Another form of communications intercept processing is cryptanalysis. Cryptanalysis (sometimes called CA) involves converting encrypted messages into plain text <u>without</u> initial knowledge of the system or key employed in the encryption. A cryptanalyst is an expert cryptologist who is knowledgeable in the techniques employed to encrypt or encode information so that even if the information is intercepted by the enemy, it will be useless. The cryptanalyst then uses this cryptology background in an attempt to "break" a code or cryptosystem. Cryptanalysis was performed by the United States in the Revolutionary War, Civil War, and World War I--and almost continually since then. From 1929 to 1932, there was a hiatus of cryptanalytic activity because President Hoover's Secretary of State, Henry L. Stimson, believed that "Gentlemen do not read each others mail," and that world peace was dependent on an atmosphere of trust and confidence. It is ironic that Stimson, as Secretary of War during World War II, was a beneficiary of the successful British cryptanalysis of the German Enigma machine cypher and by the American breaking of the Japanese "Purple" machine cypher. A key lesson of cryptanalysis was also learned during this period. When Stimson ordered the operations of the "American Black Chamber" (the code-breaking operation) to stop, the newly unemployed head of the operation,

Herbert O. Yardley, authored a book entitled <u>The American Black Chamber</u> in which he wrote:

> We solved over forty-five thousand cryptograms from 1917 to 1929, and at one time or another we broke the codes of Argentina, Brazil, Chile, China, Costa Rica, Cuba, England, France, Germany, Japan, Liberia, Mexico, Nicaragua, Panama, Peru, Russia, San Salvador, Santo Domingo, Soviet Union, and Spain.[2]

The lesson was that when these countries became aware that the United States was reading their codes, they stopped using them and began employing more sophisticated enciphering techniques. For this reason, cryptanalytic successes are perhaps one of any country's most closely held secrets, and security considerations force the cryptanalysts responsible to remain a legion of unsung national heroes.

When cryptanalysts are not successful in breaking intercepted codes or ciphers, valuable intelligence information can still be obtained through traffic analysis, or TA, as it is sometimes referred to. Traffic analysis is that cryptologic processing discipline which develops information from communication structures and the organizations they serve. The process involves the study of message traffic and related material and the reconstruction of communication plans to produce signals intelligence information. If we were to use the analogy of a letter, TA is that information on the outside of the envelope. This includes such things as call signs, precedence, frequency, communications procedures, and so on. From TA, order of battle, urgency, organizational structure, and other forms of useful information can sometimes be gained.

SIGINT ANALYSIS

J. N. Wenger summarized the signals analysis opportunities and problems in 1937 in his <u>Military Study, Communications Intelligence Research Activities</u>, which was declassified in 1982. An excerpt of the study follows:

I ANALYSIS OF PROBLEM

> 5. The far flung interests of great maritime nations today and the intensive operating schedules of their naval forces require the transmission of a vast amount of communications over channels exposed to interception. Since these communications are of necessity intimately concerned with actual policy, control, and administration they obviously constitute the most authoritative, revealing, and timely source of information accessible to our intelligence activities. Moreover, they form a source which can be tapped with the least expense and a

minimum of risk to personnel and to our own national interests.

6. To exploit properly this fertile source of information four essential steps must be performed:

    a. The communications must be intercepted and delivered to analyzing centers;

    b. All possible information must be gleaned from the communications at the analyzing centers;

    c. The information obtained from communications must be carefully collated and interpreted, since intelligence is a cumulative thing and many of the component facts are entirely without significance unless considered in relation to the whole;

    d. The interpreted intelligence must be disseminated to all who require it.

7. Information is obtained from communications by:

    a. Methods involving decryption of the text of messages; and

    b. Methods short of cryptanalysis, i.e., traffic analysis.

The first method has been successfully practiced for centuries. With the advent of machine ciphers and the adoption of increasingly effective security measures as a result of lessons learned in World War (I), it is, however, becoming steadily more difficult; and even now only highly skilled persons aided by complicated analytical machinery are able to cope with the problem. The second method is complications of the cryptanalytical problem. In time of war, codes and ciphers normally used by the enemy will doubtless be changed at once. Solution of the new systems will probably require days if not weeks to accomplish. Meanwhile, unless there be some other means of obtaining it, the flow of intelligence will be stopped at the critical period when the plan of the campaign is being laid and information concerning the enemy is essential to success. Now codes and ciphers may be readily superseded overnight upon the outbreak of war but the <u>Communication System</u> cannot be so easily changed without serious confusion resulting. Since a Navy's communication system and methods of handling traffic are dependent upon the organizations and location of its component forces, it follows that the one may be deduced from the other. Thus, if we know the enemy's communication system and methods of handling traffic, we may obtain the other more vital information. This is difficult for an enemy to prevent, because the absolute necessity for simplicity in a communication system precludes any but an elementary type of cryptographic protection.[3]

Wenger continued his report with an observation about the nature of intelligence information: "No intelligence is of more than historical value unless it is timely...Prompt dissemination calls for fast dependable communication with the Commander-in-Chief and Navy Department."4   Herein lies the classic paradox of the communications intelligence discipline. How does the intelligence organization protect its cryptologic successes in order to preserve the source of information and simultaneously prove the value of this valuable intelligence information to those decisionmakers and military commanders who can exploit the information to the national advantage? One method established in 1942 is found in the wartime files of Brigadier General Carter W. Clarke, which contain a memorandum prepared by Lieutenant Colonel Ervin for Colonel Harold L. Richey entitled "Handling of ULTRA within MIS" (ULTRA was a codeword used to describe the intercept and breaking of sophisticated German codes and ciphers). Lieutenant Colonel Ervin wrote:

> ...the stringent rules of dissemination of Ultra do and should prevent widespread distribution of such reports. Nevertheless such secret publications as the "Weekly Far East Review" are prepared by research analysts who have the benefit of Ultra in writing the report. As a consequence, if there is questionable information from Military Attaches about a situation on which we have the cold dope from Ultra, the final report that goes out on a secret level will not use the questionable information from the secret source, or will present it in such a way that the proper evaluation of the true situation is apparent. The "hidden use" of Ultra is one of the most valuable contributions that the new organization of MIS developed.[5]

ELECTRONIC INTELLIGENCE (ELINT)

The second component of SIGINT is ELINT. Hostile radar beams, beacons, and other noncommunication signals differ from communications signals in that they do not carry information. The information from a radar is developed by the radar receiver and its associated viewing scope. In the performance of the ELINT function, the source of the signal can be located by direction finding. (By optimizing the antennae of an intercept receiver, the intercept operator can derive the direction from the intercept antennae toward the transmitter being monitored. This is called Radio Direction Finding (RDF) and is applicable to all SIGINT collection components.) Recording radar signals may be as simple as an operator's recording information on a log sheet or it may be recorded on magnetic tape or other means. During the processing phase, the signal is identified and related to a certain type of unit. For example, a hostile radar signal is detected and recorded and the characteristics of the signal match those of a known type of air defense system. If we have information on the units that use this radar, we can determine the approximate location of a certain type of defense unit. If the signal is of an unknown type, it is analyzed and an initial determination made as to the function of the signal and its origin.

ELINT collection and processing can provide an Electronic Order of Battle as well as a technical data base of information which can be used in creating an electronic warfare capability. Electronic Warfare (EW) involves the use of electromagnetic energy to determine, exploit, reduce, or prevent hostile use of the electromagnetic spectrum. Malcolm W. Browne describes one application of ELINT in <u>Discover</u> magazine, in an article entitled "Video Warfare Over Lebanon." Describing the capabilities of the Grumman E2C "Hawkeye," a radar surveillance plane similar to but much smaller than the USAF AWAC aircraft, he says:

> The Hawkeye's other main sensor, its passive radar system (the ALR-59), can see twice as far (as the plane's radar). It eavesdrops on all radar emitters within about four hundred miles. Fed by antennas in the nose, tail, and belly of the Hawkeye, the passive detection system tells the computer the direction of a distant radar signal, but more important, it analyzes the signal the way a detective would analyze a fingerprint. Radar sets are engineered for specific tasks, and different airplanes, ships, missile sites, and gun emplacements emit their own radar "signatures." The unique character of each is determined by its carrier-wave frequency, the duration and shape of its pulses, and the rate at which the pulses are repeated. The signatures are so distinctive, in fact, that a computer can easily distinguish between the radars of a MiG-21 fighter, a long-range Soviet Tu-142 Bear reconnaissance bomber, or a Kresta-class Soviet warship. So the Hawkeye computer can sort out these targets, its memory contains an intelligence library with the latest and best information about the characteristics of every radar set in the world. By comparing the signals picked up by the Hawkeye's antennas with this library, the computer can instantly identify almost any radar emitter and assign it an appropriate symbol on the operator's screen.[6]

ELINT is divided into two subcategories: Operational ELINT and Technical ELINT. Operational ELINT determines the locations and readiness of target emitters. The Hawkeye example illustrates operational ELINT. Technical ELINT determines the capabilities and limitations of target emitters and provides the information for the Hawkeye's computer data base.

There is a commercial application of these two ELINT categories. Automobile drivers in the United States can readily purchase a radar warning receiver which will activate a light or buzzer when it detects speed-measuring radars, which are used by police throughout the country. When the receiver detects a policeman's radar, it tells the driver that a radar is ahead of him along the road (location) and that it is actively seeking speeders (readiness); thus, the receiver provides operational ELINT. On the other hand, the design and development of such receivers require detailed specific information on the design and operating modes of the speed-measuring radar sets. Thus, the producers of the radar warning receivers require technical ELINT to be able to manufacture and market a successful radar warning receiver.

A word of caution is appropriate to those drivers with radar warning receivers as well as military commanders. If the radar operator changes the radar's characteristics beyond the design capability of your receiver, your receiver will not recognize (indeed, may not even detect) the radar of interest.

FOREIGN INSTRUMENTATION SIGNALS INTELLIGENCE (FISINT)

In introducing SIGINT at the beginning of this chapter, a specific as well as a general definition of FISINT was provided. Although FISINT is concerned with a multitude of systems operations and development, perhaps the best and most significant subcategory of FISINT is telemetry intelligence (TELINT). TELINT concerns that technical and intelligence information derived from the intercept processing and analysis of foreign telemetry. Telemetry is an important part of a missile development program; during missile tests, data about the missile's performance are transmitted from the missile to a ground control facility. With telemetry data, the scientists involved can assess the operational performance of a missile, evaluate its overall performance capability in comparison to design specifications, and also gain insights into the probable causes of missile failures. Continued access to telemetry data from Soviet missile tests is considered to be essential to verification of compliance with strategic arms limitations treaties; in fact, the United States insisted during the SALT II negotiations that the treaty bar "the encryption or encoding of crucial missile test information."

A WARNING TO THE READER

From the above discussion, one might be impressed with the advantages of SIGINT as a source of intelligence information, since it is covert and usually reliable. However, there are some drawbacks. First, SIGINT is a passive collection discipline. If the collection target fails to activate his radars or communications transmitters, then nothing will be received. Also, certain high interest communications may be missed because receivers capable of intercepting the signal have not been developed.

Second, if the SIGINT collection target becomes aware that his signals are being intercepted, he may inject "bogus" information into his communications in order to deceive the interceptor. Heavy reliance on any single source of information will always make intelligence subject to deception--with possible disastrous results during a conflict. Also, this need for security severely limits the use of SIGINT to only those with a valid "need to know."

Third, the signals that an enemy employs during peacetime will probably be modified at the commencement of hostilities in order to deny intelligence information when it is needed most critically.

SIGINT IN THE ANALYTICAL PROCESS

The following is a case study contained in the papers from the personal files of Alfred McCormack, who was in charge of the SIGINT operations of the U.S. Army during World War II. The case study was prepared, in memorandum form, by Colonel McCormack for the Chief, Military Intelligence Service. It is reproduced here as an example of the role of SIGINT in the analytical process:

31 Aug 1944

MEMORANDUM FOR THE CHIEF, MIS:

Subject: A Case Study in Intelligence

1. The purposes of this memorandum are:

    a. To illustrate what kind of intelligence research is involved in Ultra;

    b. To show how erroneous is the view, which keeps cropping up in MIS, that there are two separate kinds and sources of intelligence, Ultra and non-Ultra;

    c. To demonstrate again why top-flight talent is required for the fact-finding work which is the foundation of all intelligence production.

2. The research problem in the case was: Are the Japanese manufacturing aircraft in Manchuria and, if so, what types and what components?

3. Evidence bearing on the problem as of 1 Apr 44 was:

    a. *Evidence pro*: Pre-war evidence of the existence of something called the "Manchuria Aircraft Company."

    b. *Evidence con*: The Airind Unit, after examining 30,000 name-plates from combat aircraft, had not identified a single plane or component as having been manufactured in Manchuria. It was considered possible that training planes might be manufactured in Manchuria, but there was no evidence on the point.

4. In April a study of Ultra items revealed a "Manchuria Air Depot" which was originating messages at Mukden.

Traffic of this Depot was assembled with a view to determining where it fitted into the Japanese air picture. Sufficient evidence was collected to establish a flow of a type of plane called "Type 2 Single Engine Advanced Trainer" out of the Mukden Depot to points in Manchuria, China, Formosa, the Philippines, Malaya and Java, and even Japan. This led to the tentative conclusion that the planes going out of the Depot had been manufactured in Manchuria and not in Japan, since Mukden was off the air routes from Japan to most of the delivery areas, and since neither trainer planes manufactured in Japan, nor planes assembled at Mukden out of components shipped from Japan, would be likely to be flowing back from Manchuria to training units in Japan.

5. The next problem was to determine whether the engines for these planes were manufactured in Manchuria or shipped from Japan. A study was made of traffic relating to shipments from Japan to Manchuria; it was determined that propellers, landing gear and other components were being shipped, but the traffic contained no references to engines. From this fact it was concluded that the engines were being manufactured locally.

6. The next problems were:

   a. To obtain information about the Type 2 Single Engine Advanced trainer, about which nothing was known except its name, and to determine the rate of production of these planes in Manchuria;

   b. To locate the factory or factories where they were being made; and

   c. To locate the Manchuria Air Depot.

7. With respect to the number of planes being manufactured, evidence was assembled to show that in a period of 25 days in May, the Manchuria Air Depot was to deliver 105 planes to its 2 principal customers; and this, plus a request for tail wheels (including a reference to salvaged wheels and to future needs of 140 per month) was thought to indicate a current monthly output of around 150 aircraft. Subsequent traffic is expected to furnish more evidence on this point.

8. The location of the factory and depot was accomplished (and Type 2 SEAT's were identified as the only planes involved) by interpretation of the first aerial photos of the Mukden area; but the point to be made here is that the photos would have told us nothing

but for the painstaking and imaginative work done before the photo reconnaissance occurred.

9. The story is a striking example of the synthesis of intelligence from many sources and of the importance of imaginative "detective work" in this kind of activity.

10. The story commenced with obscure messages employing an abbreviation "Man-Pi"--"Man" probably for Manchuria, "Pi" for some unknown word. A study of these messages suggested that Man-Pi was a manufacturer of aircraft, almost certainly in Manchuria. But no available compilation of factory or company names threw any light on the meaning of the abbreviation. Neither A-2 nor FEA could help; nor could the Japanese linguists.

11. Then a new abbreviation--"Man-Hi"--appeared in the messages. This was a little more significant, since Manshu Hikoki K.K. means Manchuria Aircraft Company, but still the evidence was inconclusive. However, the traffic did turn up a direct reference to the manufacture by Man-Hi of Type 2 Single Engine Advance Trainers, the type of trainer supplied by the Manchuria Air Depot.

12. Attention was then focused on a search for the meanings of Man-Pi and Man-Hi. All leads proved fruitless, both within and outside MIS, until the officer working on the problem chanced upon a document that solved it all at once. Digging through A-2 files on Japanese aircraft matters he came upon a translation of a letter taken from the Mitsubishi files in New York, which had been found and translated by the MIS (repeat MIS) New York Office. This letter contained the direct statement that both "Man-Pi and "Man-Hi" were abbreviations for Manshu Hikoki K.K.

13. Thus the 3 possible manufacturers of planes in Manchuria--Man-Pi, Man-Hi and the Manchuria Aircraft company--were determined to be one and the same; and that one was established as (a) the source of planes moving out of the Air Depot at Mukden and (b) a manufacturer of Type 2 Advanced Trainers.

14. A Mukden street address for the Manchuria Aircraft company was obtained. But it was in Japanese; all the available maps gave the street names in Chinese; and the linguists could not tie the Japanese name to any street shown on the map. A search was then made for either (a) a map in Japanese or (b) the address in Chinese. The latter was successful; the Chinese address was found in a Japanese yearbook. Thus the presumed location was pinpointed on a map of Mukden.

15. A search for evidence locating the Air Depot was then made. It was not successful, but it did turn up a document captured in Hollandia (translated by ATIS) consisting of instructions to a person who was going to inspect the Depot. They included a convenient sketch of the Depot and its 72 buildings, with a descriptive title for each building, e.g., "No. 9 Warehouse," "Automobile Garage," "Training Unit," "Dispensary," etc.

16. At that point we were ready for the aerial photos; and on 19 June the 14th Air Force sent a P-38 on a photo reconnaissance mission over the Mukden area. In due course the photos arrived.

17. A shot was found covering the street where the Manchuria Aircraft Company was supposed to be. It showed buildings suitable to the manufacture of trainer aircraft, with an adjacent airfield. On the field and around the factory there were 125 small planes. The first interpretation of this photo was that the planes on the field were biplanes. This was staggering news, since if the backbone of JAAF advanced training were a biplane, the training program would obviously be inadequate to prepare pilots for combat. The point was called to the interpreters' attention and the pictures were reexamined. One shot was found showing the planes in a favorable light, and they were definitely identified as monoplanes. The impresssion of biplanes had been caused by light effects on the closely parked trainers.

18. A close study of the photos showed that about 40 of the planes on the factory field had engines, while the other 85 did not. This fact, plus the fact that the factory had no vents of the type that would be expected if the operation involved the construction and testing of motors, was considered to show that the motors were manufactured somewhere else in the Mukden area.

19. A study of all the photos of the Mukden area was then undertaken, in an effort to locate the Manchuria Air Depot, by reference to the Hollandia diagram of its buildings. It was located about 7 miles W of the Manchuria Aircraft Company's factory; comparison of the diagram with the pictures left no doubt of the identification. Around the shops of the Depot were 15 planes identical with those of the Manchuria Aircraft Company's factory.

20. To summarize the principal results of the "research" outlined above:

a. The Manchuria Aircraft Company at Mukden has been established as a manufacturer of Type 2 Single Engine Advanced Trainers, and a tentative estimate of its production had been made possible.

b. A factory (and apparently the only factory) of this company manufacturing Type 2 Trainers has been pinpointed.

c. It has been concluded that the engines for these planes are probably being manufactured in Manchuria, but not at the Manchuria Aircraft Company's factory.

d. The activities of the Manchuria Air Depot have been determined; and its location, including the location of each of its 72 buildings, has been pinpointed.

e. The aircraft appearing in the Mukden photos have been identified as Type 2 Advanced Trainers, about which previously there was no information; the approximate dimensions of this type of plane have been determined; silhouettes of these planes for recognition purposes are now being prepared and will be shipped to the theaters.

f. The information now available about the Type 2 Trainers will permit interpretation of aerial photos of trainer bases on Formosa. The photos, now en route to Washington, are expected to throw light on the progress of the training program, since it is known where the trainer bases on Formosa are located and what planes their establishment calls for.

21. The preceding paragraph lists what might be called completed intelligence. However, in the course of the work much other valuable information has been picked up. The details would involve too much explanation, but among the subjects on which such information has a bearing are the following:

a. The flow of training planes to Flight Training Units;

b. Identifications of Flight Training Units and their locations;

c. Whether the Type 2 Advanced Trainer is (as it now appears to be) the only SEAT being manufactured and supplied to Flight Training Units;

    d. The ability of the Japanese to furnish components for the planes made at Mukden;

    e. Whether a twin-engine plane (now identified) is the only SEAT now being manufactured and furnished to Flight Training Units, and whether it can be shown that this plane is manufactured in Japan.

    22. This memorandum has been stencilled for use in our training program for new officers. Hence it is pointed out that the above is not an unusual case, but merely a dramatic example of what goes on every day in this work. Almost every issue of the FES contains some simple statement of fact--e.g., that two Air Divisions have moved from the Kuriles to the Nanseis; that a new Area Army has been identified; that certain ships of specified tonnages have been sunk; that a new type of unit has been identified; or that strength estimates for an area have been revised--where the basis for the conclusion may have involved at least as much painstaking and imaginative work as in the case described above--and in many instances harder work, over a much longer period of time, and with less spectacular results.

    23. Furthermore, in many cases of the hardest work, no definite results are produced, at least for a long time, but when results appear they are very rewarding.

                        Alfred McCormack
                        Colonel, G.S.C.
                        Director of Intelligence MIS[7]

From the foregoing, you can see that without SIGINT, the analysis would not and could not have been performed; however, SIGINT by itself provided insufficient information for comprehensive analysis.

You are now aware of the fundamentals of signals intelligence. Remember, however, that these fundamentals are also known to all potential adversaries. Regardless of whether you deal with political, economic, or military information, whenever you speak, someone hostile to your interests may be listening.

NOTES

1. Sun Tzu, The Art of War, trans. Samuel B. Griffith (New York: Oxford University Press, 1977), p. 144.

2. Herbert O. Yardley, The American Black Chamber (Indianapolis: Bobbs-Merrill, 1931), p. 235.

3. J.N. Wenger, <u>Military Study, Communications Intelligence Research Activities</u>, SRH-151 (Washington: National Archives, 1937), pp. 7-9.

4. Ibid., p. 8.

5. Lieutenant Colonel Ervin, <u>Handling of ULTRA Within the Military Intelligence Service (MIS) 1941-1945</u>, SRH-146 (Washington: National Archives, 1946), p. 6.

6. Malcolm W. Browne, "Video Warfare Over Lebanon," <u>Discover</u> (August 1982): 92.

7. Alfred McCormack, <u>Papers from the Personal Files of Alfred McCormack, Colonel, AUS Special Branch, G-2, Military Intelligence Branch, War Department</u>, SRH-141 Part 2 (Washington: National Archives, 1944), pp. 319-29.

4
Human Source Intelligence

Jack E. Thomas

HUMINT, the acronym for "human source intelligence," has two aspects. One is the activity which is involved in the collection of information of foreign intelligence value by the use of human sources, whether overt or clandestine.[1] The other is a descriptor of the intelligence thus obtained. This chapter deals with the collection of that intelligence.

INTRODUCTION

Acquiring information by technical means such as sophisticated cameras and electronic sensors is a relatively new development. However, using human sources to acquire information about hostile or potentially hostile nations or groups is almost as old as mankind. HUMINT was born the first time that a posted guard ceased to be a passive sentry and moved out to determine whether strangers were approaching the cave which he was protecting.

The essential nature of intelligence (i.e., information) to military success has been recognized since mankind first began to keep records. The needed information had to be collected by human sources. The instructions of Moses to the twelve secret agents whom he sent into the land of Canaan are applicable today:

> Get you up this way southward, and go
> up into the mountain.
>
> And see the land what it is; and the
> people that dwelleth therein, whether
> they be strong or weak, few or many;
>
> And what the land is that they dwell
> in, whether it be good or bad, and
> what cities they be that they dwell
> in, whether in tents or in strong holds;
>
> And what the land is, whether it be flat
> or lean, whether there be wood therein
> or not.[2]

Hannibal successfully maintained his forces in Italy for fifteen years, in considerable part because of the effectiveness of his spies. Caesar invaded England only after his scouts had gathered the information which the Roman legions needed. Napoleon's successes were built, in part, on his knowledge of enemy resources and plans, which was provided by agents of the "Bureau of Secret Police." The Prussians expanded the Napoleonic system and created a peacetime Department of Intelligence in the war office that in 1821 became an independent department which reported directly to the King. A secret agent network in France provided Prussia with the information needed for quick success in the War of 1870. General Washington ably developed intelligence sources during the American Revolution, but there was no follow-on in the young nation.[3] When the Civil War occurred neither the North nor the South was familiar with the topography or even the road systems over which their forces had to operate. Not until 1882, when the United States Navy established what is now the Office of Naval Intelligence, did the United States have an agency in peacetime to collect information about the military affairs of foreign governments.[4]

The thoroughness of Germany's intelligence-gathering capabilities stood that country in good stead in World War I. In marked contrast, the fledgling efforts that had appeared in the United States Army and Navy toward the close of the 19th century did not prepare the United States to cope with the exploding nature of intelligence requirements in a major war.

The U.S. intelligence effort as a whole, not merely its HUMINT elements, fared quite badly during the years between World Wars I and II. In terms of having intelligence organizations capable of expanding to respond to wartime needs and having the intelligence information base on which to build to meet wartime responsibilities, the United States was little better off at the onset of the Second World War than it had been in 1917. Fortunately, the British willingly shared both intelligence and trained personnel to help launch the U.S. military intelligence effort.

What has happened to United States intelligence since World War II ended and the Cold War began and the response of the United States to its postwar "super-power" status are in part the topic of this book. While the development of the United States HUMINT capabilities cannot be described as the major facet of the evolution of United States intelligence capabilities over the past thirty-five years, it has been important.

THE SCOPE OF HUMINT ACTIVITIES

HUMINT, or human source intelligence, is a simple generic term that gives no hint of the variety or the complicated nature of the activities which are conducted under its rubric.

HUMINT activities normally are viewed as either overt or clandestine. <u>Overt collection</u> occurs when the person or organization from or through whom the information is being obtained is aware that the collector is an intelligence officer; or the person or organization allowing access is aware that any information gained may be used for foreign intelligence purposes; or the information is publicly available.[5] <u>Clandestine collection</u> occurs when the person who obtains the information and passes it on to the intelligence collection organization does so as a secret agent, without knowledge or awareness on the part of the person or organization that originated the information or is responsible for its safekeeping; or the person who provides the information is deliberately kept from awareness that the recipient is affiliated with an intelligence organization; or the information or equipment is acquired by theft, by deliberate subterfuge or illegal purchase, or by use of a covert electronic "bug."

Best known is clandestine HUMINT collection--the "spy" or "espionage" operations which are featured so often in books about the CIA and in numerous works of fiction. Clandestine operators view themselves as the elite of the intelligence profession. Modern clandestine services have developed an elaborate "tradecraft" that includes not only such paraphernalia as secret writing devices, codes, miniature radios, remotely controlled cameras, and the like, but also elaborate guidelines, rules, and principles that guide the recruiting processes, govern the relationships between collectors and their handlers, and are intended to facilitate the maximum exploitation of sources.[6] Some sources are "walk-ins," persons who literally volunteer to provide information secretly, but others can only be identified and recruited on the basis of a carefully developed and executed plan.

The intelligence organization conducts its clandestine field operations through the use of "case officers," professionals who are responsible for directing and handling "agents." Normally, an agent is a foreigner who has volunteered or has been recruited to work in order to obtain, or aid in obtaining, information, documents, or technical equipment needed for intelligence purposes. In most instances the agent will have legitimate access to the information which the case officer is seeking, while the information will be passed through clandestine channels. The case officer normally operates under some kind of "cover," a protective guise intended to prevent exposure of his association with an intelligence organization. Cover is considered to be "official" if the case officer's ostensible assignment is as a government employee who is not affiliated with intelligence activities, or "unofficial" if the cover is not provided by a government agency.

Another type of HUMINT specialist is the interrogator, who systematically draws information from a person that the individual may or may not want to divulge. Prisoner of war interrogation is a specialty that attracts the services of skilled linguists in wartime. In peacetime the primary subjects of interrogations are likely to be defectors, emigres, and refugees who have left their homeland for personal reasons, who may be uncertain as to the kind of reception they can expect, and who recognize that the value of the information they provide may strongly influence the reception accorded them.

The largest peacetime interrogation program in United States history was <u>Project Wringer</u>. It involved the handling of more than a quarter million German POWs on their return from the Soviet Union after World War II and the massive follow-on program of interviewing repatriates, refugees, and illegal border crossers from Eastern Europe into West Germany in the early postwar years.

Skilled interrogators not only need native or near-native language fluency, but also the skills of a psychologist so that they will ask the right questions and will follow up on hints or leads that may be mentioned incidentally by the subject.

Markedly different from the skills needed for clandestine activities and interrogations are those required to promote friendly relations with foreign intelligence security services to obtain intelligence information. This is an activity in which the art of "horse trading" comes into play.

Another important HUMINT opportunity arises from the fact that Americans travel around the world in their personal, professional, and business lives. Valuable intelligence can be volunteered by those who have enough acquaintance with the United States Government and its information needs to recognize what is of intelligence interest when they see or hear it and who later make themselves available for interviews or other types of reporting.

Sometimes, exploiting complicated foreign equipment, particularly if it is related to new weaponry in potentially hostile hands, can pose highly technical testing and evaluation problems that must be handled under extreme time pressures. HUMINT collection organizations normally will not include the type of technical specialists who are needed. Therefore, such specialists should be readily available, virtually on an "on call" basis.

Much valuable information is contained in openly published documents, periodicals, and the news media, but the acquisition of such material is not considered to be a part of the United States human sources collection effort. Instead, the United States Diplomatic Mission in each country is responsible for procuring any publicly available documents, maps, or publications which are needed by the intelligence community.

Likewise, the monitoring of foreign radio and television propaganda and press broadcasts is not carried out as part of the activity of any organization that deals with HUMINT. Such monitoring is the responsibility of the Foreign Broadcast Information Service (FBIS).

Much adverse publicity received by the CIA in recent years has concerned its participation in covert actions, now officially referred to as "special activities."[7] While special activities are conducted, under Presidential direction, by the CIA clandestine service, they are not viewed as intelligence activities.

So much is going on in the world which has some level of intelligence interest to the United States that scooping up everything of possible value which is available to HUMINT collectors would require the time and talents of far more personnel than the intelligence community has available. It is important, therefore, that specific intelligence needs, usually referred to as "requirements," be identified and be tasked on collectors in some order of priority.

Each of the recent presidents of the United States has established a mechanism within the National Security Council structure to provide senior level guidance to the intelligence community. For the past several years, the output has been in terms of questions which concern matters of current interest and topics which warrant continuing attention. Within the intelligence community, the Director of Central Intelligence issues a coordinated listing of topics of intelligence interest and the priority attached to each. This type of guidance is of importance to analysts in production components of the community, for it is they who must determine whether the data bases already hold the necessary information or whether a collection effort is needed to fill information gaps. The problem is to assure that collectors focus on what is knowable but not yet known.

The community's HUMINT mechanism for this is the Director's Human Resources Committee (HRC), established in 1974 as one of more than a dozen committees, composed of representatives of the various community components, that advise and assist the Director of Central Intelligence in executing his community-wide responsibilities.[8] One of the basic tasks of the committee is to identify intelligence requirements that can be collected by human sources and then to develop coordinated plans under which each of the HUMINT collection components accepts responsibility for acquiring the needed information.

Within the Department of Defense, problems requiring intelligence inputs are identified on the military side by the Joint Chiefs of Staff, the Unified and Specified Commands, and their components, and on the civilian side by various elements of the Office of the Secretary of Defense and the senior levels of the military departments. The Secretary of Defense has ordered the Defense Intelligence Agency to "validate, register, assign, recommend priorities for and monitor the satisfaction of DoD collection requirements."[9] For the HUMINT aspects of these tasks, the DIA Directorate for Collection Management has a Human Resources Division.

No arrangements for planning and administering activities that are virtually worldwide in nature can be expected to function without problems. The HUMINT field is no exception. Yet the fact remains that much attention has been paid to establishing means by which intelligence information needs are identified, given relative priorities, and assigned to the HUMINT collection organization which is considered to be most capable of responding to the need.

U.S. HUMINT RESOURCES

In terms of logic, any U.S. official who acquires and reports to his parent department or agency information which concerns the activities, capabilities, or intentions of any foreign government with respect to its relationships with the United States is serving as an "intelligence officer." In actuality, however, U.S. officials who are not directly assigned to an intelligence organization do not view their reporting as constituting "intelligence," even though they recognize that the information itself is or could be of value to intelligence analysts. The distinction between intelligence and non-intelligence reporting on the basis of office of origin has come to have less and less meaning during the past two decades. This is because the problems addressed by intelligence analysts and dealt with in intelligence estimates and other intelligence publications have expanded far beyond the traditional scope of military intelligence and have come to involve ever more complicated problems of political-economic-military interrelationships.

Both historically and currently, U.S. diplomatic personnel stationed abroad have, in particular, assiduously sought to avoid any implication that they are functioning as intelligence officers, even though a very major role of diplomats serving abroad is to acquire and report to the State Department information which is needed as the basis for national-level judgments concerning the United States and the country in which the diplomats are serving.

Viewed in the narrow and legal sense, therefore, the U.S. HUMINT collection resources reside in four organizations: the Directorate of Operations of the Central Intelligence Agency; the Defense Attache System, which is operated by the Defense Intelligence Agency; the HUMINT organizations of the individual military services; and the Intelligence Division of the Federal Bureau of Investigation.

THE CENTRAL INTELLIGENCE AGENCY

The Central Intelligence Agency has the primary responsibility for collecting foreign intelligence by clandestine human sources. This is the basic function of the CIA Directorate of Operations (DDO). The home office is at CIA Headquarters in Langley, Virginia, but there are overseas bases and field stations in many areas of the world.

Ever since the CIA was created, the DDO (sometimes unofficially referred to as the Clandestine Service) and its line predecessors have been the dominant element of CIA, combining the two CIA roles on which most public attention has focused--collecting intelligence by secret human sources and conducting covert operations intended to support policy objectives abroad without any open indication of U.S. involvement.

In the entire history of the CIA, only three of its Directors have been "insiders," promoted to DCI from within the Agency, and all three were from the Clandestine Service.[10] Conducting clandestine intelligence activities successfully involves careful and knowledgeable management of people, which is viewed, apparently, as good preparation for managing CIA overall and providing leadership to the intelligence community.

Nothing in the National Security Act of 1947 states that CIA was to be directly involved in the collection of intelligence,[11] but it is reasonably clear that such a role was intended, or at least not precluded.[12]

When the Office of Strategic Services (OSS), forerunner to the CIA, was formed in World War II, it developed a Secret Intelligence Branch to conduct espionage. When OSS was disbanded in October 1945, its Secret Intelligence and Counterespionage branches were transferred to the War Department and formed the Strategic Services Unit (SSU). In 1946, this was again transferred, this time to the new Central Intelligence Group (CIG) that became the Central Intelligence Agency on passage of the National Security Act of 1947.

At CIA, the SSU became the Office of Special Operations (OSO). The SSU had maintained seven field stations established in North Africa and the Middle East by the wartime OSS, so these were immediately available to CIA with equipment, codes, techniques, and communications facilities intact.[13]

A complicating factor, however, was that although the CIA Office of Special Operations was responsible for espionage and counterespionage, a separate organization, the Office of Policy Coordination (OPC), was formed in 1948 to handle the conduct of covert operations. OPC was attached to the CIA but actually reported directly to the Departments of State and Defense. Competition between OSO and OPC became fierce, and included "competing for the same agents and, not infrequently, attempting to wrest agents from each other."[14] This situation led to the recognition that a reorganization was needed. Thus in 1952, OSO and OPC were integrated at the operational level and were focused into the Plans Directorate (DDP), which in 1973 was redesignated today's Directorate of Operations (DDO).[15]

In the early 1950s, DDP was spending nearly three-fourths of the CIA budget and accounted for three-fifths of all CIA personnel. During that decade DDP gained nearly 2,000 personnel, including support elements.[16] The prominent role of covert actions in the CIA program during the 1950s and 1960s resulted, in considerable measure, in DDP dominance of CIA manning and spending. Even though the effort devoted to covert operations has declined markedly in recent years, DDO continues to be the dominant element of CIA.

During the early years of its operations, CIA's Clandestine Service was highly dependent on acquiring information by means of close liaison with friendly foreign intelligence and security services, but by the 1960s CIA had developed its own sources. The extent of success or failure is, quite naturally, closely held. Only rarely is there any opportunity to glimpse into the inner working of the system. However, this has been provided in open publications by discussion of cases involving such persons as the Soviet GRU officer, Colonel Oleg Penkovskiy, KGB officer Yurly

Ivanovich Nosenko,[17] and GRU Lieutenant Colonel Pyotr Semyonovich Popov.[18]

The Clandestine Service has always functioned as an element isolated from the rest of CIA. The maintenance of security is the primary reason. Activities are severely compartmented, and protecting "sources and methods" is given high precedence.

Functionally, the organization of DDO is a combination of geographic offices that manage the overseas field stations and topical offices which deal with covert action, counterintelligence, and the like--matters that can be looked at on a worldwide rather than an area basis.

An important exception to the clandestine nature of DDO activities is the National Collection Division (NCD), which is responsible for the overt solicitation of information from sources within the United States. These are Americans who know that they are dealing with CIA officers and who, without compensation, are willing to provide information of intelligence interest that they pick up in the course of foreign travel or through foreign business and professional contacts.

Understandably, DDO carefully screens potential recruits. It is interested in candidates who not only have foreign language fluency or a capability to acquire such, but who also have personality characteristics that would serve the Clandestine Service well. DDO also is looking for long-term employees. A revolving-door atmosphere would not be conducive to maintaining the security consciousness that DDO fosters, and acquiring the experience and skills which are needed for effective clandestine collection through human sources takes time.

THE DEFENSE ATTACHE SYSTEM

The activities of military, naval, and air attaches provide a geographically extensive opportunity for overtly acquiring HUMINT of military importance. In the United States Government they function as a jointly-manned Defense Attache System (DAS). The Defense Attaches (DATTs) and the Assistant Defense Attaches are now assigned to nearly 100 countries. They make no secret of the fact that they are intelligence officers, diplomatically accredited to the host country, to be sure, but still there as observers and reporters on matters of military intelligence interest.

The use of military personnel as "attaches" is centuries old, but U.S. entry into the field did not occur until almost the end of the nineteenth century.[19] Not until 1880 did Congress authorize appointing military and naval attaches to diplomatic missions. The following year, there were appointments to the capitals of England, France, Germany, Russia, and Austria; to Italy in 1890; Belgium, in 1892; Spain in 1893; and Japan and Mexico in 1894.[20]

Sixteen military attaches were abroad at the start of the Spanish-American War,[21] but in 1898 Congress set the limit at ten. Service pressures grew, however, and by the beginning of World War

I, there were thirty-one U.S. attaches overseas--twenty-three military and eight naval.[22] Expansion was almost nonexistent in the postwar years, and as late as 1936 the United States had only thirty-four attaches.[23] Some expansion occurred just prior to World War II. There were nine attaches each in Berlin, London, and Paris by 1939, and even a military attache in Afghanistan, who was described as the "first American diplomat" in that country.[24] Although the Air Force did not become a separate service until 1947, even before World War II the Army had "air" attaches in London, Paris, and Rome.

A big expansion occurred after World War II. By 1948 the Army and Air Force had 258 officers and fifty-five warrant officers on attache duty in fifty-nine countries, and the Navy had 120 officers in forty-three countries.[25] Enlisted supporting staff exceeded the officer strength. By 1959 the Army alone had 476 personnel in sixty-eight overseas attache offices serving seventy countries.[26]

The proliferation of attaches and Secretary of Defense McNamara's wish to place the military intelligence responsibilities in the new Defense Intelligence Agency led, in 1964, to the Secretary's designating one attache in each U.S. Embassy as the senior Defense Department representative and to his decision to direct that these attaches report to the Secretary through the Joint Chiefs of Staff.[27]

This system remains in effect, with the Defense Intelligence Agency providing central management.[28] Thus, instead of separate Army, Navy, and Air Attaches, the United States has Defense Attaches (DATTs). Normally, there are one or more Assistant Defense Attaches in most countries of the world. The size of the attache offices ranges from a minimum of two persons--one officer and one enlisted--to more than a dozen officers and total staffing of over two dozen persons.

There was considerable bargaining in determining which military branch would provide the DATTs overseas. Logically, it could be argued that the DATT should be of the same service as the dominant service in the host country. In most areas of the world, however, that service is the Army, and the Navy and Air Force were interested in having a "balance" of DATT positions among the U.S. services. The result was a reasonable balance, both in the DATT positions and Assistant DATT assignments. Most of the DATTs are at the O-6 level, while flag officers are assigned to a number of countries of particular importance to the United States. The specific locations have varied somewhat in recent years, but currently the most senior DATTs are located in the U.S.S.R., China, France, Brazil, and Mexico.

Attaches are still nominated by the individual services, but the Defense Intelligence Agency has the right to approve or disapprove them. Within DIA, management of the Defense Attache System falls on the Assistant Vice Director for Attaches and Training, whose organization includes five geographic divisions: West/South European; East/Central European; Asia/Pacific; Latin America; and Middle East/Africa. Attache training is the responsibility of the Defense Intelligence College, which is operated by DIA.

In the U.S. system, attache service is voluntary. Training problems arise because the volunteers frequently do not speak the relevant language or are unfamiliar with the country, and often have had no previous intelligence experience.

Important as the attache can be in overtly acquiring information, intelligence collection is only one of several roles which the attache must fill.

One role is representational and includes protocol functions. The DATT is the representative of the Secretary of Defense and the Director of DIA. He and his senior assistants represent the Secretary and military Chiefs-of-Staff of the separate military departments.

Another role involves supporting the Ambassador, since the DATT functions as the military advisor to the Ambassador and serves as an integral member of the U.S. Diplomatic Mission. In a number of countries where an attache aircraft is assigned, this involves rated Air Force personnel who support the Ambassador's travel within the country.

In about two dozen countries where there is no Military Assistance Advisory Group or Mission, the DATT is designated by the Secretary of Defense to administer the U.S. Security Assistance Program, and serves under the U.S. theater commander, such as CINCPAC or CINCSOUTH.

Another complicating factor is that because of limited authorizations for attaches in some areas of the world, particularly in Africa, the attache in one country is accredited as a non-resident attache in up to three adjoining or nearby countries.

Despite his other roles, the attache is frequently an important collector of intelligence information. His military status affords him the opportunity to develop relationships with his military counterparts.

The United States does not have a professional attache corps, and most attaches have only a single tour in such duty. A small number of officers who like attache duty service are sometimes reassigned as attaches, usually serving in the same country, which results in a significant reduction of training time.

THE MILITARY SERVICES

The military services in recent years have become quite interested in expensive technical collection systems designed to collect intelligence information and have not devoted a major effort to HUMINT. The bulk of U.S. intelligence resources are spent on collection. This is not unexpected when one considers that the primary targets are tightly closed societies. Thus, technical collection costs outweigh those for HUMINT by a ratio of about seven to one, and this includes on the HUMINT side the heavy CIA investment in its Clandestine Service.[29]

After a sizeable decline during the past decade, however, the HUMINT resource curve in the Armed Forces has turned upward. Increasingly, there is a realization that, despite the high quality of U.S. imagery and signals intelligence, there is much intelligence information that can be obtained only through human sources.

The Army currently devotes more personnel to HUMINT activities than all the other services combined. The Air Force makes the next largest effort; the Navy/Marine Corps allocate the fewest. This is hardly surprising since Army operations, and hence Army interest in intelligence, tend to be more sensitive to the kinds of intelligence potentially available from human sources than is the case with the Air Force or Navy.

Organizationally, the Army's HUMINT activities are conducted primarily by the Intelligence and Security Command (INSCOM). Those of the Air Force are a responsibility of the Special Activities Center, which is an element of the Air Force Intelligence Service. The Navy/Marine Corps effort is handled by the Naval Intelligence Command. All of these organizations have headquarters in the Washington, D.C. area, but they have overseas elements in the European and Pacific theaters.

The HUMINT efforts of the services are focused primarily on two areas--support for the operational forces and for those DoD components involved in weapon systems development. These forces and components are interested primarily in detailed, factual information, much of which is the type that human sources can acquire. The operational commands need order of battle and warning data--detailed information about unit identities, dispositions, strength, equipment, and activities of potentially hostile forces. The weapons systems developers need scientific and technical details on the performance parameters, operating characteristics, and construction of those foreign weapons systems which U.S. forces might someday have to confront. The thickness of armor on a foreign-built tank and its resistance to armor-piercing munitions are examples of the type of information which is needed.

Because of the declining emphasis on HUMINT activities relative to technical collection in the recent past, the military services have been more successful than the CIA in developing a cadre of HUMINT specialists, but interest in HUMINT, including additional resources, improved training, and more career focus, appears to be on the rise.

THE FEDERAL BUREAU OF INVESTIGATION

The Federal Bureau of Investigation is a law enforcement organization, but it also has important HUMINT functions since it is largely responsible for conducting counterintelligence activities within the United States.

While the bulk of the Bureau's personnel and resources are devoted to investigations relating to violations of federal criminal statutes, the Intelligence Division--that element of the

FBI that is involved in combating espionage, sabotage, and other subversive activities--is part of the U.S. intelligence community. The Assistant Director of the Intelligence Division serves as a member of the National Foreign Intelligence Board and the National Foreign Intelligence Council. The annual budget for the FBI Intelligence Division is included in the National Foreign Intelligence Program budget which the Director of Central Intelligence recommends to the President.

The Bureau's contribution to human source intelligence is primarily a byproduct of information that its agents acquire during their counterintelligence investigations. The FBI is, however, authorized to collect foreign intelligence or to support the foreign intelligence collection operations of other agencies if it is officially requested to do so.[30]

FUTURE PROSPECTS

HUMINT, more than any of the other intelligence disciplines, has suffered from the adverse impact of the widespread publicity directed at intelligence activities as a result of the Congressional investigations of 1975-76.[31] The constant attention of some elements of the U.S. media has followed. One aspect of this was the continual efforts of critics of CIA to identify the names and assignments of the CIA's overseas personnel. This led the Congress in 1982 to adopt the Intelligence Identities Protection Act.[32] The Senate Committee on the Judiciary summarized the impact of publicity on HUMINT activities as follows:

> ...relations with foreign sources of intelligence have been impaired. Sources have evidenced increasing concern for their own safety. Some active sources and individuals contemplating cooperation with the United States have terminated or reduced their contact with our intelligence agencies. Others have questioned how the United States Government can expect its friends to provide information in view of continuing disclosures that may jeopardize their careers, liberty and lives. The result of this has been a reduction of those very relationships which are vital to obtaining high-quality U.S. intelligence. These disclosures have contributed to a perception among foreign intelligence services that U.S. agencies are unable to preserve important confidences. This perception has led to and may lead these services to undertake reviews of their liaison relationships, which have resulted in, and will result in, reduction of contact and reduced passage of information. In taking these actions in the past, some foreign services have explicity cited disclosures of intelligence identities.[33]

Efforts to rebuild and strengthen U.S. HUMINT capabilities are underway because of the recognition that, regardless of the effectiveness of technical collection capabilities, the need for a strong HUMINT capability will always remain. As William J. Casey has stated:

> The wrong picture is not worth a thousand words. No photo, no electronic impulse can substitute for direct on-the-scene knowledge of the key factors in a given country or region. No matter how spectacular a photo may be, it cannot reveal enough about plans, intentions, internal political dynamics, economics, etc. There are simply too many cases where photos are ambiguous or useless, and electronic intelligence can drown the analyst in partial or conflicting information. Technical collection is of little help in the most difficult problem of all--political intentions. This is where clandestine human intelligence can make a difference. I am personally dedicated to supporting it and strengthening it.[34]

NOTES

1. "Foreign intelligence" is defined in Executive Order 12333, promulgated December 4, 1981, as "information relating to the capabilities, intentions and activities of foreign powers, organizations or persons, but not including counterintelligence except for information on international terrorist activities."

2. Numbers XIII: 17-20.

3. James Fenimore Cooper's novel, The Spy, used the anonymity of General Washington's spies as a central theme.

4. Jeffrey M. Durwart, The Office of Naval Intelligence: The Birth of America's First Intelligence Agency, 1865-1918 (Annapolis, MD: U.S. Naval Institute, 1979).

5. U.S. Government publications which are available for purchase from the Government Printing Office are a prolific source of overt collection by foreign intelligence services.

6. The actual "tradecraft" of any Clandestine Service is classified, and no official publication is available. Insights about CIA clandestine tradecraft can be obtained from books written by "insiders" such as the following: William E. Colby, Honorable Men: My Life in the CIA (New York: Simon and Schuster, 1978); Peter De Silva, Sub Rosa: The CIA and Uses of Intelligence (New York: New York Times Book Co., 1978); Cord Meyer, Facing Reality: From World Federalism to the CIA (New York: Harper and Row, 1980); David Atlee Phillips, The Night Watch (New York: Atheneum, 1977); Harry Rositzke, The CIA's Secret Operations:

Espionage, Counterespionage and Covert Action (New York: Readers' Digest Press, 1977). A light-hearted approach is provided by Wolfang Lotz, Israel's longtime "Champagne Spy" in Egypt, in A Handbook for Spies (New York: Harper and Row, 1980). It was written after Lotz had been exposed, imprisoned, traded for nearly 5,000 Egyptian prisoners of war after the Six Day War of 1967, and retired. The first publication in "The Intelligence Professional Series" of the Association of Former Intelligence Officers (AFIO) is "The Clandestine Service of the Central Intelligence Agency" by Hans Moses (1983, 24 pp.).

7. Defined in Executive Order 12333, Section 3.4 (h) as: "activities conducted in support of national foreign policy objectives abroad which are planned and executed so that the role of the United States Government is not apparent or acknowledged publicly, and functions in support of such activities, but which are not identified to influence United States political processes, public opinion, policies, or media and do not include diplomatic activities or the collection and production of intelligence or related support functions."

8. Different from most DCI committees, the HUMINT Committee members are the heads of the organizations involved, not their delegated representatives.

9. DoD Directive 5105.21, May 19, 1877, sec. C.6.

10. Allen W. Dulles (1953-61), Richard Helms (1966-73), and William E. Colby (1973-1976). Until the appointment of DCI William J. Casey in 1981, the three DCIs who were CIA professionals cumulatively had served as much time in the position as the nine "outsider" directors combined.

11. 50 U.S.C. 401, sec. 102. (d).

12. U.S. Senate. Select Committee to Study Governmental Operations with Respect to Intelligence Activities (The Church Committee). Final Report, Book I, April 26, 1976. Senate Report No. 94-755. "VII. The Central Intelligence Agency: Statutory Authority. A. Clandestine Collection of Intelligence," pp. 127-31.

13. The Church Committee, Final Report, Book IV, p. 14.

14. Ibid., p. 37.

15. For a summary of CIA's development, including a description of its clandestine activities, see: The Church Committee, Final Report, Book IV, "History of the Central Intelligence Agency," pp. 1-107.

16. The Church Committee. Final Report, Book IV, pp. 41 and 46.

17. The KGB is the Soviet internal and external security and intelligence organization; the GRU is the acronym for the Soviet military intelligence organization.

18. See: Oleg Penkovskiy, The Penkovskiy Papers (Garden City, NY: Doubleday and Co., 1965); and William Hood, Mole (New York: Norton and Co., 1982). The latter book deals with the Popov case.

19. For historical review of the use of military attaches worldwide and an assessment of their fields of activity, see: Alfred Vagts, The Military Attache (Princeton, NJ: Princeton University Press, 1967).

20. Ibid., p. 33.

21. The Army Almanac (Harrisburg, PA: Stackpole Co., 1959), p. 282.

22. Vagts, p. 34.

23. Ibid., p. 68.

24. Ibid., p. 75, quoting Gordon Enders, Foreign Devil (New York, 1942).

25. The Army Almanac (Washington, DC: U.S. Government Printing Office, 1950), p. 14.

26. The Army Almanac (1959), p. 94. The total included sixty-eight attaches, ninety-eight assistant attaches, forty-eight warrant officers, 178 enlisted personnel and eighty-four Army civilian employees.

27. The New York Times, 13 December 1964.

28. DoD Directive 5105.21, sec. C.7.

29. The Church Committee, Final Report, Book I, p. 344. The Church Committee reported that about 87 percent of U.S. resources devoted to collection is spent on technical sensors, compared with about 13 percent on HUMINT, both overt and clandestine operations.

30. Conducted in the Senate by the Select Committee to Study Governmental Operations with Respect to Intelligence Activities, chaired by Senator Frank Church (Democrat, Idaho), and in the House of Representatives by the Select Committee on Intelligence, chaired by Congressman Otis G. Pike (Democrat, New York).

32. Public Law 97-200, June 23, 1982.

33. U.S. Congress. Senate. Report No. 97-201. Calendar No.

293. _Report to Accompany S. 391_, "Intelligence Identities Protection Act of 1981." October 6, 1981, p. 9.

34. Remarks at the International General Session of the Chamber of Commerce of the United States, Washington, D.C., April 28, 1981.

5
Imagery Intelligence
Stephen S. Beitler

>The purposes of the U.S. reconnaissance and surveillance program are: to provide strategic early warning; to monitor enemy forces; to assess weapons systems characteristics; to develop and maintain a data base for operations planning; to conduct ocean surveillance; to monitor compliance with strategic arms limitations agreements; and to support crisis monitoring and decisionmaking. The U.S. collection effort employs ground-based, airborne, and shipboard systems .... Space technology has contributed importantly to the surveillance program.[1]

In addition to its strategic applications, remote sensing is an invaluable intelligence source for the tactical commander. The tactical imaging mission provides commanders with timely, high quality intelligence for planning and support of operations. Rapid dissemination of this perishable intelligence to airborne or ground-based commanders and, when appropriate, strike aircraft or artillery is paramount. Remote sensing products include intelligence on the disposition, composition, and movement of enemy forces, enemy installations, lines of communications, and electromagnetic emitters based upon the supported unit's essential elements of information (EEI). Other imaging missions include target detection and "change" detection, terrain analysis and map corrections or supplements, confirmation or denial of other intelligence sources, camouflage detection, and evaluation of friendly camouflage techniques.

Remote sensing to acquire intelligence is either surveillance or reconnaissance. Surveillance is systematic, repetitive, overhead observation of expansive areas. Reconnaissance, however, is directed toward specific targets, does not require repetitive coverage, and is initiated because an area may possess intelligence value or affects operations. Tactical reconnaissance and surveillance missions are further subdivided as standoff, penetration, rear area protection, operations security, and cuing missions.

A standoff mission is reconnaissance or surveillance of enemy-held areas by aircraft remaining as far rearward in friendly air-space as sensor capabilities permit, reducing the danger of their engagement by enemy air defenses. Penetration missions are conducted in enemy-controlled airspace up to 150 kilometers beyond the forward line troops. Rear area protection missions assist in friendly forces security, while operations security missions identify friendly concealment and deception weaknesses. During cuing, one reconnaissance system is used to key other reconnaissance or fire delivery systems.

While visual observation, electronic reconnaissance, armed reconnaissance, forward air control, forward observation, command and control, etc., have intelligence acquisition roles, this chapter only considers imagery intelligence. Permanent record imagery is intelligence from inaccessible areas which can be studied, compared with previous imagery, and restudied. Obtained from cameras or infrared and radar sensors and recorded on film, its accuracy of form is excellent, although it is subject to the analyst's vagaries. Finally, imagery is often an important factor in identifying artillery, vehicles, industrial complexes, and installations.

Permanent record imagery also has definite limitations. It may not provide enough detail, and depending upon mission flight parameters, deception operations may appear "real." Political restrictions, air defenses, and weather may hinder acquisition. Technical difficulties are not infrequent, and terrain and atmosphere conditions may affect analysis. Effective analysis often depends upon intelligence from complementary disciplines and an analyst's skill. Accurate analysis requires well-grounded analysts with diverse backgrounds. For military analysts, prior operational experiences, knowledge of enemy military doctrine, and the area's topographic and geographic features are essential.

REMOTE SENSORS

Collection platforms, particularly aircraft, usually capture the attention of general audiences. But the sensors aboard these platforms are equally important. Remote sensors are usually classified according to the sensor's axis orientation (vertical or oblique), lens system (single, the most common, or multiple); spectral range (infrared, visible, or radar), and scanning mode (single frame, continuous strip, scanning lens panoramic, rotating prism panoramic, or other specialized modes).

Optical sensors produce high resolution imagery on black and white, color, infrared, and camouflage detection films in vertical, oblique, or panoramic formats. They also require significant illumination and are restricted by darkness or clouds. Night photography is illuminated by flash cartridges and restricted to the vertical format. Electronic imagery is acquired by infrared or side-looking airborne radar (SLAR), is recorded on photographic film, and is used in combination with other sensors, or during periods when visual observation or optical sensors are not feasible.

Optical sensors are vastly more complex than box cameras, but their basic characteristics are similar; a light free box containing a fixed focus lens (because the objects are at distances so great they may be considered at infinity), diaphragm, and shutter at one end, and a light sensitive medium at the opposite end.[2]

Framing cameras, the most common optical sensor, have a fixed lens, and either a between-the-lens shutter that exposes an entire frame simultaneously, or a focal plane shutter with a slotted curtain that sweeps across the frame, exposing the film at regular intervals. Vertical imagery is made with the camera's optical axis approximately perpendicular to the earth's surface, or with the film as horizontal as is practical. Dimensions can be precisely measured due to vertical imagery's constant scale, and with overlapping exposures, it can be viewed in three-dimensional stereo. Used for mosaics and maps, vertical imagery's advantages include determining direction as though it was a map, and its use as a map substitute by adding a grid system and marginal data. Among its disadvantages, vertical imagery is subject to atmospheric interference (for example, cloud layers), is often unobtainable due to political boundaries, does not present a natural viewing position (overhead instead of a side view), and some objects may be concealed by others (such as tree canopy concealing vehicles).

Oblique imagery is taken with the camera's axis intentionally directed between the horizontal and the vertical, resulting in a uniform scale variation. Features appear larger in the foreground and smaller in the background. In high oblique imagery, the apparent horizon appears, and in low oblique, the apparent horizon does not appear. More area is visible in high oblique than in vertical imagery, but analysis becomes more difficult farther from the sensor. Additionally, as terrain height increases, the value of obliques decreases, because terrain features may be masked.

Oblique imagery's advantages include its more natural side and exposing vertical distances and proportions, details, construction, and concealed objects. Target overflight is unnecessary, reducing the risk to the plane and crew; but due to the greater distance that light waves must travel through the atmosphere, haze becomes a limiting factor. Also, because its perspective is from a single point, an oblique is correct in direction and distance only from the point at which it was imaged. Finally, terrain features and manmade objects can cause "dead space," but these can be reduced by imaging at a steeper angle.

Panoramic cameras can scan from horizon to horizon, and, by sweeping the field of view across the line of flight, expose only a very narrow segment at any moment. A unique image results, usually four or five times as wide as it is long, covering a broad band of terrain at a constantly changing scale, oblique at its extremities and vertical under the aircraft. The point directly below the aircraft has the largest scale and as the scan view swings away from the vertical, the area within the field of view increases and the scale is decreased proportionately. Rectangular patterns (such as city streets) appear convex and converge toward the horizon.

Panoramic imagery's advantages are increased coverage and improved resolution because the area imaged is near the camera lens' optical axis. But mensuration is difficult because the scale is not uniform, and distortions make target identification difficult. Also, aircraft must penetrate enemy airspace to obtain panoramic imagery.

Sonne or continuous strip cameras have been in use since 1932. In these, the film continuously passes over a narrow slit in the focal plane (there is no conventional shutter) at a speed compatible with the aircraft's ground speed. Thus, the film is exposed in continuous strips instead of individual frames. Continuous strip cameras are ideal for long targets (such as lines of communications), since they produce an extremely sharp image on a continuous strip.

While platforms and sensors have developed, so has film. The two objectives of producing better film are greater detail and countering camouflage. Remote sensing film is panchromatic (black and white), infrared, polychromatic (color), or camouflage detection.

Panchromatic film, the most widely used film for military applications, records color brightness in continuous tones of grey, is the least expensive, and is available in versions for high altitude mapping and reconnaissance, and for daylight or night imaging. Infrared film is a black and white film sensitive to the blue-violet colors of the visible light spectrum and reflected infrared rays. Using red filters to eliminate visible light, an exposure is obtained solely by infrared radiation invisible to the human eye. Comparatively, panchromatic film is sensitive only to the visible light portion of the spectrum. Detail on infrared images is also recorded in varying tones of grey.

Polychromatic film presents all the visible colors in their natural tones, enhancing recognition and analysis. It is particularly useful for camouflage detection, underwater penetration, terrain and beach analysis, industrial studies, and hydrographic studies. However, color film has a low exposure index, is expensive, is difficult to process, and has relatively poor stability in storage. Since its disadvantages outweigh its advantages, color film is only used for special purposes.

A special color film, camouflage detection film's top emulsion layer is sensitive to infrared reflections. Vegetation containing chlorophyll registers, after it has been cut for at least six hours, in tones of red to reddish-brown, while objects without chlorophyll are recorded as blue, yellow, black/green, or white. Camouflage detection film is a useful panchromatic supplement but difficult to analyze until the analyst is familiar with its unique color representation.

Infrared sensors detect invisible infrared emissions day or night through a combination of optics, electronic, and mechanical devices to produce thermal images. An infrared imaging set contains scanner optics, a detector, and a recorder. The scanner detects ground infrared emissions and reflects them to a parabolic mirror. The parabolic mirror focuses them onto the detector, converting the collected infrared radiant energy into an electrical signal. The electrical signal is then converted to visible light and recorded on ordinary panchromatic film.

Infrared sensing is particularly useful for haze penetration, camouflage detection, terrain analysis, and at night. Infrared imaging missions are usually conducted at night since objects (unaffected by the sun's energy reflected from their surfaces) have truer temperature value and human activity, such as vehicular engines or campfires, is evident. Infrared's camouflage detection properties are limited because dead vegetation gradually loses its infrared reflectivity until it finally appears dark on imagery. Its excellent terrain analysis capabilities are due to the varying infrared reflectivity of objects and vegetation. Damp areas, for example, which are not discernible on panchromatic film, stand out on infrared film.

Infrared's advantages closely parallel its uses, and it is also a passive, real-time sensor. Infrared's disadvantages include tonal reversal, terrain masking effects, the film's special handling requirements, and platform low altitude penetration requirements.

Unlike optical sensors, which require external illumination, radars provide their own. Side-looking airborne radars transmit short pulses of energy through a narrow beam at right angles to the flight path, illuminating a narrow strip of terrain that reflects the pulses or echoes back to the antenna.[3] Sequential illuminations are recorded side by side on film to create a complete image.

Side-looking airborne radar produces fixed or moving target indication imagery. Fixed target indication imagery is a map-like presentation of the ground and moving target indication imagery presents, as an electronic signal, only moving ground objects. Its advantages include standoff imaging, a relatively fixed scale, real-time transmission, night imaging, large area coverage, and the fact that it can detect movement. Severe weather conditions may be limiting, but if aircraft can fly, SLAR will produce usable imagery that would otherwise be unavailable.

Conversely as an active sensor, SLAR is susceptible to electronic countermeasures or noise. Other disadvantages include terrain masking and the resulting radar shadow, resolution poorer than that of optical sensors, special training for imagery analysts, and a dearth of analysis keys.

Radar imaging is quite different from optical remote sensing. In particular, along-track features are recorded passing through the beam; while across-track (range), the distance from the aircraft to the object is measured. The primary differences between optical imagery and radar imagery are their methods of illumination, image formation, analysis, and terrain reflection characteristics.

HISTORY OF REMOTE SENSING

The first reported aerial observations were made by the French from captive balloons in 1793. Later, Napoleon formed a second company and deployed balloonists to Egypt in 1739 and to Italy in 1797 with his military forces. Balloons were subsequently developed and used for aerial observation and photography through the mid-1950s.

In Boston during 1860, the first American aerial image was made from a balloon at twelve hundred feet altitude. During the American Civil War, numerous observation flights were made by military balloonists, and on June 18, 1861, Mr. Thaddeus S. C. Lowe transmitted the first message by telegraph from an aerial platform.

Two Civil War aeronauts, Mr. John La Mountain and Mr. Lowe, are credited with conducting balloon imaging of a variety of Confederate positions and for using grid overlays to transfer target points from imagery to maps. Unfortunately, most Union generals remained skeptical of remote sensing. Even Generals Porter and McClellan, staunch supporters of the balloon corps, lamented the time lag between the acquisition of intelligence and its dissemination, a complaint still voiced today.[4]

On October 23, 1911, the Italian Air Force first used an airplane and made an observation flight in war, against Turkish positions between El Aziz and Tripoli; and shortly afterward on February 24, 1912, made the first imaging sortie during the Balkans War. In 1914, Great Britain's Royal Flying Corps designed the first dedicated optical sensor, subsequently used to map Egypt and the Suez Canal Zone.

On August 29, 1916, Congress appropriated the first large sum for aviation: $13,228,666.00. But on the eve of U.S. involvement in World War I, the signal corps aviation section had only thirty-five rated pilots and fewer than 3,000 aircraft, including training planes.

The interwar years, nevertheless, were watershed years for the development of aerial photography. Military remote sensing survivors conducted military and civilian mapping and the first aerial mapping units were formed. Major scientific advances included imaging with flash bombs and electric flash systems, Sonne's continuous strip camera, waterproof paper, camouflage detection film, color aerial imaging, high altitude aerial imaging, the use of remote controlled telephoto cameras, and the processing and transmission of imagery over telegraph.

After Pearl Harbor, United States remote sensing units made a poor first showing in North Africa. United States Army Air Force crews had high losses flying alone in large aircraft (the F-7 or F-9 imaging versions of the B-24 or B-17, respectively) with little maneuverability, firepower, or speed. Conversely, the Royal Air Force, using its fastest and most modern fighters, superbly accomplished similar missions.

After the invasion of Europe, imagery units were always close to the front line of troops, flying missions seventy-five miles ahead of them. Most European theater of operations imaging aircraft were unarmed, but this was impractical in the vast expanses of the Pacific theater of operations, where imaging aircraft needed the capability to destroy fleeting targets.

An interservice agreement prior to the Korean War delineated air force responsibility for collecting and processing five copies of each image and the army for analysis, production of the correct number, and dissemination. It was not until two years after the Korean War started, however, that the United States Eighth Army was able to comply with this agreement. After demobilization in 1945, imagery assets dwindled again, and neither the Eighth Army nor the United States' Far Eastern Air Force had an imagery intelligence organization at the advent of the Korean War.

The dearth of imaging assets allowed only selective target coverage. However, the Korean War marked the P-80 Shooting Star's (the first dedicated imaging jet aircraft) introduction, the first use of jet imaging aircraft in combat, and the development of panoramic and shutterless continuous strip cameras.

THE U-2

The major post-Korean remote sensing development was the first U-2 flight across Soviet airpace on July 4, 1956.[5] Developed by Lockheed's advanced development projects team ("skunk works") dozens of U-2 high-altitude remote sensing aircraft variants have been built. Its legend far outstrips its numbers. Most U-2s are single-seaters, although some are tandem. It has sailplane qualities, reaches more than 70,000 feet altitude, has a range of 3,000 miles, and its ability to maintain high altitudes for periods as long as twelve hours compensates for its relatively slow speed of 430 miles per hour. Its optical sensors can cover a 745 mile swath width with a 150 mile stereo central strip. Other sensors include a line scan camera that provides real-time imagery via a telemetry data link.[6]

Because it is difficult to fly, U-2 accidents have claimed nearly forty U-2s and the lives of several pilots. But none of these have peaked as much interest as when Mr. Francis Gary Powers' flight from Peshawar, Pakistan was shot down thirty miles from Sverdlovsk, just east of Moscow.[7]

After the incident in May 1960, President Eisenhower's June invitation to visit the Soviet Union was withdrawn. The incident became a Soviet propaganda event.

On September 9, 1961, Colonel Chen Wai-sheng of Taiwan became the first of four pilots shot down over the People's Republic of China through 1964. One of these U-2s is permanently displayed at the Chinese People's Revolutionary Military Museum in Beijing.[8] The U-2 production line was reopened in 1968 due to high attrition, and U-2Rs, a U-2C enlarged by a factor of one third, were produced.

The TR-1A, developed by Lockheed for high-altitude tactical imaging, is a U-2R derivative, first delivered to the Air Force in September 1981.[9] While its flight characteristics are similar to the U-2R's, its sensor payload and missions are not. The first tactical application of U-2 technology, the TR-1A's Hughes side-looking, high-resolution, advanced synthetic aperature radar system, can track and target enemy forces day or night, and in all types of weather. Its Lockheed precision location strike system can target hostile emitters and precisely guide conventional ordnance.10

On October 14, 1962, 928 photographs from a six minute U-2 flight confirmed the presence of nuclear-armed SS-4 Sandal medium-range ballistic missile facilities and IL-28 Beagle bombers in Cuba. Within one week, over two thousand remote sensing missions were flown over Cuba and Cuban-bound shipping. U-2s flew as many as eight missions per day, RF-101 Voodoos went in at low altitude, and Navy aircraft spent over 10,000 hours tracking ships, Soviet submarines, and their tenders. Their imagery, which the National Photographic Interpretation Center analyzed around the clock, conclusively proved that there were medium-range ballistic missiles on Cuba, even though Ambassador Dobrynin had relayed Premier Khrushchev's assurances to the contrary to President Kennedy.

Imagery was released to France, the United Kingdom, and the Federal Republic of Germany, and after the Soviet Ambassador to the United Nations, Valerian A. Zorin, had denied the weapons' presence, to the United Nations Security Council and correspondents from over 100 nations. On October 27, 1962, Major Rudolf Anderson Jr. was killed when his U-2 was destroyed by a surface-to-air missile. But Premier Khrushchev recanted his earlier position on October 28th, and agreed to withdraw all Soviet strategic offensive weapons from Cuba. Just as remote sensing detected their presence, President Kennedy subsequently used it to insure the missiles' withdrawal. On October 29th, imagery from low-level RF-101 Voodoo sorties verified that the missiles had been withdrawn.

THE OV-1 MOHAWK

Vietnam's terrain required new remote sensing techniques and methods. In mid-1962, OV-1 Mohawks were the first imaging aircraft deployed to Vietnam. Developed in the late 1950s, the Grumman OV-1D Mohawk is one of the three dedicated American tactical remote sensing platforms. This two-crew, short takeoff and landing, fixed-wing, twin turbo-prop aircraft, equipped with a forward panoramic, vertical panoramic, or square format camera, an interchangeable infrared detection system or side-looking airborne radar, has a 25,000 foot service ceiling, 265 knot maximum speed, and can loiter four hours.11 The OV-1 Mohawk is limited by severe weather, is vulnerable to enemy air defense, and its delicate electronic system requires the use of prepared runways. An old system, the OV-1D Mohawk may carry the Defense Advanced Research Project Agency's future joint surveillance and target attack radar system, a long-range, all-weather, real-time, secure link radar target locating system that can identify moving target indicators in hostile territory.[12]

The mission of the 23rd Special Warfare Aviation Detachment's Mohawks was to support the Republic of Vietnam Army with observation and remote sensing. In their first year of operation, five out of six Mohawks were lost while loitering below five hundred feet above the ground level.

THE SR-71A BLACKBIRD

The SR-71A Blackbird, which served over Vietnam, was also developed by Lockheed as a long-range, advanced, strategic remote sensing aircraft, and is America's primary strategic remote sensing aircraft today. At speeds over 2,000 miles per hour, its crew of two can image approximately 100,000 square miles in one hour at a maximum altitude of over 80,000 feet. The SR-71A has a titanium airframe, a range of more than 2,000 miles, and its crew wears astronaut suits and follows space flight pre-flight procedures. Its existence was disclosed by President Johnson in July 1964.[13]

SATELLITE REMOTE SENSING

In March 1967, during discussions on the space program's value, President Johnson declared that had it cost ten times more than the thirty to forty billion dollars invested the past ten years, it would have been worth it "simply for the photography. Before we had the photography," he noted, "our guesses were way off. We were doing things we didn't need to do. Because of the satellites I know how many missiles the enemy has."[14] Ten years later, in a speech at Cape Canaveral, President Carter officially acknowledged that the United States was conducting satellite reconnaissance.[15]

Additionally, manned Gemini, Apollo, Skylab, and Space Shuttle missions have imaged earth, and an imaging radar and large format camera have already been developed for the shuttle.[16] The SIR-B imaging radar is an experimental electro-optical sensor that can cover a fifty kilometer swath width, has fifty meters resolution at a fifteen degree look angle, twenty-five meters at fifty degrees, and twenty meters at seventy degrees.[17]

Itek Optical System's large format camera "... from a nominal flight altitude of about 278 km (150 n.mi) ... can produce a ground resolution of about ten meters with high resolution black/white film to twenty meters with color infrared film. Ground positioning accuracy will be about fifteen meters and elevation accuracy from seven to twenty-eight meters .... This is adequate for compilation of maps at scale 1:50,000 with a twenty to eighty-meter contour interval."[18]

Shuttle radar images depict a long swath of the United States and Canada, "including the streets of Montreal, nearby rivers with ships clearly visible, the regular patches of farm fields and the rugged mountains of Vermont."[19]

REMOTELY PILOTED VEHICLES

Large numbers of small pilotless aircraft have been built since World War I, when the United States Navy used a pilotless biplane as an aerial torpedo. An onboard clockwork mechanism shut down the engine at its destination, the wings fell away, and the explosive-laden fuselage dropped on its target. The first true RPV, a British radio-controlled pilotless biplane, flew from HMS Stronghold on September 3, 1924, in a flight that culminated in twelve minutes after engine failure. In July 1927, another RPV, the long-range gun with Lynx engine or LARYNX, flew one hundred fifty miles along the British coast. The Air Force and Navy also developed a drone to simulate attacks on shipping; it survived two hours of concentrated gunfire and was safely recovered during January 1933. During World War II, pilots parachuted from ordnance-laden aircraft, then controlled by radio, to their target. The Army Air Force and Navy also used over fourteen thousand target drones to replace Tiger Moth biplanes used in pre-war exercises.

During the Vietnam War, almost 3,500 RPV sorties were flown for imaging, electronic intelligence, bomb damage assessment, psychological operations (leaflet drops), electronic warfare, and forward observation for naval gunfire. The Teledyne-Ryne Firebee, the most widely used reconnaissance RPV in southeast Asia, was ground- or air-launched and retrieved, carried photographic and infrared sensors, and flew primarily where the risk was too great for manned aircraft. Three Firebees are also on display at the Chinese People's Revolutionary Military Museum in Beijing. The GTD-21, a mach three plus imaging RPV equipped with photographic and infrared sensors, and resembling a scaled-down single engine SR-71, deployed over southeast Asia from the SR-71's predecessor, the A-11, and subsequently the B-52.

Current interest in RPVs has peaked as a result of their effective employment by the Israeli Air Force and Army. In the 1973 Arab-Israeli War, the Israelis used harassment drones to saturate enemy air defense systems so strike aircraft could attack Egyptian surface-to-air missile (SAM) sites reloading. In the Bekaa Valley, in Lebanon during June 1982, RPVs were instrumental in destroying or suppressing Syrian SAM sites. Configured electronically to resemble aircraft, the RPVs drew fire, and recon aircraft imaged the firings; or, once radiating, the Israelis fired antiradiation missiles to destroy the SAM's antennas, after which attack aircraft destroyed the missiles and control vans. Tactical imaging RPVs also projected high resolution imagery in near real-time on screens overlaid with maps of Lebanon for tactical commanders. All the RPVs had a low rate of attrition because of their small size and low infrared signature, and were seemingly immune to hostile fire.

The primary mission of RPVs is real-time remote sensing. Their operators can maneuver the sensors in any direction, zoom or panoramic. Other major advantages of RPVs vis-a-vis manned aircraft are: their greater field of vision, small size, silent engine, lower safe altitudes, small radar and infrared signatures that increase survivability, variety of sensor options, long endurance, low cost, and their pre-programming ability to reduce detection or jamming.[20] Rotary RPVs, such as Canadair's CL-227 Sentinel, can also act as airborne radar pickets or raised radar platforms to enhance, for example, shipboard capabilities for over-the-horizon target designation.

Latin for "eagle," Lockheed's Aquila can perform reconnaissance and surveillance target acquisition, laser ranging/designation, artillery adjustment, and real-time damage assessment.[21] Aquila is equipped with a forward looking infrared sensor, a daylight television camera, a low-light television camera under development, an electro-optical system, and an infrared line scanner/recorder.

An Aquila RPV platoon is organic to the corps target acquisition batallion. It includes a headquarters element, two central launch and recovery sections and three forward control sections with a total of thirteen air vehicles. A section can emplace and displace very quickly. Operating from unimproved sites behind the forward line of troops, sections provide direct support to committed maneuver brigades and general support to the division.

Aquila's ground control station receives mission assignments from headquarters, controls the air vehicle and its sensor payload, and reports acquired target data to supported units. It provides real-time video monitoring, instant replays, and permanent annotated audiovisual imagery. The air vehicle is a modified flying-wing aircraft, can remain aloft three hours, has a thirteen foot wingspan, and a seven foot fuselage.[22] Once a target is located by sluing the sensor, it can be switched to automatic tracking, the boresighted laser activated, and target ranging or designation conducted. The launch subsystem is a foldable, hydraulic catapult. Its recovery system is a truck-mounted vertical ribbon barrier made of dacron webbing suspended between two arms of an extended crane-like structure. Twelve air vehicles can be launched or recovered per hour.

Aquila, which originally cost $100,000.00, was propelled by a modified go-cart engine, and landed on bicycle training wheels. Showing great promise, between 1976 and 1978 it flew reliably and effectively 150 times. While RPVs were deployed in other countries, however, Aquila's introduction was delayed for four years until 1988. Now "gold plated," this originally simple system could no longer accomplish the army's overburdening specifications.

Forty percent heavier, Aquila now has a custom engine, seven supporting trucks, and thirteen operators. Cancelled and resurrected, program costs have quadrupled over four years, the number of air vehicles scheduled for acquisition cut in half, and its mission reassigned from manuever units to divisions to justify the reduction in air vehicle acquisition. Aquila had no early competition, but the army is now exploring competitor's systems, casting doubt on its own specifications for Aquila.

Lockheed is currently developing a solar-powered RPV for continuous high altitude flight. At twelve miles altitude, "boresighted" on a particular area, its solar cells would power a giant propeller maintaining the plane's position against prevailing winds for one year. Various sensor payloads could transmit surveillance data in real-time, and would be particularly useful in a low intensity conflict. RPVs, in general, have the potential to extend the tactical commander's "eyes and ears," providing intelligence on the local situation in real-time, while reducing the tactical commander's dependence on national remote sensing systems and external agencies.

IMAGERY ANALYSIS

Imagery analysts are trained to extract intelligence from imagery produced by overhead sensors. Their specific duties include reporting intelligence pertaining to the enemy (their operations and activities, disposition, supplies, communications, and installations), reporting civilian activity related to military operations (population concentrations, industrial production facilities, and traffic networks), analyzing terrain, preparing target folders, performing damage assessments, updating maps and preparing map supplements, preparing mosaics, panoramas, and terrain models, and planning reconnaissance and surveillance missions.

The senior military analysis agency is the Defense Intelligence Agency.[23] The National Photographic Interpretation Center is the national imagery analysis body. Few imagery analysts are found in tactical echelons, which are provided imagery support by corps and above.

An imagery analyst's effectiveness depends upon experience and background knowledge about the enemy (including tactics, equipment, order-of-battle), the area of operations, area studies disciplines, collateral intelligence products, history of coverage, imagery analysis keys, sensor platform capabilities, and the commander's operation orders and essential elements of intelligence (EEI). In short, imagery analysts must have experience in two fields: imagery and the subject of the analysis.

Imagery analyst's reporting is usually in response to a commander's EEI, collection plan, or unique request. A preplanned imaging mission request is the most efficient because it allows sufficient time for coordination, planning, briefing, consolidation of requirements, proper analysis, and product dissemination. It also permits proper selection and allocation of aircraft and sensors. Requests are examined by intelligence personnel at each echelon to verify that imagery is not already available, and whether requests comply with the commander's intelligence collection plan objectives. Eventually, they are consolidated, assigned a priority, and forwarded to the executing tactical reconnaissance unit, or rejected. Imaging requests for immediate missions are forwarded as expeditiously as possible.

These requests can be executed by dedicated standby aircraft or diverted preplanned flights.

After completing the mission, the pilot debriefs and the imagery is processed and analyzed in the air force's processing and interpretation system (TIPPI) (three shelters), the mobile army ground imagery interpretation center (MAGIIC) (only two shelters), or the marine air-ground intelligence system (MAGIS) (one shelter). These facilities and the Versamat or Portable Darkroom Photographic Facility are "mobile" units containing imagery analysis, communications, and darkroom equipment for processing and reproduction, viewing, comparing, analyzing, and measuring imagery.[24]

To utilize the MAGIIC's map board and automatic features, imagery is threaded through a console; sensor data are usually manually entered or accessed on disk; code blocks are adjusted, read, and corrected by inputing a known point on the film and map; a navigation correction program interpolates additional corrections after the latter step is repeated twice, completing "initialization;" and the imagery analyst "reads it out" and reports.

The naval intelligence processing system (NIPS) incorporates processing, production, and dissemination for all intelligence disciplines supporting naval operating forces. It is afloat in the integrated operational intelligence center (IOIC) aboard attack carriers to support strike and antisubmarine warfare missions; and in the amphibious command ship intelligence center (LCC-IC) or the general purpose amphibious assault ship intelligence center (LHA-IC) to support amphibious warfare. The IOIC contains facilities for a photographic laboratory, mission planning, data processing, storage and retrieval, and multisensor analysis. Only the IOIC has a multisensor analysis facility in support of the carrier's organic airborne reconnaissance platforms, but they all can process and analyze imagery.

Imagery analysis is the process of locating, recognizing, identifying, and describing objects, activities, and terrain represented on imagery. Its product, evaluated and collated, is imagery intelligence, the quality of which is influenced by the sensor coverage, facilities, time available, and the analyst's ability. The major identification aids on overhead imagery are the "five S's:" size, shape, shadow, shade, and surrounding objects.

Size is the dimensions, surface, and volume of an object, and can often be estimated from the relative size of proximate objects. When dimensions are required, imagery scale must first be determined. A radar antenna's dimensions, for example, may indicate its operating frequency. Size is frequently distorted on radar and infrared imagery.

Shape is the configuration of an object. Although shape can be difficult to analyze, it is often the most important identification clue. Shape is also frequently distorted on radar and infrared imagery.

Shadow occurs when an intervening object prevents direct sun rays from striking certain areas. Shadows are profile views, facilitating recognition of, for example, a tall tower. Shadows on infrared imagery are caused by reflected infrared energy and resulting temperature differences. An infrared shadow or "ghost image" may persist for several hours after the casting object has moved. Radar imagery's shadows are caused by objects intervening between its source and objects farther away.

Shade is the brilliance of light, infrared, or radar energy reflected by an object. Without shade differences, an object's shape could not be discerned. Certain indicator species of vegetation (they indicate military trafficability), for example, are distinguished only by shade differences. An object's location in relation to its environment is important. Many types of vegetation, for example, are characteristically confined to specific geographic sites. Also, the repetition of general forms establishes a recognition pattern. Permanent SAM sites, for example, will normally be configured in a certain relationship to one another.

Imagery analysis keys are mnemonics or training aids for facilitating rapid and accurate identification of significant objects. Their importance becomes obvious for a military imagery analyst who must be able to recognize all natural and man-made features on the surface of the earth and deduce their significance.

Targets are classified as fixed, transient, or fleeting. Examples of fixed targets are bridges, airfield and industrial complexes, power producing facilities, buildings, and prominent terrain features. Transient targets include bivouac areas, troop concentrations, truck parks, missile and antiaircraft artillery batteries, and electronic emitters. Fleeting targets are difficult to locate and require immediate strike decisions. They include troop movements, and moving tanks, trucks, trains, ships, and boats. There are seventeen target categories for standardized reporting: airfields, missile systems, electronic installations, barrack/camps/headquarters, storage and repair facilities, military activity, river crossings/ferries, shipping, route reconnaissance, terrain reconnaissance, coastal strips, bridges, water control facilities, ports/harbors, rail facilities, industrial installations, and electric power installations.

The major standardized imagery reports are reconnaissance exploitation reports, initial photointerpretation reports, and supplemental photointerpretation reports. Reconnaissance exploitation reports (RECCEXREP) are used to disseminate, within forty-five minutes, results obtained from the initial analysis of imagery and aircrew debriefing for mission dependent EEI. Initial photointerpretation reports (IPIR) also report on mission dependent EEI, but in greater detail than a RECCEXREP. Supplemental photointerpretation reports (SUPIR) are used to report mission independent EEI, for special studies, and detailed analyses commonly conducted at national echelons where duplication of reporting is, unfortunately, endemic.

Reporting must be timely, thorough, and accurate. There is, however, a tendency to excessively apply the words "probable" or "possible" in much reporting. The unnecessary use of qualifiers discredits not only individual reports, but all imagery intelligence reports. Ultimately, the imagery analyst's report affects the lives of soldiers, sailors, airmen, and marines.

NOTES

1. U.S., The Organization of the Joint Chiefs of Staff, United States Military Posture for FY 1980, quoted in Commander Cecil B. Jones, Jr., USN (Ret.), "Photographic Satellite Reconnaissance," United States Naval Institute Proceedings (June 1980): 49.

2. U.S., Department of the Navy, Naval Air Systems Command, Naval Reconnaissance and Technical Support Center, Image Interpretation Handbook, vol. 1. TM30-245, NAVAIR 10-35-685, AFM 2000-50 (1967), pp. 2-16 and 2-20. Chester C. Slama et al., eds., Manual of Photogrammetry, 4th ed. (Falls Church, VA: American Society of Photogrammetry, 1980), pp. 283-4.

3. U.S., Department of the Air Force, Defense Sensor Interpretation Applications Training Program, Radar Imaging Principles (1983), p. 1.

4. Glen B. Infield, Unarmed and Unafraid (New York: MacMillan, 1970), pp. 19, 31.

5. Colonel William V. Kennedy, USA (ret.) et al., Intelligence Warfare (New York: Crescent Books, 1983), p. 126.

6. Bill Gunston, An Illustrated Guide to Spy Planes and Electronic Warfare Aircraft (New York: Arco Publishing, Inc., 1983), p. 30.

7. Infield, p. 170.

8. Ibid., p. 178. Jay Miller, "U-2R...TR-1: Lockheed's Black Ladies," Air International (October 1984): 186.

9. U.S., Department of Defense, Report of the Secretary of Defense Caspar W. Weinberger to the Congress on the FY 1985 Budget, FY 1986 Authorization Request and FY 1985-89 Defense Programs, p. 170.

10. Kennedy, Intelligence Warfare, p. 141.

11. U.S., Department of the Army, Reconnaissance and Surveillance Handbook, TC 34-50 (1980), pp. 45-6.

12. U.S., Department of the Army, United States Army Weapons Handbook (1984), pp. 78-9.

13. "U.S. Military Aircraft," *Aviation Week and Space Technology*, 12 March 1984, p. 136.

14. Brigadier General George W. Goddard, USAF (Ret.), *Overview: A Life-Long Adventure in Aerial Photography*, with DeWitt S. Copp (New York: Doubleday, 1969), pp. 398-9.

15. James Banford, "America's Supersecret Eyes in Space," *The New York Times Magazine*, 13 January 1985, sec-6, pp. 39, 50, 52-4.

16. Slama, pp. 961, 965-6.

17. Ibid., p. 961.

18. Ibid., pp. 965-6.

19. William J. Broad, "Astronauts, Freed From Technical Woes, Turn Attention to Earth," *The New York Times*, 10 October 1984, p. A13.

20. Lockheed Missiles and Space Company, "Army Aguila RPV Program," (no date), p. 20.

21. Lockheed Missiles and Space Company, "Aguila: U.S. Army Remotely Piloted Vehicle Program," (no date), p. 1.

22. Ibid., p. 2.

23. Defense Intelligence Agency, Division of Imagery Analysis, Organization as of July 1984.

24. U.S., Department of the Army, United States Army Intelligence Center and School, *Air Reconnaissance Target Reporting Guide* (1981), p. 2.

Part 3
Analysis

6
The Crucial Manager
Alan R. Goldman

In his classic book <u>The Intelligence Establishment</u>, Henry Howe Ransom describes the intelligence process in terms of various steps which have become known in the intelligence community as the intelligence cycle. The first step in the cycle is the Setting of Requirements, followed in sequence by Collection, Evaluation and Production, and Dissemination. Despite the fact that in any intelligence agency all these steps are continually occurring, the cycle does provide a sense of order to an often confusing process and profession.

This chapter concerns itself with step one in the cycle, the Setting of Requirements, which Ransom describes as "the crucially important task of intelligence management which determines what types of information are needed and assigns procurement to various intelligence arms."[1]

It is unfortunate for the good management of the intelligence process that so little attention is devoted to the requirements manager: what that manager must know, do, and be to perform successfully. Clandestine collection is the glamorous action in the intelligence cycle and is the stuff of fact and fiction in the literature of intelligence. This chapter briefly describes what the job of setting requirements is and what the crucial manager should be. It does not describe how to do the job.

From the organizational perspective, the requirements manager(s) stand at the nexus between external organizations and his or her own agency--the point person. The actual job of setting requirements is very simply the setting of the agenda for a military intelligence agency. It lets the employees of the agency know what they are expected to do and when they are to do it. The requirements manager analyzes the issue, asks the questions, levies the tasks, and reviews the results of completed actions to insure compliance. While the requirements manager is subject to higher level authority and guidance, that crucial individual or set of individuals must actually pick and choose (and thus set priorities) from a multitude of possible projects and tasks. Therefore, the attributes of a successful requirements manager should be of great concern to those who select such individuals, as well as to the actual individual.

WHAT SHOULD A REQUIREMENTS MANAGER BE?

(1) Be an enthusiastic student of military history and contemporary political-military issues. Yes, general knowledge of subject is more important than mastery of management principles and techniques. The setter of requirements sets priorities, and those priorities must be grounded in a sense of the military problem, the supported service need, and the threat. The manager, of course, is not expected to be the expert on a given functional or regional area. So Mr. or Ms. Manager, enjoy the vocation, read, and learn.

(2) Be a person of high integrity. The crucial manager faces temptations toward favoritism, manipulation, paths of least resistance, and pushing problems downward. By keeping faith with and drawing inspiration from the vital mission your agency performs, you will help yourself maintain the honesty and objectivity your job demands. Draw courage from a realization of the importance of your work. At no time since the Revolutionary War have the intelligence arms of the Army, Navy, Air Force, Marines, and Department of Defense been more critical to the security of the country. U.S. armed forces will either be required to fight the big war outnumbered and win or wage smaller military/political/psychological wars against highly elusive enemies. In either case, the use of constrained intelligence assets may well determine victory or defeat. You the manager will often have a decisive role to play in deciding which questions are addressed, when, and by whom--especially as the volume of requirements exceeds the capabilities of your agency to service them. Your mission, your service, and the threat are your guide to action and the gatekeeper of your conscience. Finally, draw spirit and perseverance from the heritage of military intelligence and from what you owe to those who have made the ultimate sacrifice.

(3) Be sensitive to the real needs of your consumers. Users of intelligence are often not quite sure what they want. You therefore receive the equivalent of "tell me everything I must know about country X or weapon Y." By working intimately with the actual user(s) of intelligence, you can jointly hammer out an intelligence requirement. Experienced employees, a valuable resource in your intelligence organization, will provide insight into the needs of external organizations they have supported with intelligence output. As you become thoroughly familiar with the needs of external consumers of intelligence products, you will learn to prioritize, plan, program, and task more efficiently.

One of the complexities of intelligence production management involves dealing with requirements from many consumers at the same time. Having multiple requirements means that there is competition for resources, multiple tasking of analysts, and overlapping information requirements.

The requirements manager attempts to sort out the individual needs and priorities of each consumer so that specific tasking information can be given to the analytic team that will produce the product. The intelligence requirements manager must effectively "walk" through the analytical procedure to determine the time and resources that will be required to respond to the requirement.

The person who will do the analysis must be consulted during the process of defining and refining the requirement. Before the intelligence manager can establish tasking priorities, the following things must be known about the requirement:

o   Its significance to the mission.
o   How and when the product is to be used.
o   How much time is available for analysis.
o   Which information resources will be required.
o   How the product is to be disseminated.

The answers to these questions are used to negotiate a suspense time for the product, determine the necessary level of detail and accuracy of information, and choose an analyst to perform the analysis. These issues must be agreed upon between the consumer and the intelligence manager. Sometimes, the requirement must be refined or the available resources supplemented. The intelligence manager may need to request special personnel from other organizations or special priority for the use of collection systems.

Evaluating the required information resources is a matter of determining if there is an information overlap between current or previous intelligence products, selecting an analyst (or analysts) capable of using that information, and determining if the collection plans and priorities are adequate to meet any additional information requirements.

In most cases, the intelligence manager will make these evaluations on the basis of experience with similar requirements and products. The manager frequently requires an interactive dialogue with both the consumer and the analysts who will do the analysis. This dialogue is needed to adequately refine the requirement to fit the needs of the consumer into the available time and resources.

(4) Be sensitive to the capabilities of the personnel in your organization. Know your chief's priorities and what the organization you work for can reasonably be expected to produce. Do not overtask and push impossible demands downward. You are paid to take the heat by saying no to improper or extravagant demands. At the same time, set standards; expect more, not less, from your organization. Above all, encourage initiative from the employees! Workload is never evenly spread throughout the organization. Everyone must have a real day's work to do. Intelligence professionals can generate results when no specific requirements exist. The mission is once again the guide to appropriate intelligence collection, analysis, and production. In time, product lines born of explicit and implied requirements will evolve. Acknowledge people who do good work. Say thank you!

(5) Be an evaluator and promoter of your organization. Elicit from the users of intelligence their candid evaluation of how well or badly intelligence serves their purposes. Let the users know you will be responsive to constructive and realistic criticism. Once your organization has performed, go out and advertise your product. Be bold! Be willing to try what seemed impossible a year ago. There will be imperfections, gaps, and problems, but stretch yourself and your organization to try. Again, the threat is great and the truly significant work for the military service and country must be attempted. Improvements will come in time. Praise and reward those who dare to try the difficult.

(6) Be caring of yourself spiritually, mentally, and physically. The demands on you will often be intense, conflicting, and occasionally even improper. The requirements manager is beset by pressures. To identify a few:

1. Your boss, your boss' boss, your boss' boss' boss.
2. Customer #1, customer #2, customers #3, #4, #5, etc.
3. DoD guidance.
4. Director of Central Intelligence guidance.
5. Internal organizational pressures.

There are programs to manage stress. There are exercises to keep you healthy. Talk over your work problems. When there are hard choices to be made, draw assurance and perseverance from your knowledge of the military problem and the crucial nature of the mission. You the Commander, you the Resource Manager, but especially you the Branch or Division Chief--the first line supervisor of analysts--are indeed the crucial manager.

PRODUCTION RESOURCE MULTIPLIERS

The manager's most difficult problem occurs when the resources required to satisfy the demand for information exceed the resources that are available. Managers use a set of simple heuristics (or rules of thumb) to effectively multiply their resources and improve productivity.

Removing Redundant Requirements Is A Multiplier

A most important heuristic applied by the manager is to minimize redundant analytical efforts. This situation could easily occur if the intelligence manager did not identify overlapping information needs in requirements, and tasked different analysts to provide the same information. By identifying overlapping requirements, the intelligence manager can "kill two birds with one stone" by using one analytic task or one collection mission to satisfy two or more requirements.

Exploiting the historical intelligence base is a multiplier as well. Previously collected information can apply to many new products and requirements, especially those that depend on an analysis of trends and problem areas. Managers are responsible for seeing that records are maintained on collection coverage and products for potential use in future requirements.

Managers who decide on job assignments for analysts will attempt to task the same analyst with similar requirements in order to exploit that analyst's memory of prior product information.

The most obvious tool for focusing on common information needs is the creation of shared data bases. Order of battle (OB) is one of the most familiar shared data bases used in both strategic and tactical intelligence. Other forms of data stores that represent shared information sources are maps, finished intelligence products, doctrine studies, and target files.

Although overlapping requirements can be grouped together to share common information sources, <u>the analyst must treat each requirement separately in formulating the product for the users</u>. Even if the requirements are completely overlapping in their information needs, in formulating the final product you must still consider how each product user is going to use that information. If the tailoring is not done on an individual end-user basis, the value of saving resources through combined analysis may be wasted on an inferior product.

Preparation Is A Time Multiplier

Once past, time is lost--except when you have spent that time in preparing for future information needs of clients. In the tactical environment, intelligence preparation of the battlefield (IPB) is taught as a means of preparing information on terrain, weather, and enemy capabilities for use in time-critical decision-making. IPB prepares the mind of the analyst for more rapid analytical processing as well as pre-processing much of the static information base required for analysis. The strategic equivalent of IPB is the systematic development of knowledge about the strategic war plans of foreign forces and knowledge about the battlefields and environments in which conflict might occur.

Any intelligence production unit puts substantial efforts into creating and maintaining the knowledge bases used as sources for other products. Anticipation of required information is a responsibility of the intelligence manager because time and resources must be allocated for such preparations. The anticipation of requirements allows for systematic development of common information baselines and rehearsal of analytic procedures. Preparation has the impact of multiplying the effectiveness of the analysts during situations that are time critical and/or that have limited collection assets.

Generalization Is A Speed Multiplier

Another technique used by the intelligence production manager to produce products in less time is to designate a less precise level of description for conveying information in the product.

The time required to do analysis is in direct proportion to the level of detail and accuracy required in the product. If an intelligence requirement can be satisfied with more general descriptions or with less accuracy, a corresponding reduction can be achieved in the time needed to produce that product. Especially in those cases where the required level of detail is not known, it is important for the intelligence manager (or the analyst) to find out how the information is to be used and how accuracy will affect that use.

An example of how generalization can reduce analysis time can be seen in a combat modeling application. One combat model might require a very detailed description of the operation of a particular kind of unit or weapon system in order to represent time-critical performance features. On the other hand, another model might require only stereotyped representations of overall force structure. The analyst would not be required to spend the same amount of time on analyzing force structure as would be required by someone looking at the details of a logistics application.

Phasing Analysis From General To Specific Is A Speed Multiplier

You can produce general, less accurate information more quickly than accurate, detailed information. If information requirements overlap but differ in detail and accuracy requirements, the general information should be addressed first because that information can be produced more quickly. If you try to merge both requirements into a single requirement, you may compromise accuracy on one hand or delivery speed on the other.

A classical solution for overlapping requirements is to have analysts make multiple passes over the same information, extracting greater levels of detail with each successive pass. In this way, the product information requiring less detail can be satisfied immediately and with a minimum of resource expenditure.

Exploiting All Sources Is A Multiplier Of Certainty

Dealing with uncertainty is the intelligence analyst's stock and trade. Uncertainty is reduced by information that confirms likely hypotheses and increased by information that disconfirms them. For the strategic analyst in particular, the "ground truth" is seldom if ever known. The intelligence organization deals with the issue of uncertainty by creating an "all-source" environment to bring as diverse as possible a set of relevant information to bear on the issue.

Most persons recognize intuitively that problems are more likely to yield a correct solution when one has a wider range of information about the problem. In intelligence production, information is actively pursued from any possible source that might fill information gaps, however vague or error prone that source might be. It is the diversity of information sources used by the strategic analyst that is an effective underpinning for achieving increased validity of solutions. The term "all-source environment" generally is used in the intelligence community to mean that the analyst can access information from the systems as well as from collateral and unclassified sources. Intelligence managers also arrange for access to other intelligence producing organizations as well as academic and other non-intelligence organizations. Formal access arrangements are supplemented by the individual contacts that analysts have throughout the intelligence, academic, and professional communities.

Information Source Multipliers

Information that someone else collects for another purpose may be a valuable information source for you to exploit also. The interpretations of that information may in itself become a source if its original source is known and if its credibility for your use has been evaluated.

Products should have audit trails that trace the information sources and the analysts who performed the analysis. The intelligence production manager generally establishes the procedures and guidelines by which sources are referenced in shared databases and in products disseminated within the intelligence community. References to information sources should provide the following types of information:

o   Collection mode (SIGINT, HUMINT, IMINT, Open Source).
o   Collection mission identifier or source designation.
o   Requirement reference for mission tasking.
o   Intended use of information as viewed by the source.
o   Mission parameters or standard reference.

This level of source reference makes it possible for you or other analysts to get back to the original source data to check or modify interpretations. You must always be wary of using other analyst's interpretations of information unless you know the source, the analyst, and the conditions under which the analysis was performed. If the interpretation of another analyst is to be used without going back to the original source information, the following information must be added:

o   Source credibility (belief that source is capable of providing sufficient information for this interpretation).
o   Source reliability (historical quality of source).
o   Source precision (precision level of source for this interpretation).
o   Name of analyst who did interpretation.
o   Purpose for which interpretation was made.

Evaluation of the source is a much more difficult task than simply providing a reference to the source. An interpretation for one application may not require the same level of credibility or precision as for another application. For example, the interpretation of imagery to determine the number of weapon systems in a unit does not require the same level of precision as to determine the specific model or features of a weapon.

Guidelines for evaluating sources are generally informal, and rating scales, where used, tend to be imprecise. Imagery is rated on a formal basis using the NIIRS scale, but this applies only to how the imagery was used for a specific target interpretation and not to the overall value of the imagery as a source for other uses.

In summary, sharing information sources can multiply the analyst's access to information. The intelligence manager tries to make this information source sharing as effective as possible by ensuring that source references are disseminated.

Capacity Multipliers

Problems occur when the time needed by the analyst is greater than the time available. When this happens, analysts may be formed into analytical teams to decrease the production time by paralleling analysis tasks. The way in which analysts are organized as a team is a reflection of underlying principles of information-sharing and exploitation of the personal knowledge of analysts as a resource. The capacity gains are in terms of the added background knowledge of a multidisciplinary analytical team, parallel capacity for exploiting more information sources, and ability to look at the problem from multiple perspectives.

The organizational principles applied by the typical manager include rules for specialization, rules for partitioning workload, rules for team communication, and rules for maintaining team integrity. The team leader maintains the integrity of the analytic team by defining individual responsibilities and by providing mechanisms for team communications. The rules which the manager may apply to the issues of dividing responsibility include:

o Give responsibility by geographic area (White boundaries).
o Give responsibility by collection source mode (SIGINT, HUMINT, IMINT).
o Give responsibility by different levels of Red Thinking.
o Give responsibility for end-user dialogue and product tailoring (Blue perspective).

In order to maintain analytical integrity under these rules of dividing responsibility, the team manager must ensure that all analysts in the team share a conceptual model of the general mission parameters, and that all analysts have access to the overall situation model. The analyst team is, in effect, creating a group hypothesis of a threat situation. Within their own areas of responsibility, team members contribute to the shared threat model in terms of:

o Providing background knowledge.

o Identifying missing information in model.
o Filling-in information gaps from information sources.
o Testing the model with new information.
o Testing the model against doctrinal concepts.
o Evaluating the significance of changes in the model.
o Selecting information for product reporting and tailoring it for the product.
o Cataloging sources of information and maintaining an audit trail on the methods and reasoning used in the analysis.

SUMMARY

The intelligence manager is faced with the problem of scarce time and resources to meet the information needs of product users. The intelligence manager, and you as an analyst, must weigh the demands of current production requirements against the need to prepare for the time-critical information needs of wartime operations.

A critical asset of intelligence production is your own personal knowledge. Also, the time available can constrain the types of information sources you can exploit and the procedures you can use in analysis. The management rules described in this chapter will help you maximize the effectiveness of scarce time, personnel, and information resources in intelligence production.

NOTE

1. Henry Howe Ransom, The Intelligence Establishment (Cambridge, MA: Harvard University Press, 1970), p. 15.

7
Basic Intelligence
Stephen J. Andriole

INTRODUCTION

This chapter looks at the nature and purpose of basic intelligence. It first places such intelligence within a matrix of the components and forms of strategic intelligence. It then turns to some examples of basic military intelligence, a discussion of the methods available to the basic intelligence analyst, some case studies, and some thoughts about the larger role of military intelligence analysis in the national security process.

STRATEGIC AND TACTICAL INTELLIGENCE

What is tactical intelligence? What is strategic intelligence? How are they the same? How do they differ? The Joint Chiefs of Staff's <u>Dictionary of Military and Associated Terms</u> defines strategic intelligence as "intelligence which is required for the formulation of policy and military plans at national and international levels." The same dictionary defines tactical intelligence as "intelligence which is required for the planning and conduct of tactical operations." The dictionary also suggests that "tactical intelligence and strategic intelligence differ only in scope, point of view, and level of employment." What does this all mean? First, it means that there are no fundamental differences between strategic and tactical intelligence, except those traceable to the differences which inevitably exist within individual missions. In other words, the same mission may generate different--strategic and tactical--intelligence requirements, depending upon who is asking the questions. Corps commanders worry a lot about tactics, while Secretaries of Defense worry much more about strategy.
 Tactical intelligence also differs from strategic intelligence because of its orientation to combat and operations. Hence, the often heard reference to tactical intelligence as combat or operational intelligence. Strategic intelligence, on the other hand, is frequently "mission independent," oriented to more general national, international, and global issues.

Because of its combat and operational orientation, tactical intelligence also tends to be much more communications-intensive than strategic intelligence. This too is a result of the unique requirements of tactical intelligence analysis and production. Combat operations demand the availability of reliable, secure, and reconstitutable communications, while strategic planning and decisionmaking require objective judgment, unbiased analysis, and effective communication skills.

The differences between strategic and tactical intelligence thus reduce to differences in the perspective of the individual commander, analyst, or decisionmaker faced with a specific problem. We are concerned here almost exclusively with the analysis, production, and presentation of strategic intelligence; however, many of the ideas discussed throughout this book are extremely relevant to the analysis and production of tactical intelligence as well.

THE COMPONENTS OF STRATEGIC INTELLIGENCE

It might be helpful to think about strategic intelligence as a large whole comprised of a number of related parts or components. The intelligence literature recognizes eight distinct components of strategic intelligence: armed forces or military intelligence; biographic intelligence; economic intelligence; geographic intelligence; political intelligence; scientific and technical intelligence; sociological intelligence; and transportation and telecommunications intelligence.

Armed forces or military intelligence focuses on foreign military forces, orders of battle, equipment, combat effectiveness, combat readiness, and doctrine, among other related aspects of foreign military capabilities. Biographic intelligence focuses upon the major personalities in foreign governments, personalities that may have dramatic influence upon allied or adversary decisionmaking. As might be expected, biographic intelligence is critically important to negotiations, conferences, and even routine high level decisionmaking. Economic intelligence, which deals with the natural resources, trade, finances, and industrial capacities of U.S. allies and adversaries, also attempts to identify economic vulnerabilities and the availability of strategic commodities. Geographic intelligence focuses upon weather and climate, coasts, landing beaches, and landforms, among other topographical and geographical problems and opportunities. Political intelligence involves the collection and analysis of information concerning the workings of foreign governments and foreign leadership--as well as any political factors that might contribute to allied or adversary foreign policies that could affect U.S. national interests. Political intelligence focuses upon the structures of foreign governments as well as the political dynamics which determine the effectiveness and durability of governments. The study of revolutions and coups is thus well within the scope of political intelligence analysis and production. Scientific and technical intelligence focuses on the scientific and technical capabilities of foreign governments, especially as those capabilities contribute to a nation's ability to realize its national goals. Sociological intelligence concentrates on the social structures of foreign societies as well as upon the values, beliefs, traditions, and attitudes of foreign populations. Finally, transportation and telecommunications intelligence concentrates upon intranational and international transportation networks, such as highways, railroads, inland waterways, airports, and the like. Transportation and telecommunications intelligence analysts are also responsible for assessments regarding the telephone, telegraph, and civil broadcast capabilities of foreign governments.

It is important to remember that the definitional boundaries of the components of strategic intelligence are by no means sacrosanct. At best, they are overlapping and at times even redundant. The political analyst responsible for determining the likelihood of a coup in the Philippines would by necessity enter the worlds of economic, sociological, biographical, and political intelligence. Similarly, it is extremely difficult to assess economic capabilities without spending some time studying the target country's political structure. The definitions of the various components of strategic intelligence are instructive, but by no means completely accurate.

It is also appropriate here to call your attention to some additional definitional problems in intelligence analysis and production. Note, for example, the absence of any reference above to the various "INTs" of intelligence. No doubt you have already heard a great deal about SIGINT (signal intelligence), ELINT (electronic intelligence), PHOTINT (photographic intelligence), HUMINT (human intelligence), and even LITINT (open literature intelligence). Many of you have also heard something about imagery intelligence, reconnaissance intelligence, and any number of other "kinds." While it may be useful at times to think about all of these as legitimate components of strategic intelligence, in practice it makes more sense to regard them as the means by which the eight primary components of strategic intelligence are produced.

THE FORMS OF STRATEGIC INTELLIGENCE

The components of strategic analysis deal primarily with the substance of intelligence. The forms of intelligence deal with the nature of the intelligence product. For example, there is "basic" intelligence--the subject of this chapter--and "current" intelligence. There is also descriptive intelligence, explanatory intelligence, predictive-estimative intelligence, and evaluative intelligence. Basic and current intelligence are top-level criteria for defining the various forms of strategic intelligence. The four other forms take their lead from these top two. As a result, it is possible to think in terms of basic descriptive, explanatory, predictive-estimative, and evaluative intelligence, and current descriptive, explanatory, predictive-estimative, and evaluative intelligence.

Basic intelligence is the mainstay of the intelligence community. Without it, it would be impossible to conduct any other form of intelligence analysis. Basic intelligence concentrates on past and present conditions and events likely to have an impact on foreign and international behavior. In one sense basic intelligence is encyclopedic in nature. But in another, more accurate, sense, it is the basis upon which a variety of products for the support of planning, policymaking, and military operations are produced. It may be helpful to think about basic intelligence as "general intelligence" concerning the capabilities, vulnerabilities, and intentions of foreign nations. Current intelligence, on the other hand, focuses upon more dynamic processes, upon events and conditions which are rapidly unfolding and which are potentially threatening to U.S. national interests. Current intelligence is characterized by change and the need to constantly update the conclusions, analyses, and judgments.

Unlike the distinctions among the various components of strategic intelligence, the distinction between basic and current intelligence is relatively clear. The distinctions among descriptive, explanatory, predictive-estimative, and evaluative intelligence are also straightforward.

Descriptive intelligence, whether it be basic or current, seeks to identify the nature and characteristics of a particular component of strategic intelligence. Basic descriptive political intelligence, for example, might involve describing the political structure of Poland as it evolves over time in response to Soviet domination. Basic descriptive economic intelligence might be concerned with the monetary structure of Common Market countries, while basic descriptive scientific and technical (S&T) intelligence might be concerned with whether or not Argentina has the scientific infrastructure upon which to build advanced nuclear weaponry. Current descriptive biographic intelligence was no doubt in great demand when the Soviet Union recently selected a new President.

Explanatory intelligence seeks to identify reasons why specific events occur or do not occur. It is useful to regard explanatory intelligence as more sophisticated than descriptive intelligence, though this is not to imply that one is more valuable than the other. An example of basic explanatory intelligence analysis occurred following the fall of the Shah of Iran, when virtually every part of the intelligence community wanted to know why the Shah's regime fell. Another example of basic explanatory intelligence involves the search for explanations regarding why Soviet crop yields are always so disappointing. A current explanatory scientific and technical problem might involve the search for an explanation regarding how the Soviet space program continues to progress.

Predictive-estimative intelligence concentrates on the future. Basic predictive-estimative political intelligence certainly involves analyses of long-term European, Asian, and

African political futures, while current predictive-estimative political intelligence requires analysts to issue "indications and warnings" (I&W) about impending intranational and international crises.

Evaluative intelligence is concerned primarily with assessments. Basic evaluative scientific and technical intelligence might thus be concerned with assessing the capabilities of Soviet chemical weapons. Basic evaluative economic intelligence might involve assessments regarding a particular country's ability to wage war, while current evaluative political intelligence might evaluate the viability of a new foreign political structure. Evaluative intelligence is also concerned with evaluations of the sources of intelligence information, the reliability of information, and even the viability of alternative organizational structures for intelligence production.

The forms of intelligence, when combined with the components, yield an understanding of the range of strategic intelligence for which the intelligence community is responsible. As you can see, there are a great many combinations. In response to such massive requirements, the intelligence community has organized itself according to some very general notions of divisions of labor. For example, the CIA is generally regarded as responsible for the production of economic intelligence, while the Department of State's Bureau of Intelligence and Research is charged with the production of political intelligence. The DIA is the source of much excellent scientific and technical intelligence, just as both CIA and DIA are responsible for biographic intelligence.

In practice, however, such divisions of labor are by no means clearcut. More than one intelligence agency, office, or department may produce the same kind or form of strategic intelligence. Depending upon an agency's mission, for example, it may very well find itself producing intelligence in areas for which it has never been primarily responsible. Instead of trying to match the components and forms of strategic intelligence to specific offices, agencies, or departments, it is important to remember that intelligence analysis and production are almost always requirements driven.

A STRATEGIC INTELLIGENCE MATRIX

Figure 7.1 presents a strategic intelligence matrix, a graphic way to think about how the various forms and components of strategic intelligence interrelate. The eight components of strategic intelligence appear along the left-hand side of the matrix. The various forms of intelligence are listed across the top. Each box or "cell" in the matrix represents one instance of intelligence analysis. It is thus possible to think about basic predictive-estimative political intelligence, current descriptive scientific and technical intelligence, and basic evaluative sociological intelligence, among other combinations. This matrix provides us with a convenient way to think about various intelli-

FORMS \ COMPONENTS	Basic				Current			
	D	E	P-E	Ev	D	E	P-E	Ev
Armed Forces, or Military								
Biographic								
Economic								
Geographic								
Political								
Scientific & Technical (S&T)								
Sociological								
Transportation & Telecommunications								

D = Descriptive
E = Explanatory
P-E = Predictive-Estimative
Ev = Evaluative

Figure 7.1. A Strategic Intelligence Matrix

gence combinations; it can also help us select levels and units of analysis as well as analytical methods.

BASIC "MILITARY" INTELLIGENCE

Basic "military" intelligence is of course not exclusively military. When an intelligence analyst is tasked to estimate the military capabilities of the Soviet Union at the turn of the century, he invariably relies upon a good deal of economic and scientific and technical intelligence. Any forecast of Soviet military strength would necessarily include a variety of forecasts about the state of the Soviet economy in the year 2000 as well as technological forecasts about the capabilities of Soviet weaponry. As suggested above, the boundaries that surround the forms and components of strategic intelligence are by no means fixed. Nevertheless, there are many instances of intelligence analysis and production that are clearly more oriented to military rather than any other kind of intelligence. It is on this species that we will concentrate.

What are some typical military intelligence problems? What are some examples of problems in basic military intelligence analysis? While far from comprehensive, the following list is at least representative of the nature of basic military intelligence problems:

- What is the nature and depth of Soviet military strength in Eastern Europe?;

- What are realistic military projections for the Peoples' Republic of China?;

- What is the Polish Army's capacity for internal war?;

- Develop a profile of Argentine military capabilities;

- Assess the mobility of North Korea's armed forces;

- Estimate the capacity of the Marcos government in the Philippines to militarily resist internal violence;

- What is the Soviet order of battle in Eastern Europe?;

- How long could Soviet logistics feed a mobile Soviet land attack in Afghanistan?;

- Describe the capabilities of French fighter aircraft in the order of their strength;

- Explain the military outcome of the Falklands conflict in terms of military strategy, tactics, and capabilities; and o Rank order global nuclear strength by country, region, and alliance.

As you might imagine, these questions represent a very small, though representative, sample of the kinds of basic military intelligence problems that confront the modern intelligence analyst. They should be distinguished from topics of more immediate concern such as daily or weekly troop movements, engagements, and maneuvers. More urgent questions fall within the realm of current and indications and warning (I&W) intelligence, as ably discussed by E. Luther Johnson and Timothy M. Laur elsewhere in the book.

Note also the "impurity" of the above questions; almost all of them require the analyst to integrate many of the other components of strategic intelligence in order to produce "military" intelligence. In fact, if you look closely at the questions, you will see a role for each of the eight components of strategic intelligence in the analysis and production process.

The intelligence matrix in Figure 7.1 also suggests that basic intelligence can take many forms. It is possible to conduct basic descriptive analysis, basic explanatory analysis, basic estimative-predictive analysis (which is usually long range), and basic evaluative-prescriptive analysis. These distinctions are important not only because they facilitate diagnostic problem structuring, but because they help analysts select optimal methods as well.

METHODS FOR BASIC INTELLIGENCE ANALYSIS AND PRODUCTION

There will always be considerable debate about the merits of alternative methods for intelligence analysis and production, regardless of where the analysis falls in the intelligence matrix. In fact, it is difficult to travel anywhere in the intelligence community and not find a debate raging about the strengths and weaknesses of qualitative versus quantitative methods. Over the past decade, entire offices within individual intelligence agencies have been formed to do nothing more than determine the feasibility of applying new qualitative and quantitative methods to intelligence analysis and production. Suffice it to say here that the debate is far from over, and that--as with all debates-- there is a sensible middle ground.

The sensible middle ground requires that we first develop some definitions of quantitative and qualitative methodology. Quantitative methods refer to all those involving measurement. Those employing quantitative methods are generally concerned about precisely how the measurement problem is handled. In the physical sciences, there are no insurmountable measurement problems, but in the social and behavioral sciences, a great many such problems arise. In other words, it is a lot easier to measure quantitatively the capabilities of Soviet submarines than the intentions of Soviet strategists.

Qualitative methods refer to those which handle available data in some very different, i.e., non-empirical, ways. Within the realm of predictive-estimative intelligence, for example, qualitative methodologists might rely upon intuition, wisdom, judgment, and experience in order to produce intelligence about intentions or even capabilities. Quantitative methodologists, on the other hand, would attempt to convert these judgments into some measurable, i.e., numeric, form.

Many intelligence analysts believe that intelligence is an "art," not a "science." Such analysts implicitly or explicitly regard quantitative methods as unsuited to the analysis and production of much strategic intelligence. Of course, very few arguments develop over the appropriateness of quantitative methods in certain areas of intelligence production, such as scientific and technical and economic intelligence. But real problems arise when discussions turn to sociological, political, and even military intelligence. The essence of the opposition to the application of quantitative methods to the analysis and production of sociological, political, and military intelligence can be traced to a deep-seated suspicion that many intelligence professionals have about the utility of quantitative social and behavioral science. Without question, some of the suspicion is justified. Over the past two decades, the social and behavioral sciences have not exactly made enormous strides methodologically or substantively. There are also a number of horror stories about the misapplication of quantitative methodology in strategic intelligence, stories that have of course been exaggerated over the years but nonetheless persist in the memories of many old hands. It is important that we develop a balanced perspective on the use of quantitative and qualitative methods. We should listen to the horror stories, but also remember that progress has indeed been made in the development and application of quantitative methodology over the past decade or so.

The middle ground thus suggests that you determine whether or not your problem is approachable quantitatively or qualitatively. Is quantification possible? Or can you only expect to render qualitative judgments? If the intelligence problem involves assessing the likely level of Soviet grain production, then chances are that you will be able to quantify much of the analytical process and the results. But if you are asked to estimate the likelihood that the Libyans will explode a tactical nuclear device in central Africa, then you will probably have to rely on a combination of quantitative and qualitative estimates.

To a great extent, the argument regarding the strengths and weaknesses of quantitative versus qualitative methods has been for naught. The real questions have to do with the nature of the intelligence problem and the amount and quality of available intelligence information. Scientific and technical problems are by nature much more quantitative than predictive-estimative ones. Certain forms of military intelligence are extremely "hard," while almost all political intelligence is "soft."

It is also possible to apply quantitative methods to the manipulation of qualitative data, and vice versa. For example, it is possible to convert soft information about adversary intentions into quantitative-numeric form using some Bayesian statistical techniques. It is also possible to move in the reverse direction and de-quantify hard data. So long as the decisions regarding the use of one versus another method are explicit, and so long as we are aware of the nature and liabilities of our data, we can proceed with confidence.

As stated, military intelligence analysis and production frequently flow from the application of quantitative methodology. So long as adequate empirical data are available, and so long as the assumptions that govern the analytical processes are well-conceived and explicit (sometimes even in the form of a formal model or analytical framework), quantitative methods can be applied effectively. But if available data are soft and the problem defies precise structuring, then qualitative methods may be appropriate. Estimates about Soviet naval forces, for example, can be relatively hard, while estimates regarding Soviet military intentions in the Middle East are much more difficult to quantify.

The "debate" between the quantitative and qualitative analysts is thus really not a debate at all. It more accurately resembles a popularity contest. The middle ground, of course, suggests that data, requirements, and analytical precedent determine the "best" analytical method.

What are some of the specific methods available to the basic military intelligence analyst? On the qualitative side are the standards: wisdom; intuition; experience-based judgment; and Delphi (and many hybrids). On the quantitative side are those anchored in descriptive and inferential statistics, Bayes' theorem of conditional probabilities, and cross-impact assumptions about the co-occurrence of important events and conditions. The more sophisticated quantitative techniques, like econometric modeling and multiple regression, sound a whole lot more useful than they really are. While there are occasional uses for such exotic techniques in economic and scientific and technical intelligence analysis, by and large the enormous substantive requirements of the intelligence community preclude their widespread use. There are also methodological problems. Many of the "sophisticated" techniques frequently fail to yield reproducible results, an absolute prerequisite to their defensible use. There are also major disagreements among even the champions of the methods. It is very difficult to find three or more advanced methodologists who will agree about how, when, and why to apply the techniques.

SOME CASE STUDIES

Sometimes intelligence analysts are required to assess the military capabilities and interests of the U.S. in a given area for a variety of strategic or tactical reasons. Imagine, for example, a request regarding the distribution of U.S. military forces in the Middle East or in Central America. Perhaps there is a need to determine the vulnerability of U.S. military forces in a specific area or to assess how visible the U.S. military presence is in a particular geographic region.

Such questions formed the basis of a military intelligence analysis performed nearly a decade ago by the Westinghouse Center for Advanced Studies and Analysis.[1] In fact, the study was broader, concentrating on a variety of U.S. economic, military, political, and cultural capabilities abroad.

The analysis, conducted by Jan S. Breemer and Peter H. Fenn, defined military interests by identifying a number of indicators that lent themselves to quantification. The indicators themselves included the following:[2]

- o U.S. military presence, defined as the total number of uniformed U.S. military personnel abroad;

- o U.S. military property, defined as the total dollar value of U.S. service-owned and leased property, active and inactive, industrial and nonindustrial;

- o U.S. security assistance, defined as the annual delivered dollar value of military assistance plus the annual programmed value of equipment and service so transferred;

- o U.S. military sales, defined as the annual delivered dollar value of military equipment; and

- o U.S. bilateral and multilateral military treaties, among several others.

Data were collected for a ten year period for nearly all of the countries in the world; they were then separated into regions, such as Western Europe, Southeast Asia, and the Persian Gulf. The data analysis suggested that there were high concentrations of U.S. military interests in Southeast Asia and the Middle East, but relatively low concentrations in Africa. The results reported more than just crude profiles and trends; rank orders with explicit distances among them were also reported.

Why is this analysis highlighted here? First, this case study suggests how useful well-defined, explicit indicators of U.S. military interests abroad can be. It suggests the utility of developing quantitative expressions of the indicators, and how rank ordering (high-to-low, most-to-least) can effectively summarize analytical results. The message here is not necessarily that quantitative methods are "better" than qualitative ones, but that the perception of intelligence analysis as a systematic process is always beneficial.

The second case study involves an assessment of NATO readiness in the event of a Warsaw Pact attack on Western Europe.[3] The purpose of this analysis was to determine how the NATO decisionmaking process inhibits or accelerates NATO military readiness.

The specific objective of the analysis was to determine how long it would take NATO to respond to a Pact attack; more specifically, the objective was to predict the number of days it would take NATO to respond to a Pact attack following an "irreversible 30-day mobilization cycle. Furthermore, it assume(d) . . . that the Pact is in no way influenced by NATO actions . . ."[4]

The flow chart in Figure 7.2 suggests how the analysis was conducted. The objective of the analysis was to model the process in Figure 7.2 in "such a way that the model (could) be used to predict the total mobilization lag in response to the . . . scenario."[5] In order to produce this prediction, the following steps were taken:[6]

- o A specific daily set of intelligence reports was selected that plausibly reflected a realistic series of events;

- o Predictions of SACEUR responses were made in probabilistic terms, using experts and a "rational choice model;"

- o Predictions of lags in the NAC response were also made, based upon expert judgments about NATO organizational processes;

- o Integration of additional uncertainties about the SACEUR and NAC lags due to expectations about the availability (or lack) of intelligence; and

- o Assessments were made regarding a probability distribution for the total NATO mobilization lag.

The results of the analysis suggested that SACEUR would recommend NATO mobilization seven days after the Pact began to mobilize and all of NATO would approve the mobilization fifteen days after Pact mobilization. The analysis also suggested that given intelligence uncertainties, NATO could have from nine to twenty-one days for mobilization.

This case study is highlighted here because it illustrates the use of a technique, called decision analysis, which quantifies expert judgment. It is also a model-based analysis (see Figure 7.2) that represents how military intelligence problems can be elaborately structured.

The third and final case study discussed here focuses on the use of the Soviet Armed Forces as a political instrument.[7] One of the first steps in the analysis involved identifying and defining Soviet military force, ultimately defined as being comprised of

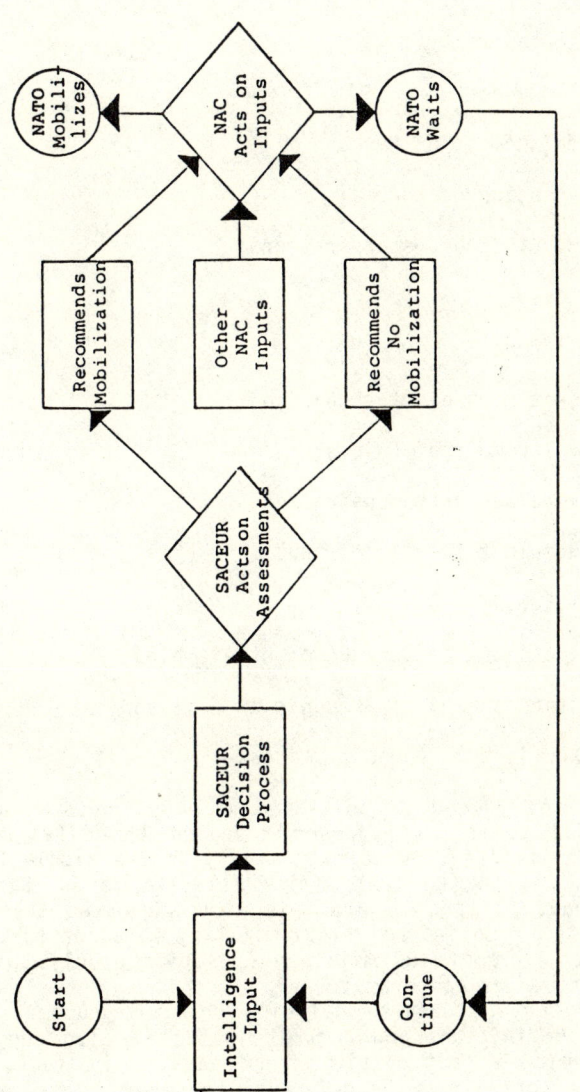

Figure 7.2. Flow-Chart of NATO Mobilization Process
(from Brown, et al)

five kinds of ground force, five kinds of air force, and three kinds of naval force, all as follows:[8]

- o Ground Force:
  - Firepower;
  - Blockade;
  - Emplacement of Forces;
  - Retention of Forces;
  - Exercises or Demonstrations;

- o Air Force:
  - Firepower;
  - Harassment of Other Aircraft;
  - Emplacement of Forces;
  - Exercises or Demonstrations;
  - Equipment Transport; and

- o Naval Force:
  - Harassment or Seizure of Other Ships;
  - Establishment of Presence at Sea; and
  - Exercises or Demonstrations.

The analysis of the data collected on the Soviet use of military might for political purposes revealed that the Soviet Union projected its military force extensively in the Middle East, the Persian Gulf, and the Horn of Africa relative to Sub-Saharan Africa and Southeast Asia. The analysis also suggested that the overwhelming amount of Soviet political-military behavior has been coercive. In fact, out of 190 military operations, only thirty-two could be described as cooperative.[9]

Like the military interests analysis, this one suggests the need for careful definitions and accurate data; it also suggests the value of developing alternative hypotheses. In fact, the original study was conceived with reference to several hypotheses. One assumed that the Soviets did in fact use their military force for political purposes. Another assumed that the bulk of this use was coercive, while the third posited that the Soviets use their military more frequently than the United States for political purposes, and with less favorable results. As problem structuring tools, hypotheses can help with the analysis and production of basic current intelligence and can keep analyses focused on their stated objectives. Hypotheses are also good assessment tools. If your data confirm your hypotheses, then your analysis can be regarded as successful, though at times unconfirmed hypotheses can yield as much information as confirmed ones.

The last case study also illustrates how difficult it sometimes is to distinguish between military and other kinds of intelligence analysis. Very often military intelligence problems are inseparable from political and economic ones; hence, the caution expressed earlier about the distinctions among the components of strategic intelligence.

The three case studies together should provide some insight into the nature of basic military intelligence. None of the analyses was concerned with events that were unfolding on a daily or weekly basis. None was targeted at rapidly unfolding events or conditions, nor were they conducted within the current intelligence environment, an environment akin to that which one might find at a daily newspaper. (In fact, much current intelligence closely resembles the daily section of the paper on world events, while other forms of intelligence resemble weekly news magazines.)

The three case studies also illustrate the various forms that military intelligence can take. The first was essentially descriptive; the second was much more evaluative and predictive; the third was descriptive and explanatory.

A number of analytical methods are illustrated in the case studies. The first and third case studies are basically quantitative-empirical, but the second utilizes a method that quantifies subjective or "expert" data. One is grounded in an explicit model, while another attempts to test a set of hypotheses.

In addition to the forms of basic intelligence analysis highlighted by the case studies, there are a variety of other products that flow from the basic intelligence community. Some of these include fact books, data about weapons and adversary doctrine, and reports on a variety of military intelligence subjects that circulate throughout the community. It is thus useful to think about basic intelligence as the analytical infrastructure of the entire intelligence community. Without it, the community would certainly grind to a halt; much more importantly, critical national security decisions would be made without the benefit of genuine analysis.

BASIC INTELLIGENCE AND THE NATIONAL SECURITY PROCESS

Basic intelligence ultimately finds its way into the national security planning, decisionmaking, and policymaking process. It is an indispensable component of successful planning. Among other things, strategic planning almost always involves identifying and evaluating alternative courses of international or global action. Some of these courses of action are intended for implementation several years in the future, while others are intended for shorter-range implementation. These courses of action might involve military, economic, or even "social" activity. When the activity is planned for near-term application, it represents the result of conventional strategic planning, but when the activity is targeted for future or hypothetical application, it should be understood as the result of contingency planning.

Examples of contingency planning abound on the international landscape. What should the United States do if the Iranians or the Iraqis block the Strait of Hormuz? How should the United States respond to the sale of Soviet natural gas to the Western Europeans? What actions should the United States and its allies take if Marcos' Philippines government falls? How should the United States respond to Cuban aggression in Central America? All of these questions involve developing and assessing plans. But without accurate and reliable intelligence about these and related problems, the plans would be extremely hollow. Intelligence breathes substance into planning, and permits decisionmakers to identify the plan most likely to satisfy U.S. national interests.

Planning, by definition, is a longer-term process than decisionmaking, which implies more immediate action. Decisionmaking almost always involves identifying goals, identifying decision options, evaluating those options, and implementing but one alternative. Comprehensive decisionmaking also includes an evaluation step, which explicitly assesses the impact of the decision outcome. Basic intelligence analysis plays a slightly larger role in the planning process, while current intelligence slightly dominates the decisionmaking process, though this is not to imply that basic intelligence is the only type used during the planning process, or that decisionmaking only relies upon current intelligence. Basic and current intelligence both play important roles in planning and decisionmaking. Short-term urgent decisionmaking requires a great deal of current intelligence, just as longer-term, slower-paced planning demands a great deal of basic intelligence.

As we move from planning and decisionmaking to policymaking, the number of players in the process begins to grow considerably. Planning is frequently the occupation of full-time analysts who often have a great deal of prior planning experience. Decisionmaking frequently involves elected officials, who tend to make decisions based on a much larger set of evaluative criteria. Policymaking involves the work of planners, elected and appointed decisionmakers, and a whole host of others with a vested interest in the policymaking process. Here the reference is to the members of Congress, each of whom has his or her own view of what U.S. national security policy ought to look like. As we move from planning and decisionmaking to policymaking, the role of intelligence begins to shrink somewhat. While in principle intelligence should play as active a role in the policymaking process as it does in planning and decisionmaking, frequently the sheer number of players and distribution of vested interests interact to dilute the impact of intelligence analysis. No doubt there are a number of legitimate intelligence failures, but how many so-called failures in intelligence are attributable to failures in policymaking? The mission of the intelligence community is to produce accurate, reliable, and timely intelligence that contributes to and fulfills planning, decisionmaking, and policymaking requirements.

If you were to trace the flow of intelligence within and beyond the intelligence community, you would find that intelligence is not unlike the proverbial water falling down the side of a mountain. In some cases it takes the path of least resistance, but in others it simply overpowers any obstacles in its path. So it is with intelligence. Sometimes solid intelligence exerts an enormous impact upon planning, decisionmaking, and policymaking, but on other occasions it is successfully resisted or deflected. It is extremely important to develop a realistic understanding of the role of intelligence in the national security process.

CONCLUSION

This chapter has covered a lot of diverse ground. It has attempted to introduce and describe basic military intelligence analysis and production, but because of space limitations has only done so via a brief overview and a few short illustrations. Nevertheless, the structure of the chapter itself should convey the nature, purpose, and flow of basic military intelligence, especially as it may be compared and contrasted with other forms and components of strategic intelligence.

This chapter has also raised as many issues as it has resolved. The question of analytical methods remains open, as do questions about the role of basic military intelligence in the national security planning, decisionmaking, and policymaking process.

Above all else, this chapter has stressed the importance of basic intelligence. Subsequent chapters deal with several forms of current intelligence. As you read them, remember that basic intelligence lies at the heart of all intelligence analysis and production.

NOTES

1. Jan S. Breemer and Peter H. Fenn, <u>Identification and Measurement of US Interests Abroad: A Quantitative Analysis of US Stakes at the Sub-Theater Level and Their Relative Vulnerability to Local Conflict</u> (Falls Church, VA: Westinghouse Center for Advanced Studies and Analyses, November 1974).

2. Ibid., pp. 1-18.

3. Rex V. Brown, Clinton W. Kelly III, Richard R. Stewart, and Jacob W. Ulvila, <u>The Timeliness of a NATO Response to an</u>

Impending Warsaw Pact Attack (McLean, VA: Decisions and Designs, Inc., December 1975).

    4. Ibid., p. 1.

    5. Ibid., p. 4.

    6. Ibid., pp. 4-5.

    7. Stephen S. Kaplan, Diplomacy of Power: Soviet Armed Forces as a Political Instrument (Washington, DC: The Brookings Institution, 1981).

    8. Ibid., p. 41.

    9. Ibid., p. 34.

8
Current Intelligence

E. Luther Johnson

The Joint Chiefs of Staff (JCS) dictionary, JCS Publication 1, defines current intelligence as "intelligence of all types and forms of intermediate interest, which usually is disseminated without delays necessary to complete evaluations or interpretations."

This definition aids in the determination of where to place the area of current intelligence in the intelligence cycle or process. Insofar as subject area coverage is concerned, current intelligence covers all topics from political to technical intelligence. From the point of view of time, it encompasses ongoing events, usually beginning at the present time and reaching back, from a practical standpoint, to whatever earlier studies exist about a topic under consideration, or far enough back to include relevant developments to a study or report recently completed or under preparation.

Almost exclusively, current intelligence reflects events created by human beings, which become "newsworthy." It can also be viewed as history being brought up to a date and, more often than not, up to deadline in an institutional context, whether it be a major or minor command or the bureaucratic framework of a major national agency. While a technical intelligence analyst may be responsible for the design and functioning of a piece of equipment, it is more in the field of current intelligence to explain how and where it is being used, reflecting the results of human decisions. Furthermore, the current intelligence analyst must integrate such events into the ongoing evolution of the region and/or countries under his or her cognizance. In contrast to basic intelligence, which should not diminish in value or importance over time, current intelligence must be almost continuously attuned to change and its impact on the environment. In essence current intelligence concentrates on change and the dynamics caused by human activity and the integration thereof into an understandable sequence of cause and effect.

A newly assigned current intelligence officer, responsible for the activities of one or more countries or regions, or perhaps just one phase of the activities thereof if a large country or region, can easily fall into a soporific routine of mechanically shuffling through the mass of information reported each day, finding items that he or she considers to be important or interesting, deciding that these should be written up in the daily intelligence summary that his or her command or agency publishes, selecting some melodious sounding and impeccably written sentences from the source cable--no copyright restriction--copying them over into command format, subject to the idiosyncracies of immediate superiors, turning in the product to the cognizant superior, who most likely will change a word here and there, and then being convinced that a good day's--or good shift's--work has been done. As undoubtedly surmised by this enumeration, a passable product may have been accomplished; after all, no one else will be going through the mountains of incoming information reports, messages, and cables that formed the basis for the output in question. On the contrary, the current intelligence analyst is expected to make a professional contribution to his or her command and agency, not supply a patchwork of inputs that others have made.

To assess and describe the current intelligence officer's position and expected contribution, it is probably more useful to look at his or her job from the point of view of the well-known intelligence process or cycle (i.e., collection, production, and dissemination). Of course, current intelligence officers are never responsible for this cycle as a whole; however, it is more meaningful and productive to examine their analytical efforts in a parallel cycle: data collection and receipt, analysis, and dissemination. It is also helpful for the individual involved to look upon his or her assignment as a mini-intelligence cycle in order to achieve the most valuable and significant output possible.

CURRENT INTELLIGENCE INFORMATION

In a bureaucratic setting the largest supply of current information will be found in the analyst's "in" basket, which may seem to be bottomless. With proper dissemination throughout the intelligence community, the analyst should have access to all information needed for a credible job performance. However, there are additional aspects that need to be considered.

The first is the knowledgeability of the analyst him- or herself. An analyst who is familiar with his or her areas as a result of formal academic training, residence abroad, relevant service schools, duty assignments, and language capabilities will obviously perform better than one who is not. Analysts should try to place themselves mentally within the framework of the country or area for which they are responsible, know how the latter has evolved, and try to acquire a basic "feel" for it. In a way, current intelligence analysts assume the role of representatives of foreign countries and areas under cognizance, and they must be able to respond to questions not only of fact but also to issues of judgments or values the local inhabitants may have on various issues. Admittedly, not every analyst is lucky enough to have this type of complete background, and if this is not the case, individual efforts through self-study are needed to complement shortcomings.

The source material the analysts receive can conveniently be broken down into two categories, classified and unclassified. The two combine synergistically to enhance the coverage of the area or country in question, if used in a thoughtful, analytical manner, as will be discussed in the next section of this chapter. The classified material comes more or less automatically to the analyst or to his or her supervisor, if the dissemination is restricted. After a review of unclassified sources available to the analyst, classified material will be discussed in more detail.

Among the unclassified sources, press reports are most easily obtained. A few U.S. newspapers carry fairly substantial foreign reporting, although coverage can vary radically from one part of the world to another. Many times an analyst may gain more information with more even coverage if he or she has access to the wire services. Some of these may concentrate on a particular area and employ veteran reporters. However, it must be kept in mind that the latter do rotate and get reassigned, which will impact on comprehensiveness and quality.

Where foreign newspapers are collected and forwarded, the analyst who is able to read them in the local language can gain considerable insight into the issues at hand. Foreign newspaper reporting and analysis is also provided by U.S. Government agencies. The analyst should remember, however, that the latter reports have been subjected to an initial filtering process, as it were, by the reporting officer who forwarded them. The latter may have selection criteria different from those used by the analyst because of different government agency missions. In this context it should be stressed that the Foreign Broadcast Information Service (FBIS) provides timely translations by wire and hardcopy. Their publications are also available to the public through regular subscriptions. It is also advisable for the new analyst to consult a basic reference manual, be it classified or not, to ensure that he or she is receiving even coverage. It should be remembered that press articles for countries with totalitarian governments can be valuable for what they do not, or will not, report.

Basically, newspaper reporters can be viewed as intelligence collectors who serve unwittingly--and without extra pay--on the staff of information providers. The well-known reporters with international reputations can be veritable godsends to the analyst. The report of a question and answer period between an Oriana Fallaci and one of her "victims," be it a Lech Walesa or a General Galtieri, will provide otherwise unobtainable insight into the latter's thinking on various issues. Knowledge of their mental processes can be most useful at a later date, when the analyst wants to supply such information to some other issue under analysis. Interviews with leaders who have recently left office can also be extremely useful as background information and for filling in past gaps; such individuals now are in a less constrained environment, both from an institutional and political viewpoint, and are apt to be more forthright.

The current intelligence analyst will also benefit from ascertaining which leading academic writers publish articles in scholarly journals and periodicals in the areas of analyst responsibility. While the academic researcher may not approach a topic with the same comprehensiveness as the analyst, the former nevertheless delves into issues of interest, providing additional insight for the latter. If an analyst reviews academic literature on a regular basis, he or she will soon discover who the cogent and/or prolific writers are. At that point an assessment should be made of the academic writer's competence as a source. This should not be too difficult because, by then, the analyst should be able to compare academic quality with similar output from other sources. For the government analyst, academic writing is all too often not timely, but it provides a means of expanding analyst understanding and filling gaps of knowledge. Moreover, the analyst may not have access to these open source publications because of the location of his or her command, or command unwillingness to underwrite subscriptions.

Another useful tool for the current intelligence analyst is the great number of reference manuals available, particularly throughout the industrialized world. Many of these change annually, and they can thus be considered as current publications rather than basic intelligence manuals. The analyst should have access to, or acquire, those published in his or her area of responsibility, even if written in a foreign language. These types of publications are not usually translated, and any English counterpart is unlikely to be as complete. In this context it should also be mentioned that many international organizations publish high quality reports and publications. Factual information contained therein is usually very accurate, particularly when it is supplied by nations with open societies where accuracy tends to be subject to a checks and balances system.

An analyst may also benefit from access to recently created commercial data bases, such as DIALOG or the Bibliographic Retrieval Services, which, albeit unclassified, can produce quickly a bibliographic summary with abstracts, if needed. This type of support can be very useful when analysts are confronted with a requirement to look into an unfamiliar subject or topic, and background information is needed to construct a framework on which to base the assigned project.

Examining more closely the classified category, the analyst must at the onset accept on faith that all required material is received automatically, since one cannot, of course, ask for what one does not know exists. After some time in the new assignment, experience and contact with colleagues in other commands and activities will educate him or her to what other information is available but not received. Contact with other analysts is fairly easy, since there usually is an informal network available for exchange of ideas and information.

With a reasonable assurance that all needed and available

information is at hand, the analyst can begin to consider analytical processes and respond to tasking. Part of this analytical process should also include assessments on the balance of classified and unclassified information. Analysts cannot expect that they can always mix the two in a project, since often they are required to produce a report or study at a particular classification level or exclusively on the unclassified level. In this case it is essential to separate classified and unclassified facts: if the latter are supported by the former, the analytical task becomes easier; if not, the analyst must resort to command or agency procedures for review and reduction of classification levels. In either case, these procedures must be followed meticulously to avoid inadvertent disclosure.

It is also necessary to keep in mind the process of change that is reported in both categories of information. In some cases the change process is slow moving, in others rapid, all of it caused by human decisionmaking, either directly or indirectly. Unfortunately more often than not, change is not reported in chronological order, but even information out of sequence is valuable, in spite of the added effort of restructuring a course of events.

To conclude this section on source material available to the analyst, the complementary aspects of classified and unclassified information are stressed again. A new analyst may become fascinated by the classified component alone, but it should be remembered that the world does not evolve in the classified sphere exclusively, although many important events will be reported only in this medium and will become known, perhaps, to the world some half-century later when a historian has gained access to the data. Unclassified events are equally important to the analyst because they often reflect the results of decisionmaking bodies that have to consider, in varying degrees (depending upon the type of government involved), the public impact of their decisions at home and abroad. This process will furnish additional information to the analyst about the outlook and beliefs of the decisionmakers involved.

CURRENT INTELLIGENCE ANALYSIS

The primary duty of current intelligence officers is analysis, as previously stated, but to perform in a superior manner they need information, as was noted earlier. Before delving into medias res, as it were, there is a need for organization of information--rigorous, stringent organization. An analyst can focus too readily upon the currently received and personally interesting news items at the expense of other information which deserves equal or more attention. The analyst must also guard against remembering one particular news item better than some others, which can warp analytical output.

To approach current intelligence analysis methodologically, the analyst should at the onset of the assignment, even before reviewing the daily accumulation in the "in" basket, concentrate upon, and assess, the dynamic structures in pertinent countries or areas of responsibility. This review should cover the whole range of activities that can initiate change (for example, political, military, economic, cultural, and foreign policy entities). Even if the analyst is responsible only for one of these areas, it is necessary to consider which influences from other areas impinge as well. It is unwise to concentrate only on vertical depth since changes and events also can result from horizontal influences from other parts of society. Human activity rarely occurs within the constraints of one discipline.

Within the various national political, military, economic, and cultural structures, the analyst should attempt to identify those forces that have in the recent past caused the greatest amount of change. These will, of course, vary considerably from one nation to another. In this regard the analyst who has a background in the area, as stated earlier, will, comparatively speaking, get settled into the assignment a lot faster than one who does not. This informed analyst will be able to isolate a lot sooner the various loci of power and will also be able to exclude personal feelings and biases from his or her analysis, as well as mirror-imaging of personal perceptions, based on personal experience and projection of the individual's cultural framework. An analyst should ask questions about why this or that particular constellation of power or power centers came into existence, who are the individuals involved and in what manner or pattern, and why have particular situations evolved the way they have. If the analyst does not have or is not able to discern the answers to these questions, additional research is in order to improve the level of understanding of areas assigned.

Once the dynamics of a nation or area are understood to the satisfaction of the analyst, the next step should be to create mentally or on paper a schematic of known interaction patterns. The bureaucratic organization chart should not be the model as these charts tend to be too static; rather, some type of flowchart should be considered that reflects who has or have done what to whom in the recent past. This can take the form of identifying the groups competing for power--they exist everywhere, including in totalitarian nations, where, admittedly, it may be more difficult to discover and evaluate them, but where intergroup contention may be far more exacerbated. The influence of these groups should be assessed on some type of scale of relative influence and past impact, in order to form an opinion of likely future evolution, activity, and/or endurance over time. These flowcharts will never be complete, but they will show relationships. As the analyst gains knowledge and experience, these flowcharts can be made more complete either through the daily stream of incoming information or as the result of judicious conclusions that point to certain linkages. When issues under scrutiny are international, two or more nations will be involved, requiring a determination of: what brought the issue about in the first place; which nations and what forces therein participated in the formulation of responses; whether these responses were satisfactory or not to those involved and even to those not involved; and if the latter should believe that their interests have been adversely affected.

Sometimes an international issue can become very elaborate. One of the best examples is the Arab-Israeli confrontation, which has been in existence during most of the post-World War II period. Here a number of nations are involved as well as a number of pressure groups and terrorist organizations with varying degrees of influence and power. In a situation such as this the analyst may find it advantageous to modify the flowchart approach, mentioned previously, in such a way that it assumes a hierarchical structure for sorting out issues, power centers involved in these issues, and the results of the latters' actions, since, over time, the analyst will find a certain pattern of action/reaction among the entities involved. In a smaller command where one analyst may be responsible for the whole Middle Eastern area, this approach may be the only way to come to grips with the problem. Moreover, this approach also allows the analyst to do rapid file coding of information received. Alternatively, a yeoman, clerk, or secretary can be trained to do the initial sorting for analyst review with follow-on duplicating, cross-referencing, and filing. Additionally, the use of clerical personnel in this manner can stimulate greater interest in their assignments.

As analysts face the daily amount of information received, they and their assistants face a large review process in order to establish some type of priority for the analytical process. However, this review process has to be tempered somewhat by assessing the quality of the source, which obviously has a great impact on the validity of the information. A primary source, such as a government publication or a statement by a prime minister or a defense minister, is, of course, authentic, although the analyst may question the accuracy of what is being written or said and for what purpose. If a secondary source, such as an attache, claims that a particular statement has been made or an event has taken place, the individual's reporting track record becomes important, and if the attache is a new reporter, it may be necessary to seek confirmation from other reports. Extreme care should be taken to avoid false confirmation (i.e., two or more reports containing the same information are received, but originate from the same source).

After this initial evaluation, the analyst will be in a good position to fit new information into the above flowchart concept and ascertain what updating is necessary, what changes have taken place, and how leaders and power brokers have acted or reacted. In this context the earlier discussion of interviews and information on leaders will aid the analyst, who should have acquired an understanding of how they think and react as events unfold.

Since every change varies in magnitude, the question arises of how to determine its impact on its environment, which can be very difficult to accomplish in an objective and empirical manner. The analyst will soon realize that, as an example, the assassination of a middle level functionary in a status quo country may have a greater impact than the same event in a nation in the throes of revolutionary turmoil. Moreover, some contentious issues have become institutionalized as a way of life, such as the Greek-Turkish confrontation in Cyprus, or the Spanish-British controversy over Gibraltar, or Sinhalese-Tamil tension in Sri Lanka, to cite a few examples of varying magnitude and intensity. These variations are important to the analyst who must determine with each incoming report of change what type of impact it may cause. The analyst must in his or her mind decide which changes fall within a certain "window" of irrelevancy, which can be wide or narrow depending on the area, the issue, and its evolution. On this latter point, the analyst must also remember that the accumulation of seemingly irrelevant events or changes can easily become the harbinger of greater and more sudden changes in the future. Areas containing, or groups showing, discontent, dissatisfaction, or unruliness may be the source of many seemingly insignificant reports, but these are areas that can cause the greatest change when accumulated frustration finds a way to escape. Most totalitarian countries fall into this category; the Polish Solidarity movement is a striking example. Unresolved problems rarely disappear, and analyst efforts to build and update a dossier on such problems will aid in determining when they may cause a major change and to what extent.

The cause of contentious issues can be manifold, such as: a disagreement over treaty provisions between two, or among three or more, nations, creating problems ranging from tension or dissatisfaction to overt military action; an international problem with a political system with feudal overtones; changing economic conditions in a one-crop or one mineral country; or the unrest created by changing social facets of life in a country experiencing rapid industrialization. In these situations the analyst will benefit by trying to pinpoint the origin of the problem, even if it means reaching far back into time, as in the case of the internal strife in Northern Ireland. It may be very useful to create a time-line, indicating what problems an issue has created since its inception, identifying what forces have been involved over time, and what was accomplished, if anything. By creating this type of foundation of the origins of a contentious issue, the analyst can gain a better understanding of the impact of current events and make more realistic assessments of the dynamics of the issue at hand, as it is updated in the contemporary setting.

In spite of a seemingly endless voluminous daily flow of information, the analyst is confronted with gaps in the flowcharts, whether they are mental or put down on paper. Analysts have to draw upon their own abilities to identify and specify gaps in needed information. By reading recently finished intelligence reports and estimates, new analysts could locate some of the needed information for filling gaps. However, once an analyst has absorbed a new issue or problem, it does not take long to discover the information gaps. If there is a critical area about which nothing is known, the analyst can request that specific collection to fill that gap be initiated, once it has been certified that the required information does not exist within the intelligence community or an open source data base. Of course, such a collection request can be very limited or very comprehensive, as well as time-consuming, in scope. Analysts may also on their own attempt to fill gaps by interchange with counterparts in another command or government agency, as stated. There are often informal correspondence arrangements with an attache, permitting an exchange of information and ideas, but the analyst should keep in mind that occasionally agency or command turf protection can inhibit the dialogue.

As mentioned earlier, not only do internal events, but also those external to a country, impact on change, adding complexities to flowcharts and timelines. In this context the current intelligence analyst must keep in mind that he or she is not a U.S. foreign policy analyst in those situations where a change involves relations with the United States. Granted, the foreign policy of the United States may have an important bearing on the unfolding of events in a foreign country or area, and the analyst must keep abreast of these to analyze the changes underway there. This can present a problem for the analyst in attempting to maintain a complete picture of a situation. While information on the U.S. part of the issue may not always be readily available, analysts in most commands do receive cable messages from the U.S. Department of State, and with those, as well as newspaper reports, it should not be too difficult to maintain an uninterrupted flow of information. On the other hand, analysts must realize that U.S. initiatives and responses to foreign events may purposely not be available, because very sensitive negotiations are conducted on high governmental levels. Information on ongoing discussions may be restricted to very few officials on a strict need-to-know basis.

As the current intelligence analyst becomes accustomed to a new assignment, the analytical techniques and suggestions above will become second nature. With this expertise the analyst now needs to give some thought to analytical results and output.

THE CURRENT INTELLIGENCE PRODUCT AND ITS DISSEMINATION

Intelligence analysts are often accused of amassing enormous amounts of information in their files, and occasionally, to their utter dismay, information handling specialists may become involved in suggesting streamlining procedures. However, this mass of information is vital to the analyst, as the results of the research efforts are based on systematic access to numerous pieces of information, arranged by the analyst in such a way that their relationship to similar events and trends will cause the preparation of reports, cable messages, and/or oral briefings, to cite a few of the most common dissemination vehicles.

In this final section the interaction between the current intelligence analyst and personnel outside the office, as it were, is commented upon in relation to the accuracy and objectivity of the research product.

As a general statement, it is safe to say that the degree of review and staffing of analyst output is directly proportional to the size of command or governmental activity. A large activity will obviously have more layers of supervisors who may decide to become involved in the approval procedures before a product is released to the command section or disseminated outside the confines of the command involved. During this process the intelligence analyst may have to guard against changes that might alter or warp conclusions. Fortunately, this is a rare occurrence, as the "chain of command" consists of professionals who have gained their experience over a long period of time. On the other hand, if the "chain of command" includes nonintelligence personnel, which could happen in a smaller command, the analyst must be particularly alert for changes and additions that may skew the conclusions, and attempt to point out deviations from objectivity and factualism in an appropriate manner.

Even among intelligence personnel, there may arise situations where it is difficult for the analyst to maintain his or her conclusions and judgments. Very often, the analyst will be assigned to interagency work groups and task forces where intelligence is produced by committee. Anyone assigned to the analysis of contemporary events and trends will be given this type of assignment as an extra duty sooner rather than later. While all members of a working group will have more or less received and studied the same raw data, there will of course be honest differences of opinion. Moreover, the analyst will often attend these meetings after having received a certain amount of counsel from superiors, which can place the analyst between the Scylla of his or her supervisor and the Charybdis of group pressure, particularly if the analyst is junior in rank, military or civilian. Additionally, a committee product tends to be watered down to a common denominator, acceptable to all the participants. The impact of group efforts in achieving positive results has been discussed in academe, and the new current intelligence analyst will benefit from a study of them.[1]

Regardless of the vehicle the analyst uses to publish research results, it should be kept in mind that the recipients of the analyst's report are often not familiar with the foreign area discussed. Consequently, there is a natural tendency for them to project their own cultural background, mores, and perceptions into a foreign area. Thus, the analyst must continuously keep in mind that his or her phraseology includes wording to guard against inadvertent misunderstanding on the part of the reader or listener. This is particularly important for areas outside the Western cultural tradition. Moreover, the analyst will do his or her command great service by being alert to developments where ignorance of cultural factors will cause needless problems, even outside the scope of normal intelligence functions. For example, unilateral planning by a command operations department of a military exercise with a Moslem country during one of its religious holidays can become self-defeating for everyone involved.

In addition to nonintelligence personnel as recipients of analyst products, there are two particular categories of analysts within the intelligence framework who are very much dependent on the results of current intelligence research. One of these consists of Indications and Warning (I&W) analysts who, through their own analytical and reporting channels, provide warning to the national command structure, as described in Timothy Laur's chapter. The early detection of unusual events or trends that do not fit a foreign area's or nation's evolution are more likely to be discovered by the current intelligence analyst than the I&W analyst. Moreover, in small commands the same individual may serve in both capacities. In the other category are estimators, who have their own procedural modus operandi for the production of defense and national estimates. The current intelligence analyst can be expected to assist in the drafting and staffing of estimates, which normally takes place on the top military command and national levels only.

In conclusion, the current intelligence analyst is an individual who is well educated and experienced in his or her area of responsibility, has a good track record with accurate, convincing, and time-tested research products, a goal that, admittedly, can only be achieved over time, but one that the newly assigned analyst must strive to reach.

NOTE

1. Irving L. Janis, <u>Victims of Group Think</u> (Boston, MA: Houghton Mifflin, 1972).

9
Estimative Intelligence
G. Paul Holman, Jr.

If intelligence products were automobiles, then estimates would be the "Jaguars" of the industry. They are prestigious, attract influential customers, and move fast when in good tune. But when badly tuned, they are cranky at best and just plain useless at worst. As all Jaguar owners know, what matters is not the year or model of one's car, but the competence of one's mechanic. The same applies to estimates. Throughout all the sensational attention they have attracted over the past few years, much has been said about the comparatively simple and mechanical problems of organization within the three-lettered bureaucracies of CIA, NSA, DIA, and INR, but next to nothing about the human beings--the estimators--who tinker with diverse and divergent data to derive confident predictions about the future.

Judging by journalistic accounts, our estimators have failed so abjectly to predict the key developments of the past fifteen years that they deserve mass sacking for incompetence, if not being put on trial for treason. Jack Anderson alleges quite bluntly that, "it's the bumblers who get promoted."[1]

This indictment of the estimators is in no way limited to muckracking journalists. Such a professional intelligence officer as retired Air Force Major General George Keegan asserts that, "the real problem of national security during the past decades has involved the serious errors, not of the so-called clandestine warriors, but of the professional estimators."[2] Ray Cline--whose combination of both collection and analytical duties in CIA as well as the State Department allows him considerable insight into the human dimensions of intelligence--agrees that the estimates have been wrong. Yet he finds less fault with the estimators:

> It does not surprise me at all that many of the predictions were wrong...intelligence is always wrong. Certainly my experience in intelligence estimates is that intelligence estimators are always wrong, and there are always plenty of people around to tell them so. The questions that are brought up for public scrutiny and even scrutiny in the high levels of the government are never the simple questions on which intelligence can give clear and precise answers.[3]

Following Cline's approach, the goal of this chapter is to give one estimator's view of his trade, less for the sake of appraising the accuracy of recent estimates or recommending organizational innovation than for the simpler purpose of demystifying the process by which estimates are written. Indeed, there are no intelligence products--and few governmental documents of any kind--on which the personal insights, creativity, education, rivalries, alliances, and ambitions of individual bureaucrats can have so much impact as on estimates.

Documentation for this subject is scanty, but the oral tradition passed from estimator to estimator is very rich. As a result, this chapter will rely more heavily on the author's personal recollections than on printed sources. It constitutes a sort of "intelligence estimator's how-to-do-it manual," whose purpose is more practical than scholarly, although some problems of broad significance are implicit.

SELECTION AND NATURE OF TOPICS

The reasons for writing estimates vary widely. Some appear annually, most often because they play a role in the various cycles of agency and departmental budgets. Many--perhaps the majority of the really controversial ones--occur in response to specific crises or changes in the international situation. And a handful take place because of a nagging sensation somewhere in the intelligence community that an issue or problem of long-term importance has not received the attention it deserves.[4]

Each of these categories of estimates imposes special demands on the estimator. The annual products tend to become institutional pillars of the intelligence community's edifice, which must appear (often at great length) whether or not much has really changed. Ad hoc estimates have the virtue of satisfying strong consumer interest--often at the highest level of the government--but their very importance leads them afoul of interagency disagreements, emotional debates among the estimators, and politically motivated leaks far more frequently than in the case of the annual estimates. As for the few that arise in response to neither a scheduled yearly requirement nor a sudden crisis, these "initiative" products have a significance which is notably disproportionate to their modest number. Less driven by budgetary or political needs, they often enjoy a more reflective spirit on the part of their authors, a more dispassionate use of the evidence, and less of a tendency to smother controversy with the warm blanket of what one former CIA analyst calls "studied ambivalence."[5]

SELECTION AND NATURE OF ESTIMATORS

In general, estimators tend to be higher ranking than other types of intelligence officers. The cause of this situation is twofold: the bureaucratic requirement for experienced people to defend agency positions and the general view that representation at interagency meetings merits senior personnel.

As a result, the competition is always keen for estimative jobs. Darwinian principles apply, and selection boards tend to hire estimators who possess area knowledge, foreign language skills, advanced degrees, and attendance at senior service schools--or, at the very least, considerable success in their previous assignments. As the authors of what is perhaps the fullest and most useful study of intelligence estimates remark, "it is apparent that a natural career progression for the best in DIA is a spot within the Directorate for Estimates."[6]

For all these reasons, estimators tend to take themselves seriously. Those with any predisposition toward pomposity will find it exacerbated by the fact that they are regularly on display as agency spokesmen, negotiators, and proponents of complex positions on controversial issues of major interest to their superiors. Reinforcing these high levels of ego gratification are several mundane considerations. Estimators neither participate in extended task forces nor work long hours as a matter of routine. They often travel to the more pleasant world capitals and do most of their work in relatively well appointed offices or conference rooms. Even so, when estimates of great importance are assigned short suspenses, the estimators' lot changes abruptly for the worse. Their psychological pressures become intense, their duties onerous, and their hours interminable--especially those spent in conference with their peers from other agencies. In such situations, an estimator's life resembles that of a pilot: hours and hours of boredom, interspersed with moments of sheer panic.

Although it is understandable why many intelligence officers regard estimates as the pinnacle of their career, they do not soon pass on to retirement. Quite the contrary, for one of the keys to understanding the good and bad traits of estimators is their unusual longevity on the job. Military officers assigned to estimates are more likely to seek extensions than their colleagues in current intelligence or research, and it is not uncommon for civilians to surpass a decade in their tenure as estimators.

Enjoying competence, self-esteem, and status, no one should be surprised that estimators worry about protecting their reputations. Such reputations, however, do not reflect individual predictive brilliance or coups in intelligence production, but rather a persistent effort over the years to shape and sway the outcomes of committee deliberations.

Such a career pattern reflects the fact that estimates are inherently the result of group, as opposed to individual, activity--perhaps more so than any other type of intelligence product. A single, unaided source may report new information of great value; a single case officer may forward it to Washington; and a lone analyst may stress its importance in some finished intelligence study (perhaps even without convincing the hierarchy of its validity, depending on agency procedures for the publication of nonconformist views). But before such information will appear in any estimate, it must undergo general, coordinated scrutiny by all interested components of at least one--and more likely several--departments or agencies.

The result of all this emphasis on collegial decisionmaking in the production of estimates is a distinctive (detractors would say "jaded") mentality. Estimators believe that split opinions among agencies arise all too frequently from excessive insistence on narrow (sometimes irrelevant) aspects of broad issues. Given time, the estimators usually hope to find language which can resolve such disputes and eliminate split positions. Representing entire agencies rather than simply offices or themselves, estimators differ sharply from analysts, who earn their promotions by tenacious dedication to novel and individualistic interpretations of the issues. The result is a perennial tension between these two sorts of intelligence officers, with the estimators sometimes being accused of favoring compromise over conflict, lacking guts or backbone, and "selling out" the agency to its rivals.

Such accusations wound the estimators' self-respect more than one might think, for much of their success depends on the relationships they have formed over the years with estimators from other agencies. Some have constructive approaches, and some are time-wasting gadflies. But what even the estimators often fail to understand is that these extremes can serve a purpose, both in raising the quality of estimates (the all-too-often forgotten goal) and supporting agency positions (the immediate source of supervisory praise and promotions).

ESTIMATIVE PERSONA

Rarely are estimative working groups the domain of colorless sycophants, who quickly and easily define their extremes and blandly compromise on the middle ground between them. Far more often, such sessions combine the worst features of the theater and the battlefield. The more important the issue, the more senior the participants and thus the more dramatic or combative they become. Specific agencies and individuals develop their own particular persona, to use a literary term, whose regular and predictable reappearance transforms the proceedings from a potential Marathon or Armageddon into something resembling a classical Greek comedy.

The "Fury" is the most feared of all estimative _persona_, since it violates the understatement and consensus favored by run-of-the-mill estimators. Through emotional pressure and sometimes insults, the "Fury" can make a heavy impact on occasional estimates, especially when major controversies are involved. However, the risks of this role are many. The "Fury" makes real enemies, loses credibility, and displays such obvious scorn for the views of other estimators as to make the resolution of minor matters more difficult than it should be. Indeed, the estimator who plays the "Fury" on one paper would do well to take pains on the next to soothe hurt feelings and restore old alliances, or simply to avoid estimates altogether for a while.

Less consistently strident that the "Fury," but still rising to carefully timed displays of emotion, is the "Curtis Lemay." Best played by an Air Force or Army officer, this persona involves a display of hairy arms on the table, and calculated outbursts of obscenity. Sometimes enhancing his act by consumption of low-grade cigars (preferably in conference rooms where smoking is nominally forbidden), the "Curtis Lemay" must be able to shed his buffoon-like camouflage at supersonic speed. No Chairman will long tolerate a "Curtis Lemay" unless his irreverence actually helps the deliberative process. Tersely played, a "Curtis Lemay" can win the affection (sometimes the admiration) of all but the most flatulent bureaucrats by cutting through dense thickets of convoluted prose and demanding clear expression of controversial matters.

A less dramatic but still rather specialized persona is the "Professor." Thanks to the Ph.D. glut and to relatively high Civil Service salaries, more holders of advanced degrees than ever before have flocked away from the universities and into the intelligence community. In theory, a "Professor" should be able to cow his opponents by intimidating displays of real erudition. At their best, "Professors" may elevate the intellectual tone of what would otherwise be a vulgar interagency brawl. They may focus attention on scholarly sources of insight outside the intelligence community, and they may (less commonly) even manage to deal with the evidence more objectively than the average analyst. At their worst, however, "Professors" may possess academic specialties so irrelevant to the issue at hand as to require careful concealment from the working group. In such a case, professorial tactics will amount to little more than correcting grammatical errors in the text, name-dropping about old students who have since attained flag rank, and pompously declaiming agency positions which the "Professor" really understands no better than any garden-variety analyst.

Any of the preceding roles can easily degenerate into a "Gasbag"--a persona which relies more on quantity than quality of verbiage to score needed agency points. Young officers are well advised to avoid attempting this role until late in their careers, when respect for their age, seniority, and wisdom may compensate for their ebbing ability in matters of substance. Even then, working group Chairmen soon learn to interrupt the "Gasbag" unless the person playing this role has a keen sense of humor, some shreds of humility, and a storehouse of genuinely entertaining anecdotes. State Department officers tend to excel at this persona, but every organization has a few. Their appearance in a working group is likely whenever an issue so divides the intelligence community that at least one agency seeks obfuscation and delay, rather than detailed discussion of the evidence.

In general, the safest aspiration for any estimator is to play the role of an "Expert." This persona requires dogged assimilation of complex details, but it can be played with spectacular results by females and by relatively young officers who devote sufficient time to substantive research. Every estimator should possess a minimum of one intelligence specialty in which he or she can at least pretend to be an "Expert," as well as knowing which of the many analysts on call to support a given estimate can perform persuasively as an "Expert" in the interagency arena. The actual function of an "Expert" during difficult estimates requires stony silence at meetings until the moment of glory arrives, when the "Expert's" field of authority comes into view. But at that point, the "Expert" can usually sweep all opposition away, unless it suffers the embarrassment of confronting another agency's "Expert" (or, far less satisfactorily for the rival organization, "Fury," "Gasbag," or "Professor"). CIA has long employed battalions of "Experts," and they were one of the reasons why CIA positions used to dominate the estimates, thanks to their intimidating numbers and the sheer mass of information with which they were eager to deluge the working group.[7]

The smaller agencies possess only a few "Experts" who can persuasively disagree with CIA's positions, but on such technical issues as intercontinental ballistic missile reliability, defense economics, or bomber design, DIA and the Services have increasingly managed to influence national estimates by fielding a uniformed "Expert" or "Curtis Lemay" who had personal experience with the U.S. version of the weapon or problem in question.[8] Rarely, however, is any agency so fortunate as to have an "Expert" as its primary representative on an estimate. This _persona_ is in short supply, by the very nature of the current, specialized knowledge it demands. Real "Experts" usually begin their careers as intelligence analysts, and as soon as they leave research behind in their advancing careers they tend to degenerate into other _persona_ ("Gasbags," all too often).

Least assertive of all the estimative _persona_, yet still effective enough to represent its agency and win an occasional promotion, is the "Silent Partner." Inappropriate for CIA or State Department, and rare for DIA, the "Silent Partner" has been known to sit for days without uttering a public word. The silent partner's function is essentially negative: to assure that nothing happens which would violate the interests or declared positions of the agency he or she represents. So long as those conditions are met, the "Silent Partner" makes no effort whatever to affect the working group or even to speed its progress. As a result, the "Silent Partner" makes few allies at the table. This role can verge on perfect somnolence for quite some time, but then becomes abruptly painful when the working group stumbles on some subject of importance to the "Silent Partner's" service or agency. Having neither substantive knowledge nor proven allies at the table, the "Silent Partner" is reduced to throwing itself on the mercy of the group. Such pleas as, "This is what my boss wants" and "I can't go home unless you give this to me" are common. If rejected, the "Silent Partner" has no choice but to threaten a footnote and summon an "Expert."

Sometimes the hardest and most difficult role--but ultimately the most effective persona--is the "Honest Broker." During non-controversial estimates, this role is safe, natural, and effective, with the result that most estimators try to employ it most of the time. Thus "Honest Brokers" come in a wider range of style and quality than other estimators, making generalization about them more hazardous. When gifted with the pen--even if a substantive ignoramus--an "Honest Broker" can suggest changes in wording that cut through intransigent views and produce either a resolution of the issue or a clearly phrased dissent. If an "Honest Broker" is modestly well informed--by reading either current intelligence reports or the New York Times, but almost never both--it can defeat a "Gasbag" or "Professor." But when confronted by a "Fury" or, worse, an "Expert" exuding facts from every pore, the "Honest Broker" consults the telephone directory for reinforcements.

Controversial estimates winnow the ranks of "Honest Brokers," and few rise to the Bismarckian potential of which this role is capable. Instead, the majority of estimators simply retreat within the sure fortress of previously established agency positions, maintaining their consistency with the past at the cost of breaking no new ground. Rare, indeed, are the "Honest Brokers" who play this challenging persona to the fullest, for it entails the risk of sparking a bureaucratic explosion within one's own agency. The consummate "Honest Broker" must be willing and able to assist the working group by redrafting paragraphs or entire sections of a paper--usually on short notice--to ensure that extraneous but contentious issues fade into their proper place, while the really important ones gain prominence for the policymaker. Such an estimator will often face the problem of supplying words to clarify a text with which he or she does not agree--behavior which will delight the working group and surely improve the estimate. Within one's own agency, however, the "Honest Broker" sometimes incurs the wrath of analysts who would have preferred the original text, in order to justify harsh footnotes or alternate language in reply, even if such a heated exchange might overstate or misstate the controversy.

At least during the early stages of a highly contentious estimate, the serious "Honest Broker" may face criticism from the low and middle ranks of its own agency. However, as the paper moves toward high-level review, an "Honest Broker" will almost always earn the Director's gratitude for avoiding any agency commitment to ill-phrased, narrow, or substantively weak positions.

None of these estimative personae is fixed or permanent, but no estimator can credibly play all of them. The most passionate "Furies" emanate too much emotion to do well as "Gasbags" and are unlikely to be accepted by their colleagues as "Honest Brokers" because of past altercations. By the same token, "Gasbags" have too much inherent good will to transform themselves into "Furies" and talk too much to be "Honest Brokers." At the opposite extreme, "Silent Partners" presumably have at least some ability to play as "Experts," or they would not have been selected for their high-paying jobs, and they have usually attended enough meetings during their careers to serve effectively as "Honest Brokers." However, years spent away from research take their inevitable toll by precluding "Silent Partners" from adopting the more histrionic or knowledgeable roles.

Each of these personae plays a necessary role in the estimative process. For quick production of routine estimates, a working group composed entirely of "Silent Partners" and "Experts," with at least one "Honest Broker," would be quite adequate. But for controversial estimates--on which hinge matters of new, changing, or astronomically expensive policy--the full range of persona is often vital, trying though it may be for the self-restraint of some members. A "Professor" tends to broaden the scope of an estimate and prevent subtle problems from being defined or "massaged" into nonexistence. A "Curtis Lemay" preserves blunt military realities against the erosion of wishful or naive civilian thinking. And a "Fury" is surely the best defender in extremis of minority views, but preferably with a "Gasbag" hovering on the fringes of the group to smooth raw emotional edges and keep the "Fury's" spleen from doing unnecessary damage to the estimate as a whole.

THE CHAIRMAN AND THE FOOTNOTE

Holding such divergent and often conflicting talents together is no easy task, and it usually falls on the shoulders of the single most important estimator in the working group: the Chairman. Whatever the Chairman's background, it will be sternly tested by service as a senior estimator. Most Chairmen previously qualified as "Experts," and if they have some ability as an "Honest Broker," they can often excel in producing accurate and timely estimates. "Professors" make even better Chairmen, since their own command of the subject reassures weaker members of the group while domesticating the more loquacious ones, but only if the Chairman does not degenerate into a "Gasbag." The persona that a working group may tolerate and even enjoy from one of its working-level participants is very different from what the Chairman may safely indulge. A "Gasbag" as Chairman will be at odds with other "Gasbags," "Professors," and even some of the "Experts" who should be his supporters, creating friction which leads inexorably to wasted time and irreconcilable differences of view.

When such divided judgments occur, the real fun begins for all members of the working group, but most especially for the Chairman and the representative of the dissenting agency or agencies. In many cases, the number and tenor of dissenting footnotes (or alternate text, as it is sometimes printed) directly reflect on the Chairman's performance. Chairmen who have been excessively weak or needlessly strong tend to see their work degenerate into a mass of opposing views, so divergent on the key issues that agency heads will refuse to accept the final product and remand it to the drafters.

The power of the footnotes is formidable, since there is a deeply rooted view that the right way to read estimates is simply to find the split judgments.[9] If the estimators are, indeed, as frequently wrong as suggested at the beginning of this chapter, then the footnotes should range from judgments which were even more grossly wrong to those which were prophetically correct. To the extent that a Chairman treats dissent as treason or an insult to his own competence, rather than exploring what may be an error by the majority, the result is a dangerous disservice to any estimate's consumers.

THE AGENCIES AND THEIR CONTROVERSIES

Individual estimators and their agencies do not think alike about all things of intelligence interest, nor even about the principle of vigorous participation in the working groups that produce them. Indeed, there are widely divergent opinions of what constitutes a useful intelligence estimate. As Richard K. Betts, a scholar who has done extensive research on intelligence estimates, observes: "An NIE (National Intelligence Estimate) that is a genuinely useful contribution to strategic decisionmaking--rather than just a compendium of numbers, conventional wisdom, or competing disagreements--will do just what busy officials often do not like; it will complicate their jobs."[10] Personnel turnover complicates this problem of reader reaction still further, creating a constantly shifting array of attitudes on the part of both consumers and producers toward the disharmony that a thoughtful footnote can cause.

Some estimators take pleasure in proposing alternative views and have the expertise to write them powerfully. With luck, they may sway the views of the table and become "the community position." Others fear the strong emotions that footnotes evoke or simply lack the golden pen that doing them right requires. Moreover, when any given estimator throws a proposed footnote into the bureaucratic channels of his or her agency for coordination and approval, its fate is never quite the same from office to office and year to year. As the Soviets would say, each footnote reflects a unique "correlation of forces" and is the product of more blood, sweat, and time than any sentence ever accepted by consensus.

Over the years, some agencies have dissented more than others, but none with more vigor than Air Force Intelligence in the mid-1970s, under Major General George Keegan.[11] Scholarly treatises have given this phenomenon at least some of the attention it deserves, as also have Keegan's irreverent estimators, who posted the following list of agency perceptions on their Pentagon walls:

-- State Department doesn't believe the Russians are coming.
-- CIA thinks the Russians might like to come here but has no opinion as to when they would like to arrive.
-- Arms Control and Disarmament Agency has found the real enemy--us.
-- FBI has no opinion.
-- NSA is confident that only its special sources can explain the full truth.
-- DIA thinks the Russians are coming but probably won't arrive until sometime next week.
-- Navy doesn't know but disagrees with everyone, especially DIA.
-- Army agrees with Air Force but does not generally disagree with DIA.
-- Air Force believes the Russians have the capability to come here and have preplanned missions to do so at any time.
-- General Keegan thinks the Russians are already here and have taken over the State Department, as well as portions of CIA.[12]

The aprocryphal perceptions in question, of course, were those of the mid-1970s, and Air Force barbs of the early 1980s would be somewhat different. Even so, their jocular testimony to widely varying opinions about Soviet intentions is in no way out of date. The durability of such disputes reflects underlying tensions within the intelligence community. One observer, with extensive backgrounds in both the executive and legislative sides of intelligence, has suggested that, "Competition among the analysts has been largely based on the conflict between the military on one side, and CIA and State on the other. The former has been waging a losing battle for its independence."[13] Interservice rivalries have had the effect of weakening the military position still further, but there are grounds for arguing that the military began to win an uphill struggle for its views by the latter 1970s.[14]

Many polarities describe this split ("hard" and "soft;" "right" and "left;" "hawk" and "dove"), but such cliches obscure more dimensions of the problem than they clarify. In part, the conflict symbolizes differing views on how to balance Soviet intentions against Soviet capabilities, with State and CIA emphasizing the Soviets' reluctance to fight, while DIA and the Services stress their increasingly impressive wherewithal for war. Yet there is no agreement about Soviet intentions, either. One side believes that some residue of Marxist-Leninist fervor still motivates Moscow, while the other sees Soviet leaders essentially as pragmatic problem-solvers, who rely on Communist ideology solely as a prop to their ebbing legitimacy. In international terms, the controversy pits those who are not embarrassed to use the concept of "geopolitics" or even the simpler notion of "national strategy" against those who find such concepts antiquated or inconsistent with the behavioral sciences. No estimative document has more publicly expressed all of these controversies than the "A-B Team" exchange concerning Soviet strategic forces, which took place in 1976.[15]

Still another controversy cuts along the line of regional specialization, confronting Sovietologists with Third World area specialists who have very different ideas about the degree of Moscow's leverage over its clients, surrogates, and allies. Perhaps the most highly publicized ramification of this dispute has come in the field of terrorism, culminating in references to "moderate" terrorists and a CIA publication which asserts: "One man's terrorist is another man's freedom fighter."[16] Predictably, such statements have drawn fire from those who would define both moral judgments and Soviet links more sharply.[17]

The cumulative effect of all these controversies is to blur the starkness of division along a mere State-and-CIA versus Department of Defense axis (although that may remain a basic reality). No agency reduces its estimators to intellectual slavery, with the result that each resembles a feudal kingdom more than a despotic empire. This situation makes the work of the estimator particularly tense. Depending on the subject of discussion, as well as the "correlation of forces" emerging within each agency, one's best ally at the table may well represent an organization from which one would normally expect derision or silence, at best. Such a situation does not occur, however, when the controversy is enshrined or petrified in perennial footnotes (for example, concerning the range of the Backfire bomber),[18] which require close adherence to previous positions and often pit the same "Experts" against each other again and again, sometimes without new data to support either side and with more emotion than insight.

But when controversy rages over a new issue, the bloodiest battles may well occur within one's own agency, while the estimator is seeking coordination from analysts who may never before have had the chance to perform in an interagency arena. Under rare circumstances, the estimator may then have the satisfaction of transforming an analyst's opinion into an agency position, and perhaps the national position as well. More often, however, the estimator finds it impossible to defend the research analyst's opinion as loudly as the author might like. Such a situation can become unpleasant, as the estimator begins by deprecating the importance of the issue. ("This is too minor to fight about.") It can escalate to criticism of the analyst's view. ("You may be right, but the rest of the working group just laughed at your data and logic.") Eventually, it will probably involve what the irritated analyst may perceive as a cowardly invocation of bureaucratic authority. ("I can't ask the Old Man to take a footnote on this, and I don't think the rest of our agency would coordinate on it if I did.") Whatever the sincerity and validity of such arguments, they add growing bitterness to the relationship between analyst and estimator, especially if either escalates their disagreement to higher levels within the agency.

However, when analyst and estimator manage to forge a position which satisfies them both, they can use the dissenting footnote as the estimator's ultimate weapon. Many regions of the world are so calm, or at least so dominated by conventional wisdom within the intelligence community, that they rarely raise a controversy worthy of a footnote. In the Soviet area, however, potential footnotes are always writhing beneath the surface of even the stillest working group. Even so, few estimators make idle talk of footnotes, for nothing can discredit a reputation or disrupt a working group more gratingly than a threatened footnote that never materializes.

The first notification of an impending dissent is usually delicate, in hopes of modifying the offending prose. ("I see a possible footnote here, unless we can tone this down.") When pressed, some estimators try to disclaim responsibility for their agency's concern. ("I don't especially disagree with this point, personally, but old so-and-so in my own agency gives me no choice.") If the disagreement does not end there with satisfactory wordsmithing, other members of the working group respond generally along the lines of the Air Force "perceptions" cited above. Some agency representatives heap scorn on the proposed dissent, while others defend it and promise to seek the support of their own organizations for the footnotes in question.

Should the meeting adjourn without resolution of the controversy, all agencies undergo a careful process of preparing for the next draft, or, if the coordination process is complete, the next session of the National Foreign Intelligence Board (NFIB). Frequently preceded by frantic telephone calls between the working group Chairman, dissenting estimators, supporting analysts, and sundry bureaucrats, their goal is to delete extraneous issues and seek compromises satisfying both sides. If no words can be found to bridge the interagency gap, then estimators brief their superiors on the issues at stake, in preparation for the DIA-Service consultation at the Military Intelligence Board (MIB). Under normal circumstances, the MIB is the estimator's last chance to put the military house in order and prepare appropriate positions for the NFIB. Carefully crafted words can still sometimes convince the heads of other agencies to modify controversial passages in the text, whereupon the NFIB votes on the estimate and the estimator's job is done.

CAN THE ESTIMATORS IMPROVE THEIR WORK?

Critics of past estimates have offered various kinds of explanations for what went wrong. Some, such as General Keegan, attribute estimative errors to high-level misuses of intelligence, as policymakers increasingly wanted "to have intelligence justify and rationalize their long-term and more hopeful undertakings."[19] Ray Cline, although generally disputing Keegan's and others' attacks on the CIA, concurs on this point:

> ...the fundamental error in the intelligence world came in those years, those Nixon years, when intelligence itself was manipulated...Its distribution was used as a tool to create power and create public opinion, and in particular to impress the media in this country with certain points of view, whether or not it had anything to do with the outside world. I think the intelligence agencies could have done a lot better job on SALT and on those kinds of estimates than they were permitted to do.[20]

The correctives to such a political problem lie well beyond the scope of the individual estimator, and thus of this chapter.

A very different sort of problem, however, is the professional competence of our estimators--including their training, their knowledge, and the way they write intelligence products. Not only is this problem capable of correction without drastic change in the intelligence community's organization, the opportunities for so doing appear to have increased. CIA no longer always enjoys the "power of the first draft," which used to put DoD representatives in the weak position of responding under pressure to CIA's words.[21] The creation of DIA in 1961 and then the formation of its Assistant Vice Directorate for Estimates nine years later had the effect of giving military intelligence an increasingly unified, articulate voice on estimates.[22] Even so, most researchers consistently suggest that DIA has not yet lived up to its full potential. In the words of Pentagon sources, too many military contributions to national estimates have been "weak stylistically," while the interest of DIA and the Services in supporting estimates "goes up and down."[23]

Current signals suggest that the direction of Department of Defense interest in estimates is up. The Ph.D. glut in academia has endowed DIA and the Services with better "Experts," "Professors," and "Honest Brokers" than ever before, while recent Directors of Central Intelligence seem increasingly concerned about the freedom and quality of estimative dissent.[24] If these trends continue, then the surest key to better estimates will be better estimators, given enough time to confront the evidence and enough opportunity to debate their views--especially when their disagreements are serious. It is their wit, tenacity, and eloquence which will determine the success or failure of future estimates.

NOTES

1. Jack Anderson, "The CIA's Real Sins," Washington Post, 29 November 1981.

2. Major General George Keegan, USAF (Ret.), "Strategic Balance: Trends and Perceptions," Washington Report (American Security Council) (April 1977): 3.

3. Dr. Ray S. Cline, "Discussion," in Roy Godson, ed., *Intelligence Requirements for the 1980s: Analysis and Estimates* (Washington, DC: National Strategy Information Center, 1980), p. 77.

4. David A. Brinkley and Andrew W. Hull provide an exhaustive description of the types and goals of estimates in *Estimative Intelligence: A Textbook on the History, Products, Uses and Writing of Intelligence Estimates* (Columbus, OH: Battelle Columbus Laboratories, prepared for the Defense Intelligence School, Washington, DC, 1979), pp. 113-168.

5. David S. Sullivan, "Evaluating US Intelligence Estimates," in Godson, p. 66.

6. Brinkley and Hull, p. 195.

7. Victoria S. Price takes note of both the competence of CIA analysts and their power of the first draft, with which Allen Dulles carefully endowed them, in Victoria S. Price, *The DCI's Role in Producing Strategic Intelligence Estimates* (Newport, RI: Naval War College, Center for Advanced Research, 1980), pp. 51-3.

8. For some examples of the growing quality of DIA and service contributions to national intelligence estimates, see John Prados, *The Soviet Estimates: U.S. Intelligence Analysis and Russian Military Strength* (New York: The Dial Press, 1982), pp. 245-68.

9. This is the approach taken by John Prados. His bibliography is one of the best available, and his introduction provides a concise explanation of the sources available, as well as their dangers. See Prados, pp. xi-xv.

10. Richard K. Betts, "Strategic Intelligence Estimates: Let's Make Them Useful," *Parameters* 4(December 1980): 21; emphasis in the original.

11. Keegan, p. 3. For a scholarly interpretation which generally supports Keegan's claim, see Lawrence Freedman, *US Intelligence and the Soviet Strategic Threat* (Boulder, CO: Westview Press, 1977), especially pp. 81-96 and 152-82.

12. Anonymous, mid-1970s.

13. Angelo Codevilla, "Comparative Historical Experience of Doctrine and Organization," in Godson, p. 30.

14. Price, p. 53. For the gradual acceptance of positions long held by DIA and the Air Force, see Prados, pp. 252 and 287-8.

15. Team A, consisting of representatives from CIA and the other NFIB agencies, produced a blander and more reassuring view of

Soviet intentions than did Team B, a group of "outsiders" chaired by Professor Richard Pipes of Harvard University. The controversy is summarized in U.S. Congress, Senate, Select Committee on Intelligence, Report, The National Intelligence Estimates A-B Team Episode Concerning Soviet Strategic Capability and Objectives, 95th Cong. 2d Sess., 1978, pp. 1-14.

16. Cited by Codevilla, in Godson, p. 33.

17. Most notably Claire Sterling, who amply documents Soviet support for international terrorism without arguing for total Soviet control. "It was never part of the Soviet design to create and watch over native terrorist movements, still less to direct their day-to-day activities." See Claire Sterling, The Terror Network: The Secret War of International Terrorism (New York: Holt, Rinehart and Winston, 1981), p. 291.

18. Prados, pp. 257-68.

19. Keegan, p. 3.

20. Cline, in Godson, p. 79.

21. Price, pp. 57-8.

22. For a concise, thoughtful account of DIA's history and fortunes, see Freedman, pp. 21-6.

23. Price, p. 58, citing interviews with members of the Office of the Director of Net Assessments. John M. Collins explains such problems largely in terms of DIA's difficulty in developing and retaining high-quality analytical personnel in U.S. Defense Planning: A Critique (Boulder, CO: Westview Press, 1982), pp. 128-9.

24. Price, p. 59. Richard H. Giza of the House Permanent Select Committee on Intelligence presents some useful comments on DIA's future, with direct applicability to estimates: "Since its inception...DIA has been able to develop relatively few senior specialists and managers from within its ranks; it has had to go outside for senior level vacancies. Legislation giving DIA the same hire and fire procedures as CIA and NSA would help. However, a Secretary of Defense truly interested in developing a first class Defense Intelligence Agency is just as important." Richard H. Giza, "The Problems of the Intelligence Consumer," in Godson, p. 200.

10
Scientific and Technical Intelligence

Bernard J. Grundy

INTRODUCTION

Scientific and technical intelligence plays a key role in national security by providing critical information to national- and department-level policy officials and planners, military research and development organizations, and operational military units. Finished intelligence is derived from in depth processing, integration, and analysis of raw data collected through various means, technical and human, as well as from exploitation of open source literature and acquired foreign materiel. Within the Department of Defense (DoD), resources that support scientific and technical intelligence production are contained in the General Defense Intelligence Program (GDIP), an integral component of the larger, community-wide National Foreign Intelligence Program (NFIP) under the authority of the Director of Central Intelligence.

In addition to general military intelligence and target intelligence, scientific and technical intelligence is a principal type of military intelligence. It is defined to include (1) foreign developments in basic and applied sciences and technologies with warfare potential, and the military implications of technology transfer; (2) technical characteristics, capabilities, limitations, and vulnerabilities of all foreign weapon systems, subsystems, and associated materiel, research and development related thereto, and the production methods employed for their manufacture; and (3) overall foreign weapon systems and equipment effectiveness.

Scientific and technical intelligence is critically important to national-level consumers, including the White House, U.S. Congress, Department of State and the Arms Control and Disarmament Agency, Department of Commerce, Department of Energy, and the National Aeronautics and Space Administration. From a DoD perspective, it is essential to numerous elements within the Office of the Secretary of Defense, Joint Chiefs of Staff, unified and specified commands, and the military departments to support such efforts as arms control negotiations and compliance verification, technology transfer evaluations, net assessments of U.S. and foreign weapon systems, U.S. weapon systems and countermeasures development, force structuring and operations planning, wargaming, targeting, military operations, training, and simulator development and validation.

The principal thrust of the DoD scientific and technical intelligence analysis and production effort is clearly against what are perceived to be the overriding threats posed by the Soviet Union, other Warsaw Pact nations, and China, although growing possibilities of local insurgencies or low intensity conflict in Third World regions dictate that attention be given to weapon systems and military capabilities of other nations as well. Unlike other types of intelligence, scientific and technical intelligence is not produced on a geographic basis; rather, it is primarily subject- or systems-oriented, covering a wide spectrum of sciences and technologies, weapon subsystems, and weapon systems, including missile, ground, naval, aerodynamic, and space systems. In addition to assessments of the military implications of foreign accomplishments in the various sciences and technologies and engineering analyses of individual weapons systems or subsystems, the DoD production effort provides for multi-weapon system integration assessments to determine the effectiveness of various weapon systems as they interact in real warfare scenarios and to derive total force capabilities.

SCIENTIFIC AND TECHNICAL INTELLIGENCE PRODUCTION

Within the Department of Defense, the entire range of scientific and technical intelligence analysis and production addressed above is the responsibility of the Directorate for Scientific and Technical Intelligence (DT), of the Defense Intelligence Agency (DIA), operating in concert with selected elements of the military departments. The analysis and production efforts of these organizations are conducted within the general framework of a production management system established and operated by the Directorate for Scientific and Technical Intelligence of DIA in coordination with the military departments. DIA is responsible to the Secretary of Defense for managing this production program and, although not in the command authority line, executes this responsibility through that chain of command. As a result, the management approach that has evolved can best be described as "participatory" in nature; its success is heavily dependent upon close interaction and cooperation between management and analyst personnel of the Directorate for Scientific and Technical Intelligence of DIA and their counterparts at the production organizations of the military departments.

The basis of the production program, and foundation for the governing management system, is a set of specific "primary" production responsibilities unique to each production organization. These responsibilities are generally based on the research and development mission of the respective military department. While such assignments are fundamental to a structured and orderly production program, provision is made for necessary flexibility and adjustment. That is, production responsibilities can be, and on occasion are, modified to reflect realities of resource and capability constraints and, more importantly, to satisfy unique operational threat or countermeasures development requirements. In this regard, the concept of "complementary" production allows a particular production center to perform analyses in an area that would normally be the primary responsibility of another. This, however, requires DIA review and approval on a case-by-case basis and, once approved, continuous coordination with the primary producer to avoid unnecessary duplication of effort.

POLICIES AND PROCEDURES

Based on the existence of a well-defined community of scientific and technical intelligence producers with clearly documented production responsibilities that can be modified if necessary to satisfy unique consumers needs, DIA, in close coordination with the military departments, has developed a common set of production policies and procedures that are binding on the agency and the military departments. Collectively, these policies and procedures form a production management system operated by DIA that includes six key elements: production requirements evaluation and processing, production tasking, production scheduling, product review and approval, product publication and dissemination, and production resource review and evaluation. This system involves technical management as well as administration of a production control system. The principal job of technical management is performed by scientists and engineers (production task monitors) in the Directorate for Scientific and Technical Intelligence of DIA, who also do analyses and production in selected areas, while the production control operation is the responsibility of a small core of management and administrative personnel. The distinct advantage of this system is that it brings scientific and technical resources to bear on all aspects of the scientific and technical intelligence production operation, from evaluating of incoming requirements to disseminating finished products, including review and evaluation of production resources throughout the programming and budgeting cycle and operating year. In addition, overhead management and administration resources are kept to a minimum.

Each aspect of the production management system has been designed to afford DIA an element of production control, consistent with its mission of managing the defense-wide production program, while avoiding the imposition of unnecessarily detailed management practices on the military departments. The Directorate for Scientific and Technical Intelligence, DIA evaluates incoming production requirements. If the data are already available, the requestor is advised immediately. If production action is required the requirement is approved for production and either integrated into existing production tasking or new tasking is created and levied on the appropriate Military

Department production center in accordance with assigned production responsibilities.

The DIA scientists and engineers who function as technical managers of the production effort are also actively involved in the scientific and technical intelligence planning, programming, and budgeting process. With a small core of management personnel as the focal point, this staff collectively participates in identifying and assessing intelligence gaps that are documented in the Defense Wide Intelligence Plan (DWIP) and provides substantive and programming guidance to the GDIP Program Managers Guidance Memorandum (PMGM).

SUMMARY

Scientific and technical intelligence plays a very critical role in alerting decisionmakers to the possibility of technological surprise through in depth assessments of foreign advancements in the various sciences and technologies with military implications, in providing U.S. weapon systems and countermeasures developers with assessments of the characteristics and capabilities of operational and future foreign weapon systems, and in supporting U.S. force planners and operational forces by focusing studies on the effectiveness of foreign weapon systems, and combinations of weapon systems, in real warfare scenarios and deriving total enemy force capabilities.

This is accomplished by a group of producers under a production system, managed by DIA, that has been developed and modified over the years in full coordination with the military departments. "Participatory management" is the fundamental underlying concept, with effectiveness dependent upon cooperation and working relationships between DIA and the military departments, including the production centers, their parent commands or agencies, and departmental intelligence staffs. This production system enables DIA to perform one of its primary functions, "... the maintenance of a strong DoD scientific and technical intelligence program," without adopting burdensome and resource intensive micro-mangement techniques. Operating in this manner, the Department of Defense is able to maintain the flow of accurate and timely scientific and technical intelligence that is responsive to the critical requirements of a growing and more sophisticated consumer community.

11
Principles of Warning Intelligence

Timothy M. Laur

INTRODUCTION TO WARNING INTELLIGENCE

Indications and warning (I&W), or, simply warning intelligence, is an interdisciplinary field comprised of several types of intelligence and academic disciplines. In the intelligence arena, I&W includes current, estimative, scientific and technological, and other types of intelligence. In respect to academic fields, warning analysis encompasses history, political science, international relations, geography, and environmental science.

One of the purposes of this chapter is to discuss the multidisciplinary nature of warning. More importantly, the scope of the research, the application of examples, and the application of warning parameters in analysis will be discussed. The intent here is not to confuse or complicate the business of warning, but to suggest that warning is all of the above things intertwined. Too frequently, the warning process is narrowed to its simplest part-- a warning--and a failure to understand the entire analytical process will produce a lack of appreciation of exactly what warning is. A successful farmer may be interested only in the prediction of rain or no rain, but he has gained an appreciation, through his experience, of the complex nature of producing a weather forecast. Therefore, he knows how to interpret official forecasts for his purposes. A similar situation exists in the warning field, but too frequently the decisionmaker wants a simple invasion or no invasion prediction, with no appreciation of the numerous variables which contribute to a probabilistic forecast of (future) events. This chapter will address the warning process in terms of its concepts, systems, and analytical techniques.

Warning comes in many shapes and is expressed in many different ways. Cigarette smokers have at least a cursory knowledge of the Surgeon General's warning of the hazards of smoking. Or do they? Ask the first person you meet who smokes cigarettes to quote the warning verbatim. The chances are that he can't. This same problem of not hearing or heeding warnings exists in the formal warning business. How many of us really pay attention to railroad crossing warnings? You can think of other, day-to-day warnings that are taken for granted and essentially ignored.

In some regards, this ambivalence toward warning may be described as a "cry wolf" response. Once an individual is exposed to the same or similar warnings for a period of time, he becomes anesthesized to the threat and ignores it. This problem also occurs in the intelligence warning business. When Marshall Tito, already in his 80's, was seriously ill, warning analysts issued alerts to prepare decisionmakers for a change of government in Yugoslavia. After several months of the tenacious Tito's "imminent death," our leadership simply did not want to hear any more about the president's eventual demise.

Another example of repetitious warning which dulled the senses of leaders occurred during early 1940. After the foreign minister of Norway had been warned several times of a German attack and nothing happened, he essentially stopped listening. Then, when the invasion did occur, the Norwegians were caught by surprise.[1]

Two forms of warning actually exist. The first type, more important to us, is the warning that results from the analytical process of assessing indications and producing a warning statement for decisionmakers. The other type works almost in reverse; it is the warning statement made by national leaders intended to evoke a response or action by another leader. This type of warning may be an indication in itself. Very frequently, this type of warning is issued publicly as its impact depends on public consumption as well as soliciting a response from the intended target.

In February 1982, Prime Minister Menachem Begin of Israel warned the U.S. "not to arm Jordan." A newspaper article stated that "Begin warned repeatedly of the Jordan-Iraqi axis," thus providing a clear statement by a national leader.[2] Numerous warnings are provided continually in the press that should be noted by warning analysts for potential indications. For example, an article from the New York Times stated that the Chief-of-Staff of the Soviet Armed Forces, Marshal Nikolai V. Ogarkov, "has issued a stern warning that the Soviet Union must keep its military machine, economy and people in total readiness and that any letup in weapons development could have 'serious consequences.'"[3] Most likely, this warning was intended for Western consumption as much as for the Soviet people. The warning professional must have sufficient knowledge of the Soviet thought processes to interpret such a statement accurately and place it in proper context to accurately discern intentions. What were the likely intentions when the Libyan government warned the U.S. that "a third world war is imminent" if planned naval maneuvers in the Mediterranean took place?[4] This warning by the Qaddafi government was issued six months after the Gulf of Sidra incident, when U.S. Navy jets shot down two Libyan aircraft. To this date, the warning has not been followed with action, but analysts are still attempting to discern Qaddafi's ultimate intentions.

Iraq used a different technique to warn Iran during the Gulf War. Rather than a public statement, the Iraqi government sent an official communique to the United Nations Secretary General "warning that it now has the right 'to use all means at its disposal' to protect itself from Iranian attacks."[5] Certainly the analyst may detect a clue about intentions in this statement issued through a third party.

Open sources should be reviewed constantly to derive warnings of intentions. In a speech on March 16, 1982, President Leonid Brezhnev warned that the U.S.S.R. would undertake "retaliatory steps" if the United States deployed medium range missiles to Western Europe. General Nikolai Chervov echoed a similar warning on Soviet television a week later to demonstrate Moscow's attempt to alert U.S. leaders to the Soviet posture towards Western defense programs. Brezhnev's statement, according to Soviet sources, was "intended to raise the possibility of introduction of Soviet nuclear arms in Cuba."[6] These warnings were perhaps a clear expression of intentions.

Whenever the leadership of a nation changes, analysts will search for statements by the new leader which may suggest a shift in policy or a continuation of the status quo. Following the death of Yuri Andropov, Brezhnev's successor, analysts were quick to suggest possible shifts in Soviet foreign policy. Konstantin Chernenko, who was to be named the new leader, published what proved to be a timely article on his political philosophy. Chernenko, Brezhnev's closest aide, stated "the Soviet people and the Soviet Communist Party harbor no secret intention or malicious designs."[7]

The importance of warning and warning analysis should now be evident. Secretary of Defense Caspar W. Weinberger certainly tried to convey his view of warning in the Annual Report to the Congress, in which he stated that there are four tasks which have to be undertaken "with a high degree of urgency." The first of these was to "make more realistic the manner in which our forces respond to warning."[8] This clearly places the burden of warning on both the analyst, to properly present viable warning to leaders, and on those leaders, to properly receive and respond to warning. Secretary Weinberger demonstrated his awareness of the problems of warning analysis, stating "we ought to expect a massive and skillful effort at deception." The importance of understanding Soviet (and others') use of deceptive techniques to mask intentions is suggested by his statement that "it is likely that skillful deception could deprive us of clear warning."[9] Indeed, Soviet military doctrine puts great emphasis on deception and surprise.

The role and importance of warning intelligence was also reflected by the former Deputy Director of the CIA, Admiral Bobby R. Inman. He stated, "There are few jobs more important to our country than to recognize the earliest indications of future international problems and to alert our national leaders quickly."[10] Essentially, this statement summarizes the raison d'etre of a warning system. The primary role of warning analysis and a warning system is to allow our leaders and decisionmakers to avoid surprise.

Earlier, warning analysis was discussed in terms of providing timely warning of hostilities prior to initiation. In fact, two types of intelligence warning exist, strategic warning and tactical warning.[11] Strategic warning is simply warning conveyed to a decisionmaker in time for a decision to be made. The decision may be to take a counteraction, to maintain the status quo, or to withdraw from activity; a decision must be made, even if the decision is to take no action at that time.

The other type of warning, tactical warning, is actually an operational response to the initiation of hostilities. The "balloon is up" and the strategic warning process is over. Tactical warning employs sensors to detect a strategic launch. At this point, the warning analyst has or has not done his job. As can be seen, the type of warning involved has nothing to do with the types of weapons systems employed. That is, tactical warning is involved with warning (with minimal lead time) of a strategic launch, whereas strategic warning may be assessing indications of tactical as well as strategic activity.[12] To carry the cigarette smoker analogy to this concept, the Surgeon General's warning is strategic; the hacking cough after inhaling is tactical. Our earliest tactical warning was exemplified in Paul Revere's ride.

STRATEGIC WARNING SYSTEMS

An introduction to indications and warning intelligence often begins by referring back to Pearl Harbor and World War II. The role of history and past international crises and wars as a foundation for I&W Intelligence is very valuable. A future crisis situation will probably not reproduce a classic scenario we have observed in the past; however, certain analogues, patterns, and precedents should emerge as prerequisites to action. In fact, it was Pearl Harbor which forced national leaders to first realize the necessity for some type of warning system and the need to properly analyze information for warning signals. Nevertheless, within the Department of Defense, the development of a formal warning structure received a real boost when the United States Air Force took the initial steps to establish a warning network. This seminal system consisted of the then Air Defense Command, the Strategic Air Command, and an office of the Headquarters of the U.S. Air Force. This Air Force Indications System, formed in the 1950s, was primarily a response to the growing fear of the Soviet strategic threat. After the Defense Intelligence Agency was formed in the early 1960s, DIA took control of the eight Air Force Indications Centers which then existed.

There are actually two warning "systems" in existence which provide strategic warning to top government and military decisionmakers. The more formal organization of the two is the Department of Defense (DOD) Indications and Warning System. This consists of warning centers at various echelons of the military operational and management commands. It is this system which evolved from the post-World War II Air Force system. Each center, although autonomous in its mission of providing warning support to its local commander, also participates in the overall Department of Defense system.[13]

The management responsibility for the System rests with the Defense Intelligence Agency (DIA) and the Director, DIA is the system's supervisor. As the system grew, all Unified and Specified Commands, several of their component commands, Joint Commands, and the Headquarters of each Military Service were included. With this growth came a lack of central direction. Therefore, by the mid-1970s, DIA began several management and operational steps to promote close integration of the individual members. As a result, unprecedented standardization within the strategic warning network now exists.

As of the summer of 1984, regardless of the level, each is an around-the-clock operation. Each is an autonomous entity of the system, which is "structured and manned to provide direct support to major military commanders as well as to function as a node in the indications and warning system."[14]

The system, in its dichotomous support role, uses a series of reports to keep decisionmakers apprised of warning situations. The reports may be threat estimates, assessments and rationale for a particular warning judgment, or an analysis to be exchanged with another center in the system. Members of the system have the capability of exchanging timely information between centers.

Naturally, the optimum design of an Indications and Warning System has not yet been formulated. A basic warning system will always be necessary for a concerted effort. However, the question of membership will continue to be a management problem. How many centers and what operational level should be used in a viable warning system? The high number in the DOD system, now almost 30, could turn out to be too many for effective alerting during a crisis. As we will see below, the national warning system has been limited to optimize its effectiveness. Conceivably, we may see a reduction of primary centers in the DOD System, perhaps limiting essential warning responsibility to the I&W Centers.

Although we can assume that other countries have some type of warning system or network, few publicize such information. An open warning system has been organized in Yugoslavia which was developed for both military and civilian threats. The Observation, Reporting, Notifying and Alert Service, or OJOU, was developed in 1980 to serve as "an important component of the system of nationwide defense and prevents the surprise which a potential aggressor would strive for."[15] The service is obviously different from our I&W System; however, its wartime mission does sound familiar. To achieve the objective to "prevent any surprise and to avoid undesirable consequences," the service will discover and monitor "all types of activities and threats by an aggressor."[16]

The other U.S. strategic warning system has a less rigid structure than the DOD system. This is the group of centers which participate in the national decisionmaking process. The centers are linked into a secure teleconferencing system called the National Operations and Intelligence Watch Officer Net (NOIWON). This so-called National Warning System consists of warning centers at the CIA, DIA, NSA, State Department, White House, and the

Department of Defense Command Post (called the National Military Command Center, or NMCC). The DIA warning center is named the National Military Intelligence Center, or NMIC, and represents the Department of Defense in the national system (Figure 11.1). When a situation dictates the activation of a NOIWON conference, the NMIC, upon termination, will notify the appropriate warning centers about the details of the conference.[17]

The participation of the NMCC in the NOIWON insures that the operational decisionmakers at the national level will be in the warning loop. Dr. Thomas G. Belden, who designed the NOIWON, has pointed out that, prior to the NOIWON system, operations personnel were not getting timely critical intelligence information. Likewise, operations would not, as a rule, coordinate activities with intelligence. The importance of an operations-intelligence dialog cannot be overemphasized.

THE WARNING PROCESS

Warning analysis has the fundamental goal of providing <u>timely</u> warning; in essence, warning is a forecast of activities of potential enemies or of foreign governments inimical to U.S. interests. Once the activity is initiated, the warning analyst has (hopefully) done his job and he turns to assessing other warning problems. At this point, the war or crisis or hostilities are analyzed by the area experts, the current analysts. The warning analyst is concerned with action before it occurs.

Warning analysis is analogous to weather forecasting in several ways, and the analogy helps explain the role of the people who try to provide accurate warning. Rather than analyzing atmospheric variables and parameters to provide a weather forecast, the warning analyst evaluates military, political, economic, and other "social" indicators to formulate a warning. These "indicators" are our warning factors. At this point, the terms should be defined. "Indicator" and "indication" have many different connotations. In the warning lexicon, each has a specific definition. An <u>indicator</u> is a hypothetical event or action that may be necessary to establish a threat. For any potential threat, various indicators may be necessary. For one case, certain indicators may be observed; yet in another situation, different indicators may be expected. These potential actions are referred to as indicators, and lists of indicators have been developed to aid the warning analyst. When an indicator is observed to have actually occurred, then it is referred to as an <u>indication</u>. An indicator may be the deployment of artillery to forward areas; when this action is actually observed, we have an indication.

Indicator lists may be established for a specific country, an area, or a functional problem. Lists that are applicable to one or a few countries may have no or limited utility to others. Some similarities may be expected for military indicator lists for the U.S.S.R. and the Peoples' Republic of China, for example, but little similarity would be expected for the U.S.S.R. and Angola.

Functional lists may be developed to address a threat that is not related to a specific geographic area; international terrorism is an obvious example.

The challenge to developing useful indicator lists is the determination of accurate sources of indicators. There are many sources of indicators, and as an analyst develops experience with a warning problem, other sources will become evident. The value of particular sources will vary from country to country. For example, one source of indicators is the collective doctrine of a nation. For the Soviet Union, which publishes extensively on political, military, and economic doctrine, a rather voluminous collection of information is available to the analyst.[18] Other countries generally provide fewer clues about their doctrine.

Another source of indicators is the state of readiness of a nation's military. The steps a country takes to prepare for a military action provide us with indicators. Similarly, previous crises and exercises also should be studied for indicators. A word of caution is necessary, however. The fact that a nation took certain steps prior to initiating hostilities in the past is no guarantee that it will take the same steps again. The previous activity should be used as a point of departure for developing new indicators for future crises and exercises. Obviously, as a nation's capabilities improve with new weapon acquisitions, personnel training, and so on, our indicator lists will have to be amended to reflect these changes.

United States analogues provide another source of indicators, but again, they must be used with discretion. The preparatory steps to a military action that our forces would take may not parallel the steps another power would follow. Certainly, there are basic actions that are necessary, and these form the foundation for our lists. We should ask, "What would we have to do to invade Poland?" After answering, we should then ask, "What would the Soviets have to do?" Just because we would take certain steps is no assurance someone else would take the same steps.

Some other sources of indicators are even more nebulous. Abstract factors such as common sense, hunches, and continuity are intangible yet vital for fitting pieces into the puzzle. These are related to another source, experience. Frankly, as a rule, common sense comes with experience. We tend to temper our impressions with our own experiences. Granted, too much moderation may prevent us from taking a chance on a high probability prediction, but with experience we are better prepared to substantiate an extreme warning. Likewise, gut hunches can only be developed after years of exposure to different scenarios. After years of reviewing message traffic and literally seeing almost every possible type of activity, an analyst can better develop a sixth sense of warning. There will always be that little obscure factor that tugs at a nerve that has become sensitized over the years.

Finally, continuity is extremely important, both with individual analysts and among a warning center's personnel. If a developing situation has to be reassessed weekly, or even annually, because of personnel turnover, the wheel will be reinvented repeatedly. Acclimation, which must be developed over a period of time, is a prerequisite for thinking about warning. Unfortunately, establishing continuity, as well as the experience level necessary for optimizing analyst perceptions, is very difficult because of the nature of the job. A warning operation, by definition, is an around-the-clock, day in and day out responsibility. A watch analyst will work shift work, holidays, and weekends. After some exposure to the rotating schedules and concomitant pressures inherent in the duty, most watch personnel are screaming to go to the relatively sane, stable, and more predictable world of another intelligence discipline.

Once indicators are established and the process of monitoring lists for indications begins, the analytical technique of indications and warning takes over. In the past, the existence of indicator analysis as a unique discipline was seriously questioned. The process would be discussed very generally, at best. Now, however, some techniques have been developed and, although still in its infancy vis-a-vis other forms of intelligence analysis, the "science" of warning is in fact a distinct research area. Although indicators are varied and multidisciplinary, the analytical process for warning, when reduced to its lowest terms, may be expressed in the symbolic formula:

$$\sum I + \sum C = T,$$

where I represents the intentions of other states/governments/leaders, C represents the capabilities of particular states, and T is simply the estimated probable threat. The summation notation is used to show that the equation is derived from at least several indicators. The absence of indications is an indication in itself; however, to derive another's intentions, an analysis of several indications is necessary. No single warning indication will provide definitive strategic warning. Very simply, a nation must undergo at least some decisionmaking process and military preparation prior to hostilities, and these processes will provide indications.

Actually, the symbolic expression may be carried further for clarity and accuracy. That is,

$$I = \sum \text{Indications} = \sum \text{Ind}_P + \sum \text{Ind}_M + \sum \text{Ind}_E + \sum \text{Ind}_O$$

where Ind_P represents political indications, Ind_M and Ind_E represent military and economic indications, respectively, and Ind_O represents other indications, which could be terrorism, insurgency, and so on. These "other" indications could fall into one of the three basic categories of indications, but for certain cases, they may be analyzed in greater detail by placing them into their own "other" category. The reader should be cautioned to exercise care in keeping the terms "indicator/indication" and "intention" separated.

The estimated intentions of a potential aggressor, then, equal (or approximate) the sum of the political, military,

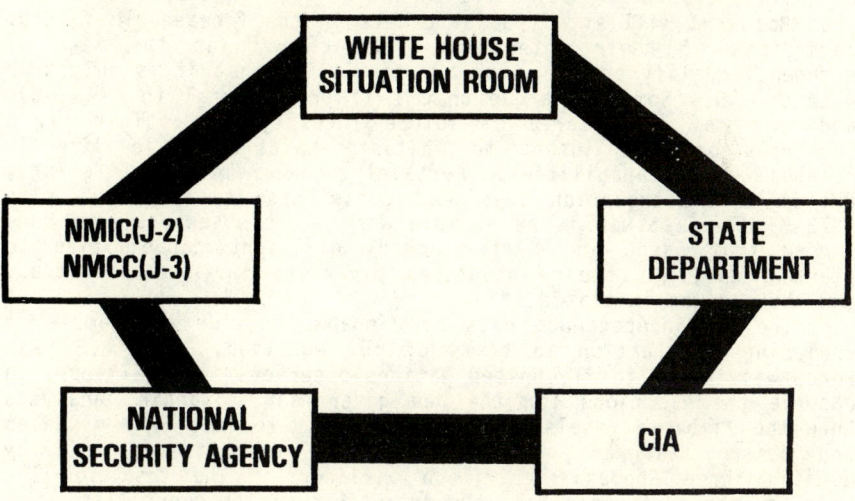

Figure 11.1

economic, and other indications. The relative worth of each indication in the equation (that is, the weight of each toward the total value of the estimated intentions) is a subject beyond the scope of this chapter, but it should be emphasized that all indicators make a relative contribution toward the final war/no war, threat/no threat prediction. The movement of combat aircraft to a forward area should be given more weight than a conference of squadron commanders at the regional headquarters, which likewise would probably be weighted more heavily than an increase in recruitment goals for the next year. All might be indicators of a potential increase in threat, but their importance in the overall equation must be considered.

The capabilities part of the relationship is "calculated" into the equation, but these factors are more computable, and not in the purview of the warning analysts. A country must have the capability before an estimative threat exists. There is no chance that Botswana will attack U.S. borders in the foreseeable future, regardless of their intentions. We could, for the sake of argument, qualify the equation by stipulating that it is only true when $C > 0$. Some may argue that I is proportional to C ($I \sim C$), and this may be an area of future investigation. That is, a country's probable intent to initiate hostilities is directly related to its capabilities. Certainly, some relationship exists, but it is the exception that most contributes to surprise. The 1973 Middle East War is an example where most observers were convinced that Egypt and Syria lacked sufficient capabilities to start a war, yet their intentions overruled their capabilities, and the war was initiated.[19]

The pre-independence days of Zimbabwe provide an example of analyzing a situation in terms of our equation. The U.S. Air Force was tasked to fly United Nations observers into Salisbury to observe the elections for the new government. Warning analysts knew the Zimbabwe rebels had the capability to fire SA-7 missiles and destroy aircraft; they had already demonstrated this by downing three Rhodesian civilian airliners. The task for the warning people was to assess the intentions of the guerrillas.

Needless to say, the warning process is much more complicated than simply plugging in values for various indications and calculating a threat. The role of the analyst in the warning business is more subtle, more complex, and, most of all, more frustrating than that. Analysts, however, can take heart in the perceived importance of the warning process at the national level. The 1981 presidential Executive Order states "Timely and accurate information about the activities, <u>capabilities</u>, plans, and <u>intentions</u> of foreign powers, organizations, and persons, and their agents, is essential to the national security of the United States."[20]

THE WARNING ANALYST

A warning analyst must be a generalist, in both his approach to analysis and use of collection resources. The analysis done for warning actually encompasses many analytical disciplines, yet is none of them by themselves. Warning analysis includes current and estimative intelligence analysis. It is different from current intelligence analysis in that warning analysis evaluates variables to determine intentions, that is, to predict the near term potential actions of other nations. It must be timely and probabilistic, be operationally related, and be received and recognized by the receiver as a warning.

Similarly, warning intelligence is different from estimative intelligence in that the latter is designed for long-term assessments of foreign activities that are of interest to U.S. policymakers. Although at times the differences between the two may be blurred, particularly when conducting postmortems of past crisis events, the urgency of warning intelligence is considerably more critical than estimative intelligence. The importance of timeliness is considerable; one rarely hears of a failure of estimates, but, unfortunately, failures of warning are frequent. The fall of the Shah of Iran, for example, was described by the House Permanent Select Committee on Intelligence as "a warning failure, in that the attention of top policymakers was not brought forcefully to bear on Iran...."[21] The report also helped to reflect the difference between warning and estimative intelligence, finding that as a result of the Iranian crisis, "In a fast-moving political situation like Iran, analysts and senior intelligence officials increasingly regarded the National Intelligence Estimate (NIE) as a distraction from more pressing business."[22]

The House study also described the problems with current intelligence analysis during the Iranian revolution. The essential conclusion implied in the study verified the differences between warning intelligence and both current and estimative intelligence. The Iran crisis provided a textbook example of the timeliness and responsiveness that only warning intelligence can provide. During fast moving events, current and estimative disciplines must support, but are second to, warning. The House study reflected the relative ease which hindsight can provide in determining failures by intelligence agencies. The role of warning was suggested in the observation that "while the events were occurring the 'signal to noise ratio' tended to obscure their significance to analysts who, caught up in a series of fast-breaking situations, tended to overlook the immediate past in assessing the present."[23] Clearly, this was the role of the warning analysts, and, unfortunately, demonstrates why the failure was one of warning, and not of other intelligence disciplines. The study also highlighted another difference between warning and other areas of intelligence: the acknowledgement by the receiver that he has been warned. In its conclusion the study noted "the importance of user attitudes in any warning process."[24] Therefore, if the decisionmaker is not aware that he has been warned, the cycle, and the warning analyst's job, is incomplete.

The warning analyst must be a generalist regarding the use of collection resources. Warning can hardly exist if all sources of information are not exploited--from the most open unclassified sources, such as broadcasts and press reports, to highly technical, sensitive systems, and all types in between. The indications and warning analyst depends on specialists in the various analytical skills and collection systems to support the warning effort, but the specialized nature of the warning process requires the synthesis of all of the contributing factors to accomplish accurate warning.

Warning analysis should not be focused strictly on a war/no war prediction. Viable warning analysis will alert leadership to developing situations with potential impact on U.S. national security interests, regardless of whether war is imminent. For example, a deteriorating economy accompanied by devastating droughts may produce widespread famine. These economic indications and other factors may develop to incite a revolutionary movement which culminates in the overthrow of the national government. If the country was aligned with the U.S. prior to the revolution, a good possibility exists that we could be blamed for contributing to the population's deprivation. Ultimately, relations may be terminated or severely limited.

A scenario similar to this took place in Ethiopia in the middle 1970s. Economic conditions led ultimately to the overthrow of Emperor Haile Selassie, who had ruled for about forty years. The new government grew increasingly pro-Soviet and our strategic presence in the country was eventually terminated. This is just one example where an accumulation of indications produced a significant shift in big power postures in a critical region. None of the events in Ethiopia yielded indications of a war/no war dichotomy vis-a-vis the U.S.S.R., but the situation certainly warranted effective warning analysis to prepare decisionmakers for potential shifts in our national security interests. These more subtle political and economic indications may have extremely serious ramifications, although they have little to do with the prediction of war between the U.S. and another nation. The Iranian revolution provides another classic case of strategic indications and warning affecting our national security interests, yet in a context independent of the "Big W" military warning problem associated with the U.S.S.R., Warsaw Pact, People's Republic of China, and North Korea.

Although warning will continue to emphasize the analysis of military factors, obviously the importance of incorporating other types of indicators in the overall analysis must be stressed. Likewise, we must analyze the "Little W" threat for those areas outside of the U.S.S.R., Warsaw Pact, People's Republic of China, and North Korea.

A serious problem with providing warning to policymakers is the situation where observed indications are in response to U.S. actions at a decisionmaking level unavailable to warning analysts. Covert diplomatic activity could produce actions which analysts observe but cannot explain. We provide warning to a decisionmaker who understands because he knows what precipitated the observed activity. Betts cautions against leadership forcing analysts to work in a vacuum, the "one-way flow of intelligence traffic from producers to policymakers. Too seldom do top officials share with professional analysts the results of the trips and high-level exchanges with foreign leaders."[25] Imagine the chagrin of the China analyst who was trying to provide accurate assessment of China's intentions in the early 1970s as our leadership was secretly reaching a rapprochement with Peking. Certainly some covert diplomatic activity is necessary at the highest levels of decisionmaking; however, the need for our intelligence analysts to provide accurate assessments dictates that they be kept in the decision loop as much as possible.

Related to this is the necessity of knowing the operational activity of the United States and its allies. It is insufficient to observe indicators which an aggressor is activating, when its action may be in response to an action on our side. United States and allied operational summaries are provided routinely to DOD warning centers so that a potential enemy's activity may be placed in proper context vis-a-vis our own military operations.

Another problem associated with warning is the use of deception. The concept of deception normally brings to mind the notions of cover, concealment, and camouflage, and therefore the role of the photo-interpreters. While this is true for these classic roles, there are other areas of deception which are particularly important for the warning analyst--the areas of disinformation, propaganda, and similar techniques.

The warning analyst's mission is to preclude surprise, and deceptive techniques are the primary means an aggressor uses to achieve surprise. Although most experts agree that the achievement of complete surprise is essentially impossible, the effective employment of deception optimizes the extent to which a victim is caught unaware. Soviet literature confirms their view of the difficulties of achieving complete surprise, "yet they believe that most warning indicators can be eliminated by comprehensive efforts to maintain secrecy in their use of deception."[26] Likewise, deceptive ruses in propaganda and false information releases may be exceedingly effective for masking intentions, the critical variable of indications and warning analysis. The Soviet Union has historically been active in deceptive measures, using "forgery, disinformation actions, and political operations designed to denigrate the United States and its allies, build empathy toward the Soviet Union, and generally influence public opinion throughout the world in support of Soviet goals."[27]

THE WARNING CYCLE

The entire function of indications and warning analysis may be explained as a cycle, in which raw information is analyzed to determine another's capabilities and intentions, to be weighed against indicator lists. When sufficient indicators have been assessed as indications of a potential threat, a warning is issued to the appropriate policy or decisionmaker. This simplified routine is graphically shown in Figure 11.2.

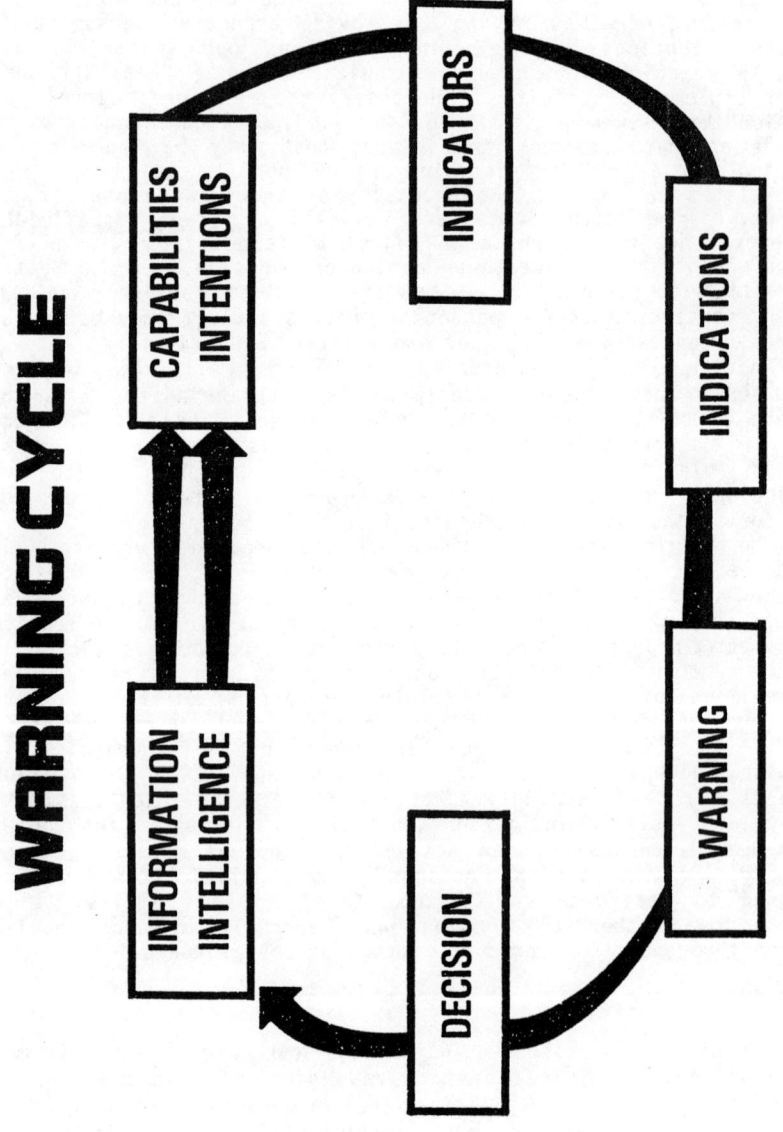

Figure 11.2

In theory, the cycle is not completed until the policymaker receives the warning, knows he has been warned, and makes a decision. Operational action may not be necessary to complete the cycle. The decision could be to maintain the status quo, to retreat or withdraw forces, or to attack. Each of the possible alternatives would solicit a response from the opponent, and a new decision process will begin. Although some arguments require a response to warning for the cycle to be complete, the belief here is that if the warning is received, accepted, and the decision is made to take no action, the cycle is completed. But, the warning analysis process nevertheless continues.[28]

RESPONSE TO WARNING

The importance of a decision to complete the warning cycle has just been discussed. But what kind of response by the recipient may be anticipated when a warning is issued? There is, in fact, a psychology of warning which creates an inherent negative attitude in the receiver. Basically warning is, by definition, bad news. When General Robert E. Huyser, former Commander-in-Chief of the Air Force's Military Airlift Command, would enter his briefing room for the latest intelligence information, he would routinely ask, "Well, what bad news do you have for me this time?" The problem of how warning is received is nothing new. In the environmental arena, how many weather forecasters are _more_ popular after they accurately forecast snow? People, by their nature, simply do not want to hear bad news. The paradox of warning only increases the warning analyst's reluctance to "cry wolf."[29]

Related to this is the problem of abusing the messenger for delivering the warning--the "killing the courier" syndrome. "If the analyst insists on perpetually bearing bad news, he is likely to be beheaded."[30] This type of attitude certainly inhibits the warning analyst faced with reluctant bosses and their preconceptions, the burden of proof, and the negative psychosis applied to bearers of bad news. No wonder analysts try not to stay in the warning business any longer than necessary. The odds simply are stacked against them.

The media also can experience the "bad news" syndrome. The vivid portrayal on television of the bombing of the U.S. Marine Headquarters and barracks on October 23, 1983 produced a generally unfavorable reaction. Many people questioned the value of showing the death and destruction. Ernest Schultz, executive vice-president of Radio-TV News Directors Association, described the public's reaction as the tendency of viewers "to take out their frustrations on the messenger bearing the bad news."[31]

Regardless of the success of the warning, the chances are that the person who provided it will face chastisement. Consider the table below. For a warning to have a "completely" favorable outcome, you would have to "warn" or predict a favorable occurrence and your prediction would have to be true, _in the eyes of the receiver_. If, for example, you predict that someone will win $100 and they receive only $50, your forecast was essentially favorable, but the receiver would nevertheless probably be disappointed with your optimism. Of course, if the reverse occurred and $100 was received against your prediction of $50, you still have not completely succeeded in successful warning. If the reader gets the impression of a "damned if you do, damned if you don't" attitude toward the forecaster, that is true. That is why many of those with warning responsibilities are reluctant to warn, playing the odds that the disaster won't occur. If it does, the chances are the bosses will be too preoccupied with responding to the crisis to take retribution. And when they eventually do, the likelihood is that you will be out of the warning business; so what's the loss?

The psyche of a warning analyst must be prepared to be exposed to a considerable amount of negativism. Odds favor a hostile attitude on the part of the person receiving the warning. As the matrix in Table 11.1 demonstrates, only under the condition of predicting good news that comes true is there a favorable outcome to the warning process. In all other cases, the result can be, at best, neutral.

TABLE 11.1 Warning Response Matrix

PREDICTION/WARNING	OCCURRED	FAILED TO OCCUR
GOOD NEWS/EVENT	FAVORABLE OUTCOME	UNFAVORABLE OUTCOME
BAD NEWS/EVENT	UNFAVORABLE OUTCOME	NEUTRAL (FAVORABLE & UNFAVORABLE)

The neutral result is quasi-favorable since the bad event that was forecasted did not occur; however, this is offset by the unfavorable responses which result from the preparations taken to plan for the crisis which never occurred. The mental trauma, the "cry wolf" syndrome which results, can negate the favorable impressions. If no actions were taken by those who were warned, then the chances are the outcome would tilt toward favorable. For example, a warning of twenty inches of snow is not followed by emergency preparations because the impact would be so devastating that no preparations are really feasible. Therefore, if no snow occurs, people generally would be pleased, but would still doubt the warning analyst's capability. However, if six inches of snow is warned, and snow removal equipment is mobilized, and people rise earlier in the morning, and no snow occurs, the forecaster has still made skeptics (at best) even though his bad news prediction failed to materialize. Again, the odds favor being damned if you do, and damned if you don't--but most frequently damned if you do (warn); therefore, the reluctance to issue warnings.

SUMMARY

The ultimate irony in the warning business is that after all the judicious data collection and analysis are completed, some events just do not occur in spite of the correct conclusions. A key factor must be appreciated when trying to predict social activities and events that are predicated on human decisions. As the indicators are being assessed and the predictions formulated, the warning analyst must remember that perhaps the decisionmaker on the other side--the one whose decisions we are trying to predict--may not in fact have decided which course of action to take.

Nevertheless, there is a role for the indications and warning specialist. In summary, there are a few basic points to recall. First and foremost, the warning analyst is a different breed, with different techniques and objectives than other areas of intelligence analysis. He must think in terms of probabilities, predictions, near-term future courses of action, occasional gut-feelings or hunches, and, always, the relevance of analysis to the operational mission. The latter may be at the tactical, battlefield level or up to the national decisionmaking level.

The fundamental difference between the warning analyst and others in intelligence is the requirement to discern the <u>intentions</u> of others, whether the others are presidents, prime ministers, terrorists, or guerrilla leaders. Similarly, the warning analyst must guarantee that the warning cycle is completed by insuring that the decisionmaker knows he has been warned and makes a decision. The problem that the warning officer faces with an unreceptive audience is unique because a decision is required. Policymakers are handicapped by their preconceptions and inhibitions, which the warning analyst must overcome. This is the "don't confuse me with the facts, I have my mind made up" attitude that the warning analyst frequently faces.

Naturally, the flow of sufficient information is necessary for the analyst to formulate a warning. Inherent limits on traffic flow impede this process. Considerable amounts of important information never get to the watch officer because of the centralization process. Key information is frequently limited in its distribution and never gets to the operational level where it is needed. All too often intelligence that is pertinent at the unit level is restricted to the Washington area. This notion, often called the "green door" syndrome, is the mind set where valuable information is guarded and never passed to those who need it. Compartmentation is related to this. Compartmentation is the technique where certain intelligence is limited in distribution to certain categories of people, often excluding the operational types who need it to accomplish their mission.

Along with all of these other problems, the warning analyst is faced frequently with negativism just by virtue of providing warnings. Rarely is a "forecaster," be he concerned with weather or international relations, greeted with enthusiasm by his audience. Unfortunately, most of the time the warning to be conveyed is bad news and the person doing the warning is blamed for it.

Despite all of these difficulties, the warning business is challenging, frustrating, and, on occasion, rewarding. Because of the paradox of warning, the warning analyst may never know how many of his warnings were actually successful. Nevertheless, successful warning provided to a receptive audience provides a singular satisfaction that is unparalleled in any other area of intelligence. This satisfaction must be earned and rarely comes easily. But, it makes the many frustrations that were faced along the way a little easier to remember and to face in the future. Hopefully, you won't be the courier of the 1980s to be shot for the message you're delivering.

NOTES

1. Richard K. Betts, "Surprise Despite Warning: Why Sudden Attacks Succeed," Political Science Quarterly (Winter 1980-81): 559.

2. William Claiborne, "Begin Warns U.S. Not to Arm Jordan," Washington Post, 16 February 1982, p. 1.

3. Serge Schmemann, "Top Soviet Soldier Urges Readiness," New York Times, 11 March 1982, p. 13.

4. "Libya Warns U.S. About Planned Navy Maneuvers," Christian Science Monitor, 18 March 1982, p. 2.

5. "Iraq Sends Warning on Iran to the UN," Journal of Commerce, 27 February 1984, p. 11.

6. Dusko Doder, "Soviets Stress Missiles Threat by Brezhnev," Washington Post, 21 March 1982, p. 22; and, "Soviet Warns U.S. on Nuclear Balance," Washington Post, 28 March 1982, p. 28.

7. "Chernenko Says East-West Thaw Depends on U.S.," Washington Post, 13 February 1984, p. 13.

8. Casper W. Weinberger, Secretary of Defense, Annual Report to the Congress, Fiscal Year 1983 (Washington, DC: Government Printing Office, 1982), p. I-11.

9. Ibid., p. I-12.

10. Bobby R. Inman, Admiral, U.S.N, "Forward," Signal (October 1981): 9.

11. The definitions which are provided are the commonly accepted uses of the two types of warning, particularly within the Department of Defense. Another approach to strategic warning,

with more extensive criteria, may be found in Steve Chan, "The Intelligence of Stupidity: Understanding Failures in Strategic Warning," The American Political Science Review (March 1979): 171.

12. For a good summary of tactical warning systems, although it is a little dated, see "Improved U.S. Warning Net Spurred," Aviation Week and Space Technology (23 June 1980). Also useful on the subject is the more recent James V. Hartinger, "The Resurgence of Strategic Defense," Defense 82 (June 1982): 30-36.

13. The term "warning center" is used in a generic sense as centers may be called "alert centers," "operations centers," "situation rooms," "watch offices," and so on. For convenience and standardization, the term "warning center" will be used here.

14. Wallace D. Henderson, "Surveillance and Warning," Signal (November-December 1978): 42.

15. "Observation, Reporting, Notifying Alert Service Charted," JPRS Translation of Belgrade FRONT, 30 May 1980, pp. 34-5.

16. Ibid.

17. A more detailed, excellent article describing crisis management at the national level and the NOIWON system and development is available in Thomas G. Belden, "Indications, Warning, and Crisis Operations," International Studies Quarterly (March 1977): 181-97.

18. Just one example would be the USAF Translation Series on Soviet Military Thought. For more on the utility of doctrine as a source of indicators and the importance of precluding surprise in doctrine analysis, see Betts, "Surprise Despite Warning," pp. 568-71.

19. Richard B. Parker, "Prisoners of a Concept," Air University Review (January-February 1981): 54.

20. "Intelligence Activities," Executive Order 12333, 8 December 1981, p. 59941 (emphasis added).

21. U.S. Congress, House, Subcommittee on Evaluation, Permanent Select Committee on Intelligence, Iran: Evaluation of U.S. Intelligence Performance Prior to November 1978 (Washington DC: Government Printing Office, 1979), p. 1.

22. Ibid., p. 5.

23. Ibid., p. 4.

24. Ibid., p. 7.

25. Richard K. Betts, "Strategic Intelligence Estimates: Let's Make Them Useful," Parameters (December 1980): 23.

26. Jiri Valenta, "Perspectives on Soviet Intervention," Survival (March-April 1982): 52.

27. "Disinformation: War With Words," Air Force Magazine (March 1982): 85.

28. Betts, "Surprise Despite Warning," p. 551, for example, argues: "Warning without response is useless." His argument is that a counteraction is required to respond to the warning of an aggressor's action. This is true for the ultimate, discrete warning of a definitive action (invasion, missile launch, etc.); however, most often the warning process is in reality a continuum of "mini-warnings" if the process is effective, each of which has been received by the policymaker. For some of these, the status quo option is an acceptable choice. And, of course, completely successful warning of activity of interest to our leadership because of our overall strategic objectives, but representing no threat to our resources or national security, would most likely require no operational response. The other extreme example is when an accurate warning is passed to a leader who decides to take no action because doing so would reveal the collection capabilities to the aggressor--that he had the information of intentions beforehand--which could jeopardize future collection efforts.

29. The "paradox of warning" is the situation where an accurate warning is issued to a decisionmaker, who then takes steps to offset the action which was warned. This counteraction is observed by the aggressor, who then changes the preparations for the action. Consequently, the activity which was forecasted never takes place, and in the eyes of the leadership, another forecast was "blown."

30. Richard K. Betts, "Analysis, War and Decision: Why Intelligence Failures are Inevitable," Studies in Intelligence (Fall 1979): 50. Also published in World Politics (October 1978).

31. USA Today, 28 October 1983, p. 4A.

12
Counterintelligence and Combatting Terrorism

Stephen S. Beitler

...A soldier's musket lay near him; his hands were pressed upon his breast, and one of them contained a substance that glittered like silver. Dunwoodie stopped, and removing his limbs, perceived the place where the bullet had found a passage to his heart. The subject of his last care was a tin box, through which the fatal lead had gone; and the dying moments of the old man must have passed in drawing it from his bosom. Dunwoodie opened it, and found a paper in which, to his astonishment, he read the following:

"Circumstances of political importance, which involve the lives and fortunes of many, have hitherto kept secret what this paper now reveals. Harvey Birch has for years been a faithful and unrequited servant of his country. Though man does not, may God reward him for his conduct."
George Washington

It was the SPY OF THE NEUTRAL GROUND, who died as he had lived, devoted to his country, and a martyr to her liberties.[1]

The Spy, James Fenimore Cooper

COUNTERINTELLIGENCE

A fictional member of an authentic Revolutionary War counterintelligence net in New York, Harvey Birch's archetype remains unknown. But at George Washington's behest, John Jay and Nathanial Sackett had operated this particular net, the precursor of U.S. counterintelligence activities. After the Revolution, foreign intelligence activities were sharply curtailed. Federal counterintelligence activities were precluded until the Civil War, as a consequence of the Tub Plot of 1799. The plot involved the misapprehension and incarceration of Toussaint L'Ouverture's representatives. This misapprehension was based on specious intelligence along with calumny, linking the early Republicans in the plot with these representatives (who had come to the United States seeking aid from sympathetic Federalists for support of the slave rebellion in Santo Domingo).

The United States, thus vulnerable to penetration by foreign intelligence agencies, became the staging area for two ill-fated attempts to invade Canada by the Fenians (an Irish-American paramilitary organization that favored Irish independence) in 1866 and 1870. In addition, the United States was the target of significant British penetration, which continued into the early twentieth century.

Until Brigadier General La Fayette C. Baker formed the National Detective Bureau of the War Department in 1862, there had been no central organization in overall charge of the very fragmented counterintelligence efforts during the Civil War. The Bureau's missions included the protection of President Lincoln, in which it failed (although its officers subsequently did arrest John Wilkes Booth). President Johnson eventually disbanded the National Detective Bureau in 1866, when he learned that General Baker had maintained a clandestine intelligence net within the White House. However, the Bureau was resurrected in 1873 during Reconstruction as the Secret Service of the Department of the Treasury to combat rampant counterfeiting activities. The Departments of War and Navy then went again without counterintelligence apparatuses until the establishment of the Office of Naval Intelligence in 1882 and the Military Information Division in 1885.

During the Spanish-American War of 1898, even though the War and Navy Departments had been expanding their foreign intelligence activities, the Secret Service was responsible for counterintelligence. Lieutenant Ramon de Carranza, the Spanish Naval Attache to the United States prior to the War, directed Spanish military intelligence in the United States from Canada. In 1898, after apprehending Carranza's Montreal Spy Ring, the Secret Service became diplomatically ensnarled and the Department of State intervened on their behalf. This led to the Department of State's taking a lead role in intelligence operations from then on through World War I.

Between 1915 and 1918 German intelligence operated freely in the United States. Captain Franz von Papen, the German Military Attache, for example, ran sabotage and clandestine operations from a Wall Street advertising agency front in New York City. The Secret Service, using messages deciphered by the State and War Department's Black Chamber, was able to disrupt German espionage activities. In 1917, the Bureau of Investigation (later to become the Federal Bureau of Investigation) significantly increased its counterintelligence activities, as had the Office of Naval Intelligence and the Military Information Division in 1915. The Corps of Intelligence Police was also created by the Army during World War I to conduct tactical counterintelligence and interrogation. At its zenith it numbered 400 strong, but by 1919 it had been reduced to six personnel and would remain severely understaffed until World War II.

After World War I, the Red Scare gripped the United States and internal security operations, including the infamous Palmer Raids of January 2, 1920, were performed mainly by the Bureau of

Investigation, trailed by other counterintelligence agencies and local police forces. Interestingly enough, the excesses of this period caused the formation of the American Civil Liberties Union.

In 1935, the Bureau of Investigation finally received its charter as the Federal Bureau of Investigation, just as the finishing touches were put to the demobilization of the Military Information Department from approximately 1,500 personnel to seventy. Again, military counterintelligence capabilities were being sacrificed to spare foreign intelligence activities from the budget knife. On the eve of World War II, the Department of State failed to assume leadership of United States intelligence activities, as it had done during World War I. Thus, the Federal Bureau of Investigation expanded its counterintelligence capabilities and formed the Special Investigative Service (1940-1947) to combat the new threat.

On January 1, 1942, the Army Counterintelligence Corps, whose mission was investigative and tactical counterintelligence, was formed out of the Corps of Intelligence Police. It eventually grew to 300 detachments with 13,000 personnel. When World War II ended, the Army Counterintelligence Corps was given responsibility for the apprehension of war criminals. Counterintelligence Corps personnel prevented the attempted suicide of and arrested General Hideki Tojo, who was subsequently tried, convicted, and executed. The Office of Strategic Services, which was formed on June 13, 1942, also played a role in counterespionage duties through its X-2 division.

After World War II, the Cold War caused military counterintelligence strength to remain constant, and to this capability was added the newly created Central Intelligence Agency. Six days prior to the Korean War Inchon landings, the 441st Counterintelligence Corps Detachment in Japan arrested the members of a North Korean intelligence net and prevented them from forwarding information they possessed pertaining to that operation. In 1961, the Defense Intelligence Agency was formed to provide direction and centralization of counterintelligence efforts of the service intelligence departments.

During the 1960s, the growth of military intelligence-conducted domestic collection operations paralleled the growth of the antiwar and civil rights movements. Counterintelligence operations used similar tactics to those of the Secret Service during the Spanish-American War and the Bureau of Investigation during the Red Scare, when they committed crimes and violated the civil liberties of Americans in the name of national defense, and during World War II, when thousands of Americans of Japanese ancestry were interned. Among the techniques employed were physical and electronic surveillance, opening mail, burglary, maintaining files on U.S. citizens, infiltrating and recruiting agents among dissident and youth groups, and surveilling members of domestic political groups.

While the use of questionable countersubversion techniques was again bringing counterintelligence agencies under close scrutiny, it should also be noted that these same agencies had not ceased to protect the United States from foreign intelligence threats. But the public was outraged, and a series of commissions and congressional investigations culminated by imposing new controls on the intelligence community and, in particular, on counterintelligence activities. These included the Foreign Intelligence Surveillance Act of 1978, a series of executive orders on intelligence activities, and the Attorney General Guidelines.

Counterintelligence or Foreign Intelligence

The two major contemporary intelligence disciplines are foreign intelligence and counterintelligence. Foreign intelligence is the basis for national decisions. Counterintelligence, its antithesis, is the identification and neutralization of any threat presented by a foreign intelligence service or the manipulation of these services for the manipulator's benefit. Executive Order 12333, <u>United States Intelligence Activities</u>, states that

> <u>Counterintelligence</u> means information gathered and activities conducted to protect against espionage, other intelligence activities, sabotage, or assassinations conducted for or on behalf of foreign powers, organizations or persons, or international terrorist activities, but not including personnel, physical, document, or communications security programs.[2]

The Hostile Intelligence Threat

To discuss the intelligence community's counterintelligence missions, it is first necessary to be aware of the scope of the hostile intelligence threat to the United States. Collection methods do not vary much from country to country--about ninety percent of all techniques are the same. But the Soviet model bears discussion because it is the primary intelligence threat to the U.S.; in addition, the East European and Cuban services are modeled on the U.S.S.R.'s, the Soviets advised and trained the services of the People's Republic of China and many lesser developed countries, and the Soviets can expect or demand support from the communist parties of various countries.

The Soviets operate with a different set of values, and although any country's objective is to minimize losses and maximize gains, the basic difference between the Soviet Union and the United States is accountability. Soviet oversight is couched only in terms of success or failure, not methods or legality. Furthermore, the Soviets operate in the United States, which is an open society, and believe in multiple coverage of targets (which they do not necessarily subject to a cost-benefit equation), providing them with a distinct advantage vis-a-vis more meager U.S. counterintelligence assets.

Agent types include: penetration agents who have direct access to targets; mass recruited agents who are usually low level and are, for example, inserted in a refugee stream or prisoner-of-war group; confusion and provocation agents, whose mission is to send counterintelligence agencies on wild goose chases or engage in a deliberate plan to discredit an American official or another defector; and "frozen" (zamorozhennye) agents, who are inactive and await the outbreak of hostilities or an interruption in relations before being activated. After World War II, most of these agents were organized along the lines of a party cell. The Soviets now use better compartmentalized agent nets, in which agents know their case officers, but not the identity of other agents.

Agents generally engage in either legal or illegal operations. Legal operations are conducted by officers or agents who are identified as Soviet representatives and who usually have diplomatic status. In illegal operations, agents have no legal status or identifiable connection with the Soviet Union. These operations can in turn be run internally or externally (for example, using Mexico City, Mexico as a base for operations against the United States).

KGB (Komitet Gosudarstvennoy Bezopasnosti or the Committee of State Security) operational methods are characterized by rigid compartmentation and highly centralized control from "The Center" (KGB headquarters).[3] This extends to all facets of their operations, including recruitment and case files, all of which are maintained in Moscow and not in referenturas (local KGB stations).

Local Communist Party, TASS, AMTORG, Aeroflot, and United Nations mission employees are used as spotters, but they do not recruit their subjects. Extensive analysis of a subject is completed in Moscow. There it is decided whether or not the KGB or GRU will attempt to recruit the subject. If it is decided to attempt a recruitment, the "little hook" method may be employed, whereby the subject will become obligated as the result of some small favor, such as a loan of money for which a receipt is asked and from which a paper record is established. The Soviets prefer to use ideology as their main recruitment technique, but they are quite successful at fiscal cooptation (usually for paltry sums) and are also expert at using leverage (based upon known sexual deviance or infidelity, alcoholism, or indebtedness).

Extensively prepared, elaborate covers are created for recruits. Natural cover is most preferable (for example, a native with no Communist Party connections), but artificial covers can be fabricated in great detail with five or six backstops. Recruits are inculcated in tradecraft, but no more than is necessary for them to accomplish their missions. During their training, operational security is stressed; although this may be very good, it is often not good enough (particularly before clandestine meetings, where elaborate signal and recognition systems are employed).

U.S. counterintelligence agencies can only conduct full investigations on "criteria" countries and organizations, the list of which is classified. If a counterintelligence target is not on the criteria list, Department of Justice and Department of State authority must be obtained, on a case-by-case basis, prior to initiating an investigation. In the United States, generally thirty-five to forty percent of the official representatives of all criteria countries are intelligence officers. Additionally, thousands of official delegations from criteria countries, each with a considerable number of intelligence officers, visit the United States yearly. There are even forty deep-water ports in the United States open to Soviet shipping. Most Soviet sailors get forty-eight hours shore leave to do what they want. Students, visitors, non-official delegations, and tourists from criteria countries also number in the thousands. Emigres number in the hundreds of thousands; 175,000 Soviets alone emigrated to the United States between 1978 and 1982. If only one percent of all Soviet emigres were illegal intelligence officers, the security consequences for the United States could be dangerous.

Counterintelligence agencies attempt to identify hostile intelligence officers through defectors, friendly services, other U.S. agencies, and, of course, when agents or officers are caught in the act. After identification, the next step is to penetrate or neutralize their operations. The hostile intelligence officers fit certain profiles; KGB/GRU officers generally hang out with other intelligence officers, have large sums of money available, own an automobile, and probably live on the economy. Their Ministry of Foreign Affairs counterparts rarely enjoy any of these privileges.

Information pertaining to hostile intelligence officers can be obtained from U.S. assets, with whom the intelligence officer may be friendly. Such sources can provide valuable personality assessment data (such as, whether or not the subject is happy or what will make the subject happy).

Once enough information is amassed, an operation may be launched to recruit the hostile intelligence officer, and if that fails, to try to persuade the subject to defect. A subject of intelligence value can defect, while a subject of no intelligence value is an asylee. Recruiting the subject is preferable; a recruit can provide current information, while a defector can only provide information until the subject's debauchment.

It is, of course, of the utmost importance to neutralize any hostile intelligence service operating in the United States. This can prove exceedingly difficult, inasmuch as more than ninety percent of the information acquired by hostile intelligence officers is already public. For example, several years ago one highly sought item by Soviet intelligence officers was a Revell Polaris submarine model built precisely to scale. Methods for neutralizing a hostile service can be either passive measures (such as personnel security and document security) or more active measures (such as the disruption of their activities, feeding them misinformation through double agent cases, prosecution of agents without diplomatic immunity, exposing Soviet activities, and controlled operations).

The Counterintelligence Community

The intelligence community is charged with the:

> Collection of information concerning, and the conduct of activities to protect against, intelligence activities directed against the United States, international terrorist and international narcotics activities, and other hostile activities directed against the United States by foreign powers, organizations, persons, and their agents.[4]

Among the members of the intelligence community, eight are involved in operational counterintelligence and three in nonoperational counterintelligence. Among the operational counterintelligence agencies, the Federal Bureau of Investigation, the navy, and the air force are primarily involved in law enforcement and criminal investigations, whereas the Central Intelligence Agency, the army, and the marine corps engage in activities that cover the full spectrum of counterintelligence activities. The National Security Council, the Office of the Secretary of Defense, and the Defense Intelligence Agency are the nonoperational counterintelligence agencies. The myriad of decentralized counterintelligence agencies causes, as might be expected, differences of opinion, fragmentation, coordination problems, and ambiguous doctrine. There are four major perspectives on counterintelligence within the intelligence community:

> (1) the "law enforcement" view (sometimes disparaged as the "cop mentality"); (2) CI as an "adjunct to collection" (emphasizing counterespionage for positive intelligence purposes); (3) CI to identify and neutralize hostile activity; and (4) CI to enhance operational security (to safeguard, for example, military operations and exercises, sensitive installations, personnel, and equipment).[5]

Within the United States, the Federal Bureau of Investigation is responsible for coordinating the counterintelligence activities of all intelligence community members and for conducting all counterintelligence investigations, unless the subject is Department of Defense-related. It may also conduct counterintelligence activities outside the United States in coordination with the Central Intelligence Agency. It is responsible for producing and disseminating counterintelligence information, and for investigating all violations of the Atomic Energy Act of 1954 which might have counterintelligence implications. The Federal Bureau of Investigation currently has special agents dedicated to counterintelligence activities.

Central Intelligence Agency counterintelligence duties include coordinating all U.S. overseas counterintelligence activity and foreign liaison with the counterintelligence services of other countries. The Central Intelligence Agency may conduct counterintelligence activities within the United States in coordination with the Federal Bureau of Investigation, but it may not perform any internal security functions. It is also responsible for disseminating counterintelligence information.

The Department of the Treasury's Secret Service has a very limited role in counterintelligence activities. Its main objective is executive protection. While that is not a counterintelligence function per se, Secret Service activities to protect the President and other protectees from surveillance equipment are such a function provided that information is not intentionally acquired through these activities except for the purpose of protecting against the surveillance.

The Secretary of Defense is responsible for insuring that the Department of Defense collects, produces, and disseminates military and military related counterintelligence, and for guaranteeing that the Department coordinates its counterintelligence activities with the CIA outside the United States and with the FBI internally. The Department of Defense is the government's executive agent for communications security activities. The National Security Agency, the Defense Intelligence Agency, and counterintelligence elements of the army, navy, air force, and marine corps are charged with implementing these policies.

The Defense Intelligence Agency is responsible for the "collection and provision of military intelligence for national foreign intelligence and counterintelligence products."[6] It provides a counterintelligence support staff as directed by and for the Joint Chiefs of Staff, and overseas service counterintelligence elements which are responsible for meeting DIA information requirements.

The National Security Agency is responsible for the "collection, processing and dissemination of signals intelligence information for counterintelligence purposes" and for "executing the responsibilities of the Secretary of Defense as executive agent for the communications security of the United States Government."[7] It is particularly important to note, however, that the latter duty of the Director of the National Security Agency is not a counterintelligence function.

There are few significant differences among the various armed services' counterintelligence programs. However, the navy and the air force are generally law enforcement oriented and have smaller personnel pools. The number of personnel devoted to counterintelligence in the ground forces is greater since battlefield contact between opposing forces provides the enemy with chances to penetrate U.S. forces and because displaced populations in an area of operations pose a significant intelligence threat.

The Director of Naval Intelligence is responsible for counterintelligence, law enforcement, information and physical security, investigative services, and anti-terrorism in the navy. The Deputy Director of Naval Intelligence for Security is dual-hatted as the Director of the Naval Investigative Service, which is staffed primarily by civilians, many of whom are special agents. The Naval Investigative Service implements the stated missions and is composed of an Investigations Department and a Sabotage, Espionage, and Countersubversion Department.

In the air force, investigative services (for law enforcement and counterintelligence), counterintelligence, anti-terrorism, and personal protective service operations are Air Force Office of Special Investigations missions. The Office of Special Investigations is composed of special agents, most of whom are military. Eight hundred are support personnel. It is significant to note that the air force's Electronic Security Command, a major command, is responsible for operations security, that the Air Force Office of Security Police is responsible for information and physical security, and that neither they nor the Office of Special Investigations (which reports to the Inspector General, United States Air Force) reports to the Assistant Chief of Staff for Intelligence, United States Air Force.

Counterintelligence Investigations

Since the excesses of the 1960s, greater emphasis has been placed on issuing and enforcing investigatory guidelines and statutes. Investigatory restrictions include the Posse Comitatus Act of 1878, which prohibits the use of federal troops to enforce civilian law unless specifically authorized by the United States Constitution or legislated by Congress. Every agency in the United States Government also issues directives on the conduct of investigations, and although service regulations are important, Executive Order 12333 and the United States Attorney General Guidelines in combination with the Foreign Intelligence Surveillance Act of 1978 are the most important.

Executive Order 12333 makes it clear that collection activities in the United States will be conducted by the Federal Bureau of Investigation, and can only be conducted by others for "significant" foreign intelligence purposes, provided information concerning the domestic activities of United States persons is not acquired. Collection may also be conducted by the Federal Bureau of Investigation for the purpose of protecting sources and methods and may be conducted by other agencies during the investigation of present or former employees, contractors, or applicants. Searches by military counterintelligence agencies can only be directed against military personnel and must be authorized by a commander "empowered to approve searches for law enforcement purposes, based upon a finding of probable cause to believe that such persons are acting as agents of foreign powers."[8]

Counterintelligence investigations are conducted using techniques similar to those employed in law enforcement, but are directed at detecting, preventing, and neutralizing actual or potential threats to security. Counterintelligence investigations must be conducted in accordance with the Attorney General Guidelines, which distinguishes between United States and non-

United States persons (permanent resident aliens are considered United States persons).

There are three types of counterintelligence investigations that may be conducted against U.S. citizens. The first is a limited investigation that must be conducted within a 120-day period (two ninety-day extensions are allowed). It is left up to the Department of Justice to determine whether the person is or is not a threat. The case is closed if the subject is deemed not a threat; but a complaint investigation, the second type of counterintelligence investigation, may be conducted if the opposite conclusion is reached.

Complaint investigations are generally of incident cases, which concern acts committed by or involving an unknown person or group, or personal subject cases, which involve known persons. Complaint investigations are initiated to determine the extent and nature of an action that occurred, and what, if any, countermeasures are required. Complaint investigations are conducted when sabotage, espionage, treason, sedition, criminal subversion, desertion (Article 85, the Uniform Code of Military Justice) or absence without leave (Article 86, the Uniform Code of Military Justice--only when classified defense information may have been compromised), sedition, aiding the enemy or spying (only during wartime), and misconduct as a prisoner (Article 105, the Uniform Code of Military Justice) are suspected.

Sabotage, Title 18 U.S.C. Sections 2151-2156, is the deliberate injury, destruction, or defective production of physical facilities vital to a nation's total military or industrial power by either an act of commission or omission. Espionage, 18 U.S.C. 792-798, is conducted for the purpose of obtaining classified defense information or permitting it to be pilfered, knowing that this action will be detrimental to the United States or to the advantage of a foreign power. Sabotage cases usually begin as incident cases, while espionage cases are usually personal subject cases.

Article 3, Section III of the United States Constitution provides that "no person shall be convicted of treason unless on the testimony of two witnesses to the same overt act, or on confession in open court." To be accused of treason, 18 U.S.C. 2381, the accused individual must owe allegiance to the United States and either levy war against it or provide aid to its enemies during a congressionally declared war.

The sedition and criminal subversion statutes, 18 U.S.C. 2384-2390, and Article 94, the Uniform Code of Military Justice, which make it criminal to conspire to overthrow the United States Government, are distinct from conspiracy to advocate overthrow, and do not require commission of an overt act toward fulfillment of the conspiracy's objective. The Smith Act, 18 U.S.C. 2385, makes it seditious to advocate or teach violent overthrow of the United States Government, produce or provide written matter advocating the same, organize a group advocating the same, and become a member of such a group, when done with the intent to overthrow the United States Government through force or violence.

Aiding the enemy, Article 104, the Uniform Code of Military Justice (one need not be a declared enemy), is effected by providing the enemy with arms, ammmunition, or supplies, harboring or protecting the enemy, providing the enemy with intelligence, or communicating with the enemy without proper authority.

Spying, Article 106, the Uniform Code of Military Justice, is a wartime offense. Its conditions include that it must be clandestine, there must be a breach of United States lines, the subject must be apprehended in a United States area of operations, and an attempt must have been made to gain information with the intent to communicate it to the enemy.

The last type of counterintelligence investigation is the suitability investigation, which determines whether an individual is a security risk based on non-criminal offenses (for example, excessive indebtedness, mental illness, unexplained affluence, drug abuse, sexual perversion, etc.).

Tactical Counterintelligence

United States Marine Corps counterintelligence doctrine is similar to army doctrine, and the marine corps counterintelligence resources repose in interrogator-translator teams and counterintelligence teams. Interrogator-translator teams are organic to the headquarters battalion of a division or headquarters company of a brigade, and operate for the G2. Presently, there are nineteen regular and six reserve interrogator-translator teams, each composed of one officer and ten enlisted personnel. Interrogator-translator team personnel are qualified in a language of their contingency area and are also trained as analysts. Their primary mission is to exploit human resources and documents of intelligence interest.

Counterintelligence teams, which usually include five officers and eleven noncommissioned officers, can be divided into a headquarters and four subteams (each comprising one officer and two noncommissioned officers), with each subteam allowed to act independently. Their mission is to provide tactical counterintelligence support to marine forces, to detect and neutralize hostile intelligence collection measures, and to provide classified defense information and installation security. There are currently eleven active and three reserve counterintelligence teams. Three counterintelligence teams are normally assigned to each Marine Amphibious Force, one to Headquarters, Fleet Marine Force Atlantic, and one to Headquarters, Fleet Marine Force Pacific, for general support.

The United States Army Intelligence and Security Command maintains resident and district offices throughout the world to conduct counterespionage and countersubversion investigations and operations and has responsibility for providing counterintelligence support to army echelons above the corps level. The military intelligence battalion (counterintelligence), an element of the military intelligence groups (echelons above corps), is the largest Intelligence and Security Command counterintelligence unit, and has a headquarters company, technical support company, and two counterintelligence companies. Each counterintelligence company includes headquarters and technical support sections, and also field operations, signal security support, and operations security support platoons. There are, additionally, counterintelligence personnel in echelons above corps intelligence centers.

Corps counterintelligence assets include a counterintelligence company in the tactical exploitation of the military intelligence group (combat electronic warfare and intelligence corps), and additional counterintelligence personnel in the counterintelligence analysis and operations security staff sections of the all-source analysis center. Divisional counterintelligence assets are located in the headquarters, headquarters and operations company, and the intelligence and surveillance company of the military intelligence battalion (combat electronic warfare and intelligence-division). Below the division level, counterintelligence forces are only found in the operations support section of the military intelligence company (combat electronic warfare and intelligence) of separate brigades, groups, or regiments. Each operations support section has a headquarters, an interrogation team, two counterintelligence teams, and a communications security team. The interrogation team is usually located at the enemy prisoner-of-war collection point, while an operations security support team is usually organized from a counterintelligence team and the communications security team.

The mission of tactical counterintelligence is to prevent hostile intelligence collection through the use of active and passive counterintelligence measures. Passive counterintelligence measures are adequate security control measures and can include personnel, document, installation, and signal security, movement control, resources control, noise and light discipline, border and frontier security, population control, censorship, camouflage and concealment, and electronic counter-countermeasures. Active measures are employed to directly stop enemy attempts to collect information or engage in sabotage or subversion; such measures include counterespionage, countersabotage, countersubversion, deception, and electronic countermeasures. Active and passive measures generally fall into three functional categories: counter-human intelligence; counter-imagery intelligence; and counter-signal intelligence. Tactical counter-human intelligence activities can include: counterintelligence special operations; liaison; counterinterrogation; security measures; and countervisual, counterolfactory, and counteracoustical measures. Although they are not human intelligence collection threats, countersabotage and countersubversion also usually fall into this area.

Counterintelligence special operations include counterespionage investigations, the use of line crossers, technical support measures, offensive counterintelligence operations, defensive source nets, black, grey, and white lists, and counterinterrogation. Offensive counterintelligence operations are actions to neutralize hostile espionage or subversive organizations and may include, for example, penetrating them or "turning" their members. Line crossers include refugees, defectors, and enemy prisoners-of-war. They are identified during initial screening in accordance with their possible value for return to hostile territory as United States agents. Defensive source nets are utilized to observe vulnerable members of a target of espionage by sources within the threatened target.

Black, grey, and white lists are developed at all echelons to identify persons who have been selected as counterintelligence targets because they possess some type of information. These individuals run the gamut of attitudes, from hostile to obscure to favorable. Black, grey, and white lists can also include installations, organizations, or groups that may prove a threat, and documents and material wanted for exploitation.

Technical support measures can include use of the polygraph, electronic surveillance, locks and locking devices, technical surveillance countermeasures, photography, and laboratory analysis. Electronic surveillance is the employment of electronic devices ("bugs") to monitor conversations, activities and sound, or electronic impulses. Photography is useful in the identification of individuals and for recording incident scenes and the activities of suspects. Photographs are valuable evidence since they present facts and are readily accepted as proof. Laboratory analysis is used to detect false documentation and secret writing. And, finally, the polygraph can be utilized as an investigative aid or for personnel screening, and must be administered by a qualified operator. Its results are viewed in terms of the possibility or probability of the examinee's truthfulness. Polygraph tests are conducted to uncover deception, obtain leads, compare conflicting statements, and verify statements.

Liaison is generally conducted with foreign counterintelligence services, but may be conducted with anyone or any organization when pertinent. Counterinterrogation measures are taught to all personnel by counterintelligence personnel to prolong their resistance to enemy interrogation. This instruction includes the Geneva Convention, the Code of Conduct, and hostile interrogation techniques training. Countervisual, counterolfactory, and counteracoustical measures are really just a one-hundred-dollar way of describing the use of, for example, light, litter and noise discipline, camouflage, and terrain masking--the responsibility for which really rests with unit commanders.

Security, which really extends to all three disciplines and, according to Executive Order 12333, is not a part of counterintelligence, includes personnel security programs, security advice and assistance, operations security evaluations, automated systems security, and security education and training. An example of a comprehensive all-source operations security program is the Sensitive Activity Vulnerability Estimate. It includes signal, imagery, and human intelligence personnel in an on-site survey team whose mission is to identify vulnerabilities and recommend countermeasures.

Counter-imagery intelligence activities include actions to determine enemy imagery collection capabilities and activities, the assessment of friendly operations to identify patterns or signatures and the vulnerabilities they create, and the development and recommendations of countermeasures. A signature is an indicator unique to a particular unit or piece of equipment, for which countermeasures should be developed. Pattern analysis is the study of stereotyped actions which habitually occur and may betray a unit's type, disposition, activities, and capabilities. Examples of undesirable patterns include conducting reconnaissance overflights at approximately the same time prior to an operation, or always moving particular units in the same order during a specific type of operation. It should be noted that counter-imagery activities are conducted by imagery interpreters, not counterintelligence personnel.

Counter-signals intelligence is the analysis of the enemy signals intelligence threat, the assessment of friendly electronic vulnerabilities, the use of signals security (communications security and electronic security) techniques to protect friendly emitters, and the use of offensive techniques and countermeasures to directly limit hostile intelligence collection.

Communications security is comprised of protective measures to prevent unauthorized use of United States Government telecommunications, including the use of codes, secure voice equipment, radio-silence, radio-telephone procedures, and traffic analysis. Electronic security includes the use of radar masking techniques and the use of reduced power. Both communications security and electronic security include tempest, or the elimination of compromising emanations generated by communications or electronic equipment. Signals security surveys are conducted for counterintelligence purposes, but by electronic warfare/communications-electronics personnel, not counterintelligence personnel.

An Example: Brigade Counterintelligence Operations

Prior to hostilities, a brigade's interrogators move with and support advance elements. Until contact is made and enemy prisoners-of-war are available, their information will be limited to that acquired from refugees, line crossers, and other noncombatants. The separate brigade's operations security support and counterintelligence teams are deployed in the area of operations for communications security purposes and to detect security violations.

In the attack, counterintelligence personnel are located in forward units to neutralize or exploit counterintelligence targets. Interrogators are also located forward in direct support of battalion task forces, where they conduct brief interrogations of enemy prisoners-of-war, line crossers, and refugees for primary intelligence requirements. Operations security support and counterintelligence teams continue to insure that operations security and deception plans are implemented and that recommended countermeasures are employed; they also conduct communications security monitoring, as they will throughout the battle.

Counterintelligence personnel are normally deployed in rear areas to conduct civilian and enemy prisoner-of-war screening, to develop human source programs ("stay-behind"), and to provide for installation security in rear areas (particularly against guerrillas). Some counterintelligence elements will, however, remain forward to conduct activities such as recruiting individuals for insertion into refugee groups and enemy prisoner-of-war channels, exploiting known enemy agents, and for deception operations. Interrogators are generally deployed at the brigade collection point during defense, but can be deployed with battalion task forces to assist in screening operations.

Rear Area Protection Operations

During rear area protection operations, counterintelligence elements engage in normal intelligence activities focused on the rear area. They also exploit or neutralize hostile intelligence agents, enemy sympathizers, and enemy special operations forces, conduct liaison, develop civilian human source networks to provide information, conduct surveillance and investigation of suspected persons or areas, engage in security or technical surveys, recommend countermeasures, and, in coordination with other activities and units, attempt to deny sustenance or support to hostile groups.

An analysis of multiple incidents can often reveal enemy plans and intentions. Defensive source nets can be established to provide indications and warning information on potential rear area activity. They are usually composed of local nationals with access that allows them to be aware of potential activities against friendly facilities. Additionally, as a long-term recruitment objective, "stay-behind" personnel are identified in case an area becomes denied.

Stability Operations

In stability operations, counterintelligence activities are conducted to deny intelligence to insurgents and to identify and neutralize their infrastructure. Aside from operations similar to those for rear area protection, population and resources control operations are also conducted. Population control techniques include, for example, nationwide registry and identification issuance, travel and curfew restrictions, censorship, and control of public gatherings. Resources control techniques include control of the production, storage, and distribution of foodstuffs and control of commodities such as arms, ammunition, medicine, and money.

Many activities which may sound like counterintelligence measures in stability operations are performed by other sectors of the armed forces or government (for example, special operations forces or the police, as part of a general plan for combating the insurgency). But these operations are clearly linked to counterintelligence. Thus, during a stability operation it is the responsibility of counterintelligence to recommend to other sectors of the government and armed forces measures that they might employ.

COMBATING TERRORISM

Terrorism is often misconceived as novel, a dangerous threat, and the response of the oppressed to injustice. While the intensity of terrorist activities has varied throughout history, terrorism has been a constant factor in politics. Terrorist acts have rarely been remembered with the passage of time. But in the mass media state they have attracted undue attention, have been proclaimed a modern phenomenon, and have been pronounced a threat to the very fabric of society.

The Sicarii, perhaps the earliest of the known terrorist groups, was a religious sect involved in the Zealot struggle in Palestine (66-73 AD). Their favorite weapon was a short sword known as the sica (hence the sect's name), which they kept under their coats. They used unorthodox tactics, such as attacking by day during a holiday in crowded Jerusalem.

The Assassins, an oft-romanticized Ismailis Muslim offshoot, appeared from the eleventh to thirteenth centuries and operated in secrecy, using terror and disguises. They used a dagger for their assassinations (hence the derivation of that word). They had a desire for martyrdom (as do many Iranian Shi'ites today), and saw themselves as a means of defending their religious order from the Soljuks.

The Narodnaya Volya, perhaps the most famous and doctrinally "perfect" terrorist group, conducted operations from June 1878 through March 1881. Two of its members, Emelianov and Rysakov (both nineteen), assassinated Tsar Alexander II on March 1, 1881. Soon after, most of the members were apprehended by the police, ending nearly two decades of terrorist operations against the Russian monarchy. Narodnaya Volya's members were idealists opposed to the monarch. They never practiced indiscriminate murder and were, for the most part, upper class or aristocratic. They used terror against a despotic regime, whereas today most terrorist activity is "directed almost exclusively against permissive democratic societies and ineffective authoritarian regimes."[9]

The United States has had to deal with terrorism almost from the time it became a nation. The United States ships Maria and Dauphin were captured in 1785 by the Dey of Algiers, who ransommed the crews. These and other crews taken prisoner were not released until 1796, when the United States Government acceded to the ransom demands, as it would consistently do throughout the nineteenth century.

Even in 1932, the United States paid a ransom to secure the release of a U.S. riverboat captain who was kidnapped by Chinese bandits on the Yangtze River in Hupeh Province. This contrasts sharply with the precedent-setting reaction of President Theodore Roosevelt when in 1904 a Moroccan chieftain, Raisuli, seized the American citizen, Ion Perdicaris. The incident, loosely immortalized in the movie The Wind and the Lion, involved Roosevelt asking for "Perdicaris alive or Raisuli dead." The President never considered the payment of ransom as an option.

More recently, for example, Lieutenant Colonel Donald J. Crowley, the U.S. Air Attache to the Dominican Republic, was kidnapped by terrorists on March 24, 1970 and released two days later, after the Government of the Dominican Republic freed twenty political prisoners and flew them to Mexico.

On November 4, 1979, Iranian students captured sixty-six Americans (primarily diplomats) and the United States Embassy in Tehran in what was to become one of the longer, most publicized, and best known hostage incidents. Among the captor's demands of the United States Government was the return of the Shah to Iran from the United States, where he was undergoing medical treatment. In reaction the United States ended delivery of military supplies on November 9, froze Iranian monetary assets in the United States on November 14, and assembled naval forces in the Indian Ocean. As result, three hostages were released on November 19, and ten more the next day. Meanwhile, six managed to escape the takeover and find shelter at the Canadian Embassy.

However, United Nations support and two favorable International Court of Justice rulings were not enough to gain the release of all the hostages. On April 7, the United States broke relations with Iran and prohibited travel there as of April 20. A rescue attempt on April 25 by U.S. forces failed. On July 10, a hostage in poor health was released. And soon after the Shah's death on June 27, Iran began to modify its conditions for release of the hostages. The hostages were "turned over" to the Iranian government on November 3, and negotiations for their release began on November 10 in Algiers. An agreement was reached between all parties and on January 20, 1981, only minutes before President Reagan was inaugurated, the hostages were released. Although touted at the time as the longest hostage incident in U.S. history, the crews of the Maria and Dauphin were imprisoned for a much longer period.

Definitions

Many authors offer different definitions of terrorism. It is possible that there may never be total agreement on a definition. However, the Department of Defense definition is:

> The unlawful use or threatened use of force or violence by a revolutionary organization against individuals or property, with the intention of coercing or intimidating governments or societies, often for political or ideological purposes.[10]

For our purposes this definition is more than adequate, and is in any case the framework within which all military intelligence officers work.

There is also a great deal of confusion about the concepts of antiterrorism and counterterrorism. Journalists particularly tend to use the terms interchangeably, although they are different in meaning. Antiterrorism is "defensive measures used by the Department of Defense to reduce the vulnerability of DoD personnel, their dependents, facilities, and equipment to terrorist acts;" counterterrorism is "offensive measures taken to respond to a terrorist act, including the gathering of information and threat analysis in support of those measures."[11]

The Terrorist Threat

Terrorist incidents may include, but are not limited to, kidnapping, barricade-hostage situations (the seizure of a facility with hostages), bombing, armed attack (upon a facility or individuals), hijacking (an airplane, ship, or other vehicle), assassination, sabotage, exotic pollution (nuclear, chemical, or biological contamination; for example, the introduction of mercury into oranges shipped from Israel), threat hoaxes, thefts and break-ins (illegal entry), and arms smuggling. Between 1968, when the United States Government first began recording terror incidents, and 1981, about three-fourths of all terrorist incidents occurred in Western Europe, Latin America, and the Middle East. Almost one-half of all recorded incidents within this timeframe occurred in only nine countries: the United States of America; Argentina; Italy; France; the Federal Republic of Germany; Iran; Turkey; Greece; and Israel. Citizens of 131 different countries were terror targets, but attacks against U.S., Israeli, British, German, French, and Soviet nationals accounted for over sixty percent. United States citizens were targeted most frequently (thirty-eight percent). Approximately forty percent of these attacks were against diplomats, twenty-five percent against businessmen, and ten percent against military targets. Bombings and assassinations accounted for seventy percent of the attacks that produced casualties. U.S. citizens, however, were victims of only twenty percent of all attacks that produced casualties, while they suffered almost forty percent of all terrorist incidents.

From January 1968 to June 1982 there have been 684 skyjacking attempts, of which 108 were terrorist hijackings or politically motivated. This was about nine percent of all terror attacks during the same period. More than one-third of these resulted in casualties (212 dead, 186 wounded). Seventy percent of terrorist hijackings resulted in diverted aircraft, even though, in many cases, the terrorists were not able to achieve their demands. Forty-eight terrorist groups, almost half of which were Palestinian or Latin American, claimed credit for all the aircraft hijackings during this period. It is interesting to note that in January 1973 the United States Government implemented full screening of aircraft passengers, and the Federal Aviation

Administration reports that 2,000 firearms have since been confiscated.

In retrospect, more than 670 terrorist groups have claimed credit for attacks against Americans since statistics were first collected. This figure is certainly inflated inasmuch as some names are aliases, and some are used by common criminals or psychotics. But the list includes groups and states and runs the spectrum of ideologies, classes, cultures, and races.[12]

A Sampling of Terrorist Organizations and Support

One approach generally sees six types of terrorists/terror groups: (1) ethnic, religious, or nationalist; (2) Marxist-Leninist; (3) anarchist; (4) pathological groups or individuals; (5) neo-Fascist and extreme right-wing; and (6) ideological mercenaries. These terrorists and organizations clearly fall on all sides of politics or anarchy, and are in favor of different causes or no causes. But their strategies remain the same: to provoke a desired response. Consequently, these individuals and organizations have common characteristics.

The size of terrorist organizations is critical. The larger they are, the greater their potential for detection. While some organizations may be quite large (the Irish Republican Army (IRA), for example), only a small number of its members are involved in terrorism. The excessive size of the Tupamaros in Uruguay led to the group's downfall. The more compartmentalized a terrorist organization is, the better its chances for survival.

Finances are critical. Terror operations are complicated and require substantial financing. This can come from a supportive government, voluntary donations, or through illegal criminal activities (for example, kidnapping, robbery, protection, etc.). Intelligence is also critical. Terror operations require extensive planning, which is impossible without detailed target intelligence. This can be gathered through informers or penetration agents.

Weapons are important. The Narodnaya Volya was the first terror orgnaization to use dynamite on a wide scale. Terrorist technology has since improved, particularly in terms of miniaturization. Aside from self-production and development, weapons can be purchased on the international arms market, supplied by sympathetic governments or groups, or they can be stolen--often from the adversary government.

Popular support is also important and is usually forthcoming from some sector of society, no matter how large or small, how left or right, and regardless of class. Peasants, the working class, intellectuals, the middle or upper class, and the clergy have all provided popular support for terrorist movements.

The media are, however, the most crucial element to terrorist success. Terrorism thrives on publicity--which the media provide--and this affects the choice of targets, which will be those that prove to be of interest to the press. Of course, this tactic is not effective in a country with censorship.

The media, with their inbuilt tendency toward sensationalism, have always magnified terrorist exploits quite irrespective of their intrinsic importance. Terrorist groups numbering perhaps a dozen members have been described as "armies;" their "official communiques" have been discussed in countless television shows, radio broadcasts, articles and editorials. In a few cases even nonexistent groups have been given a great deal of publicity. All modern terrorist groups need publicity; the smaller they are, the more they depend on it, and this has, to a large extent, affected the choice of their targets.[13]

Terrorists are the pervasive few who disrupt the normal functions of society. Their tactics include assassinating public figures, particularly government officials (the oldest manifestation of terrorism), and indiscriminate terror, which has evolved only recently--simultaneously with the availability of effective explosives and the ability to manipulate the mass media. Other tactics include: expropriation or robbery (both of which are good operations for testing recruits); operations to gain the freedom of captured terrorists (always a top priority); kidnapping for political purposes; extortion of ransoms (one of the oldest tactics); and hijacking. Hijackings are usually of aircraft but can be of other conveyances. This tactic is not only engaged in by armed political terrorists, but also by refugees, defectors, and common criminals.

The Euzkadi Ta Azkatasuna (ETA or Basque Nation and Liberty) is an example of a separatist party dedicated to achieving independence, in this case for the Basque region of northern Spain. It is linked with Basque groups in southern France, which it uses as a safe haven, and has kidnapped foreign diplomats in Spain. The ETA was linked to the murder of Admiral Carrero Blanco, then the Spanish Prime Minister, in Madrid on December 20, 1973, and had had an advance group in the capital for one year prior to the operation. They maintain contacts with Basque students all over Spain, although they operate principally in the Basque region and have contacts with other terrorist groups, including the Ejercito Revolucionario del Pueblo (ERP or People's Revolutionary Army) in Argentina, from which the ETA received sophisticated training.

The Movimiento de Liberacion Nacional (MLN or National Liberation Movement) was popularly known in Uruguay as the Tupamaros after Tupac Amaru, an Inca chief who led a rebellion against the Spaniards. They were an ultraleft Marxist group that began as rural guerrillas in the early 1960s and quickly moved their operations into Montevideo, Uruguay's capital. The Tupamaros kidnapped numerous foreign diplomats, among them the U.S. and British ambassadors, whom they held for eight months in 1971, and a U.S. Public Safety adviser, whom they murdered on August 10, 1970. The Uruguayan government began a very effective crackdown on the Tupamaros in 1972. Although some escaped to

Argentina, where they continued to work with Argentine terrorists, they are now inactive. Their legacy was to drive a long-standing democratic nation to totalitarianism.

The Red Army Faction in the Federal Republic of Germany, better known as the Baader-Meinhof Gang (after their early leaders Andreas Baader and Ulrike Meinhof), was one of the most active anarchist groups in Europe. They probably looked to the new left rather than to the old anarchists for ideology, if one wishes to ascribe an ideology to them. They were responsible for numerous bombings at United States military bases in Germany, including those of May 1972 at Heidelberg, and United States Army, Europe, Headquarters in Frankfurt, in which two were killed and fifteen wounded. Many of its members committed suicide in prison, including Baader, Meinhof, and Ennslin.

Pathological terrorism is more a phenomenon of individuals than groups, but most groups that manifest it appear to reside in the United States, where it has become a way of life for them. The Weathermen and the Symbionese Liberation Army (SLA) are such examples (some could argue that the Baader-Meinhof Gang would also qualify as a pathological group). Groups such as the Weathermen or the SLA are motivated at this point in time less by "acquired" ideology than by reputed personal psychological inadequacies. The Weathermen were a spinoff from the radical Students for a Democratic Society (SDS). Although they carried out no act of international terrorism, they reportedly had contact with two Palestinian terrorist organizations (the Popular Front for the Liberation of Palestine (PFLP) and Al Fatah) and the IRA. The 1981 Brink's Robbery in New York was committed by a coalition of members of the Black Liberation Army, old Weathermen, and the May 19 group.

In the United States and most western European countries, neo-fascist organizations do not appear to pose a threat, but they are potential problems in Spain and Greece and recurring problems in Portugal and Italy. In Italy, the neo-fascist groups Avanguardia Nazionale, Ordine Nuovo, and Rosa dei Venti have been implicated in a number of violent terror attacks, including the 1969 Milan bank bombings and the August 5, 1974 Italicus express bombing, which killed twelve people. Although organizations such as Ordine Nuovo were banned earlier, General Ugo Ricci was arrested in 1974 as the leader of a neo-fascist plot to assassinate leading politicians and trade union leaders and (apparently) to poison the water supply.

Ideological mercenaries share a common ideology that crosses national frontiers; generally, they do not conduct operations strictly for fiscal considerations. Rengo Segikun (the Japanese United Red Army), an offshoot of the Zengakuren (a militant left-wing student movement), began urban guerrilla operations in 1969 and pioneered modern transnational terrorism. An ignominious transnational terrorist action was committed by the Rengo Segikun on behalf of the PFLF when it provided three of its members for an operation in which they machine-gunned passengers at Lod Airport in Tel Aviv, Israel, on May 31, 1972.

State-Sponsored Terror

The most ominous turn of events in terrorism to date may well be the national support of terrorist groups by countries with objectives that may be similar to those of the groups they support. These countries often provide all types of support services as well as sanctuaries from arrest. During World War II, the IRA, for example, collaborated with Nazi Germany.

Between January 1968 and June 1982, the United States Government list contained 129 state-sponsored terrorist incidents, a statistic which the U.S. Government considers to be an underestimate. Almost forty percent of these incidents were assassinations or attempted assassinations, roughly six times the rate of assassination in non-state-sponsored terrorist attacks. Forty-four percent of all these incidents resulted in casualties, with sixty persons injured and sixty-one killed. The majority of incidents occurred in the Middle East, were carried out by Middle East nations, and were directed against Middle Eastern expatriates and diplomats.[14]

United States Government Organization for Combating Terrorism

There has been considerable evolution in U.S. policy since the late 1960s, when official policy was not to give in to terrorist demands, but at the same time to secure the safety of hostages even if the host government had to make concessions. But compromise with terrorists is transitory and always detrimental in the long run. A sovereign government cannot allow itself to be dictated to by criminals. A terrorist victory just encourages more such acts. Therefore, present policy is not to pay blackmail, or release prisoners, or bargain. In essence, no concessions will be made to terrorists.

The Interdepartmental Group on Terrorism is the principal policy and programs body on terrorism for the Government. It is chaired by the Department of State and its Deputy Chair is the Department of Justice/Federal Bureau of Investigation. Its other members are the Department of Defense/Joint Chiefs of Staff, the Department of Energy, the Department of Treasury, the Department of Transportation, the Central Intelligence Agency, the National Security Council, and the Office of the Vice President. The group generally meets twice per month. The State representative and chairman also serves as the Director of the Department of State's Office for Combating Terrorism.

The Advisory Group on Terrorism, which reports to the Interdepartmental Group on Terrorism, is composed of the following members: the Agency for International Development; the Arms Control and Disarmament Agency; the Bureau of Alcohol, Tobacco, and Firearms; the Center for Disease Control; the Central Intelligence Agency; the Defense Intelligence Agency; the Department of the Army; the Department of Energy; the Department of the Interior; the Department of Justice; the Department of State; the Department of Treasury; the Department of Transportation; the

Federal Aviation Administration; the Federal Bureau of Investigation; the Federal Emergency Management Agency; the Federal Protective Service; the Immigration and Naturalization Service; the International Communications Agency; the Joint Chiefs of Staff; the Metropolitan Police Department of the District of Columbia; the National Security Agency; the Nuclear Regulatory Commission; the Office of Justice Assistance, Research and Statistics; the Office of Management and Budget; the Office of Undersecretary of Defense; the United States Coast Guard; the United States Customs Service; the United States Postal Service; and the United States Secret Service.

Within the borders of the United States, the Department of Justice/Federal Bureau of Investigation is the lead agency for countering terrorism, including the gathering of intelligence to that end. Overseas, the Department of State is the lead agency for countering terrorism. And the Federal Aviation Administration is the lead agency when there are skyjackings of U.S. flag carriers within the United States.

The Principal Deputy Assistant Secretary of Defense for International Security Affairs is the Defense representative for the Interdepartmental Group on Terrorism, as well as the main focal point for anti-terror policies within the Department of Defense. Unified and specified commanders and chiefs of military assistance and advisory groups are responsible for local anti-terror policies and protection in their areas of operations.

In the event that force is required to resolve a terrorist situation, the United States Government has several organizations from which to choose. Most major cities have special weapons and tactics (SWAT) teams that are trained to respond to local emergencies and criminal hostage crises. Each Federal Bureau of Investigation district has its own SWAT team for responding to a wide spectrum of criminal and terrorist incidents. For overseas actions and terrorist crises of extreme dimensions, the armed forces retain a wide spectrum of units capable of responding.

One other unusual organization whose responsibilities include responding to a terrorist threat is the Department of Energy's Nuclear Emergency Search Team (NEST). NEST includes approximately 250 volunteers, from nuclear physicists to aviation mechanics, who have responded to more than twenty blackmail threats and two nuclear accidents. In 1976, for example, Green Peace claimed it had placed a nuclear device in a van parked in front of the White House. NEST responded and found a fifty-five gallon drum filled with concrete and a ticking device.

The best and historically most common collection method against terrorism is the use of informers or agents or human intelligence. Major Le Caron, a British police agent who infiltrated Irish terrorist organizations for the British government between 1865 and 1885, was the UK's most successful font of information. James McParlan, an agent of the Pinkerton Agency in the United States, was responsible for the destruction of the Molly Maguires in the 1870s.

International and United States Laws Pertaining To Terrorism

There are numerous international conventions on various manifestations of terrorism, including the Convention on Offenses and Certain Other Acts Committed on Board Aircraft (Tokyo Convention) of September 14, 1963, the Convention for the Suppression of Unlawful Seizure of Aircraft (Hague Convention) of December 16, 1970, the Convention for the Suppression of Unlawful Acts Against the Safety of Civil Aviation (Montreal Convention) of September 23, 1971, the Convention on the Prevention and Punishment of Crimes Against Internationally Protected Persons, including Diplomatic Agents (New York Convention) of December 14, 1973, the Bonn Declaration (between Canada, the Federal Republic of Germany, France, Italy, Japan, the United Kingdom, and the United States of America) of July 14, 1978, the Convention Against the Taking of Hostages (which opened for signature on December 18, 1979), and the Convention on the Physical Protection of Nuclear Materials. All of the above conventions and declarations provide for penalties for committing terrorist acts, cooperation between governments, and extradition procedures.

Until recently, 18 U.S.C. 1385, use of the army and air force as Posse Comitatus (power of the country), proscribed the use of military forces to execute United States law unless authorized to do so by the Constitution or the Congress. While the navy and marine corps were specifically excluded, they are now included as a result of a departmental regulation promulgated by the Secretary of the Navy in 1974. It is not clear, however, how the United States Coast Guard is affected as part of the Department of Transportation (since it only chops to the navy in wartime). Additionally, while the act prohibits the use of federal troops, it does not prohibit the loan of military material to federal law enforcement agencies during periods of civil disorder.

Within Title 18, the United States Code, are statutes covering traditional crimes terrorists commit, including assault, kidnapping, etc., as well as statutes covering these crimes when they are committed against foreign officials, official guests of the United States Government, and internationally protected persons. 18 U.S.C. 878 now authorizes the Attorney General, in the event of kidnapping, assault, or conspiracy against foreign officials, official guests of the government, and internationally protected persons, to request assistance from any federal, state, or local agency, including the armed forces. This is the only exception to the prohibition of the use of military forces as Posse Comitatus.

The Federal Aviation Act, 49 U.S.C. 1301 et seq., includes amendments specifically dealing with air piracy. It allows for the death penalty if a death occurs during commission or attempted commission of that crime. The President can also suspend air service by any air carrier to a country that allows or condones terror.

Additionally, a number of laws prohibit military, economic, and other forms of aid to countries that engage in or support terrorism. For example, the International Security Assistance and Arms Export Control Act of 1976 prohibits assistance to countries providing sanctuary to terrorists. However, the President can generally waive most of these requirements.

CONCLUSION

Many counterintelligence activities are conducted under the rubric of operations security, which includes document, personnel, physical, and communications security, all of which are specifically excluded from counterintelligence in Executive Order 12333. In peacetime, these activities are the primary responsibility of military counterintelligence personnel, particularly within the United States. Operations security, simply stated, is the identification of friendly force vulnerabilities, recommending countermeasures, applying them, monitoring them, and adjusting them. The major responsibility for operations security is usually borne not by counterintelligence personnel but by the unit commander, operations officers (S3), and intelligence officers (S2).

Operations security activities are not, however, conducted to the detriment of more traditional counterintelligence activities such as counterespionage. But the lead counterintelligence agency domestically is the Federal Bureau of Investigation and the comparable agency internationally is the Central Intelligence Agency. Most of the traditional counterintelligence activities repose with these agencies. Armed forces counterintelligence activities concomitantly assert themselves during tactical operations. Their mission is to enhance the mobility and survivability of maneuver units during combat through the employment methods previously discussed.

A Confucian philosopher stated that the goal of terrorism was to "Kill 1, Frighten 10,000." One may now multiply the latter figure significantly in an age of instant mass communications methods that include television and radio. Terrorist movements can only hope to be successful against nonterrorist governments. If a group uses the tactics of terror against a democratic government that will not use repressive measures, its chances of success are reasonable. On the other hand, if a terrorist group attempts to undertake armed resistance against a totalitarian regime which applies totalitarian tactics, it is unlikely that the terror group will succeed. Political terrorism still utilizes, as it always has, the threat of violence to achieve political goals. In our democratic society, the best method of combating it is still the penetration of terrorist adversaries by human sources. The United States Government and its intelligence officers still have much to learn to accomplish this effectively.

In October 1983, James Durward Harper, a freelance computer engineer who worked in California's Silicon Valley, was arrested for passing along to the Soviets extremely sensitive documents during a series of fourteen meetings over a period of four and one-half years. Mr. Harper received $250,000 for providing the

Soviets with, among other documents, details of a research and development project to protect U.S. Minuteman missiles from destruction by a Soviet nuclear strike without setting off a nuclear blast. Mr. Harper's source for the documents was his alcoholic wife, the late Mrs. Ruby Louise Schuler Harper, who was the executive secretary to the President of Systems Control, a computer company owned by British Petroleum.

Mr. Harper passed his information through the Poles to the KGB. The FBI was tipped off to Mr. Harper's activities by a high ranking officer in the Sluzba Bezpieczenstwa (SB), the Polish intelligence service, who was a double-agent for the United States and is now being debriefed in the United States by the CIA. The Polish SB is second to the KGB in presence in the United States and has more freedom to operate. The Polish intelligence officers involved even received a personal commendation from the late Soviet Chairman, Yuri Andropov. Although the FBI apprehended Mr. Harper before he could pass another 150-200 pounds of documents to the SB, the documents he did pass have unfortunately caused grievous damage to the United States.

Meanwhile, halfway around the world, on October 23, 1983, the United States Marine Corps Headquarters of the Multinational Force in Beirut, Lebanon was bombed by a terrorist, who drove a truck laden with 12,000 pounds of explosives wrapped around gas cylinders and tamped to direct the blast upward. Two hundred and forty-one military and naval personnel were killed in the blast as a result of inadequate security measures. (In April 1983, the American Embassy in Lebanon had been similarly destroyed.) Concertina wire designed only to stop humans was easily snapped by the terrorist's truck, gates were open for it to drive through, and sewer pipes that should have been in place were pushed aside. Additionally, 350 personnel were centrally located in the headquarters building, and while intelligence was abundant, it was poorly evaluated. Although the marine corps element of the Multinational Force may have wanted to maintain its visiblity, it could have done so while taking adequate security measures. Numerous security measures implemented after the bombing could easily have been implemented prior to its occurrence.

Why was the bombing able to occur? How was Mr. Harper able to pass along such sensitive documents? Is it primarily because Americans do not understand the threat facing them? Is it because Americans have lax security habits or because they are treacherous? Is it due to a preoccupation with technology and ignorance of less mechanical but more effective intelligence collection procedures? Problems similar to these face every intelligence officer. Obviously, most Americans are not traitors and, in fact, most love their country. But how can the Harpers be ferreted out before they damage the security of the United States? How can major terrorist incidents be prevented? Technology is important and holds some of the answers for coming to grips with these problems. But in the near and perhaps long-term future, "the Spy of the Neutral Ground" holds the key to success against the foreign intelligence and terrorist threats facing the United States of America.

NOTES

1. James Fenimore Cooper, *The Spy*, with a foreword by Curtis Dahl (New York: Dodd, Mead and Co., Inc.), p. 333.

2. *46 Fed. Reg. 59953* (1981).

3. The Soviet Union's military counterpart to the KGB is the *Glavnoye razvedyvatelnoye upravleniye* (GRU) or the Main Intelligence Directorate of the Soviet Army.

4. *46 Fed. Reg. 59943* (1981).

5. Arthur A. Zuehlke, Jr., "What is Counterintelligence," in Roy Godson (ed.), *Intelligence Requirements for the 1980s*, Vol. 3, *Counterintelligence* (Washington, DC: The National Strategy Information Center, Inc., 1980), p. 24.

6. *46 Fed. Reg. 59947* (1981). The duties of all counterintelligence agencies are specifically noted in this Executive Order.

7. Ibid., 59948.

8. Ibid., 59951.

9. Walter Laqueur, *Terrorism* (Boston: Little, Brown, and Co., 1977), p. 219.

10. U.S. Department of Defense, *Protection of DoD Personel and Resources Against Terrorist Acts*, Department of Defense Directive 2000.12, February 12, 1982, p. 1.

11. Ibid., pp. 1-2.

12. U.S. Department of State, *Combatting Terrorism*, Department of State Bulletin (August 1982), p. 15.

13. Laqueur, *Terrorism*, pp. 109-110.

14. U.S. Department of State, *Combatting Terrorism*, p. 20.

13
Basic Communications Skills for the Intelligence Analyst

Gerald W. Hopple

In a modern, complex society, everyone must play many roles simultaneously. The president of the United States, for example, for whom all analysts work ultimately in his role as Commander-in-Chief, wears many hats of different colors and sizes. Introductory American government textbook writers like to talk about the president's multiple roles. He (or, in the future, she) must be head of his political party, the Chief Diplomat, the Chief Legislator (in reality, if not constitutionally), the Tribune of the People, the substitute Constitutional Monarch, and so on (including, of course, the role of the Great Communicator). Presidents, the textbook sages tell us, must play all of these roles at once and have great difficulty trying to balance the multiple, demanding, and conflicting roles of the office.

An intelligence analyst must also wear many hats (and it is critically important that analysts measure their hat sizes and determine what their strengths and weaknesses are). There are at least six distinct roles that must be mastered.

One is the role of scientist. An intelligence analyst is a scientist searching for the truth, boldly conjecturing when he or she develops theories and models and carefully testing and (hopefully) trying to refute (rather than prove) empirical hypotheses.[1] Analysts rarely wear white coats in work labs, but that emphatically does not mean that they are not scientists. However, the typical analyst is more of an applied than a basic scientist, concerned with the nature (and tractability) of the real world much more than with underlying theoretical structures. But that does not mean that the procedures and methods of <u>science</u> do not apply; they do apply, and they are violated or ignored at one's own (and one's country's) peril.

Second, it should have become clear from the preceding chapters that a good analyst is a good researcher. Again, this does not necessarily mean "basic" research. But in producing strategic intelligence, it is necessary to do a great deal of hard, solid research--and to follow the canons of researchers across the board to come up with reliable, valid intelligence products.

A third hat is the one worn by the applied problem solver. An analyst is a scientist doing research, but in many ways he or she operates as an intuitive scientist, a person who studies the real world on a daily basis in order to solve problems that need answers as soon as possible.

In everyday life, people are problem solvers who are constantly collecting and assessing information or data (description), determining what accounts for something else (explanation), and attempting to project into the future (forecasting/prediction). The analytical processes of describing, explaining, and predicting are at the heart of intelligence analysis problem solving. The problems--in the form of intelligence topics and scheduled products--emanate from users or consumers, and analytical priorities are driven by changing real world conditions (thus, Central America is a "hot" topic in the 1980s, but was relatively neglected in the early 1970s--when Southeast Asia was high on the agenda). The emphasis therefore is on applied problem solving. There is a large literature in psychology on how people go about this--and what the pitfalls and fallacies of such analysis are.[2]

Fourth, an analyst must be like a detective (as well as a scientist, researcher, applied problem solver, and even a first class newspaper reporter). You rarely have all of the pieces of any major analytical puzzle; nor do your "subjects" (the Soviet Union, China, Eastern Europe, countries in the Third World, even U.S. allies) want you to get the information that straggles in incrementally and unpredictably and deals with targets that are uncooperative at best and hostile at worst. Also, always remember the dog that didn't bark in the night!

Fifth, increasingly, the analyst must be (or become) a cyberneticist. This fifty cent word (with which you can regale friends and associates at cocktail parties) simply means a person who knows how to use and exploit the power of machines. By machines, we mean primarily (although not exclusively) computers. Computers, already important in tactical and strategic intelligence production, will become increasingly vital. There are all kinds of computer-based problem solving aids and systems; work at the frontiers of artificial intelligence promises to produce more such systems--at higher levels of sophistication.[3] As computers and computer-based analysis proliferate, analysts must learn to feel comfortable with computers and know how to talk to and live with them. One certainly does not have to retool as a programmer or computer scientist of any kind, but it is necessary to adjust to this reality.

Finally, the sixth hat is the analyst as communicator, the focus of this chapter. This may be the single most important hat. All of one's hard work goes down the drain if the analyst cannot communicate and present it effectively and efficiently. And quickly--the essence of intelligence dissemination is the timely distribution of the appropriate products to the users who need them. This chapter will focus on the general communications process. This very central topic will be addressed in terms of the audience for an analyst's work, the vital art of listening, and the effective use of <u>brainstorming</u> and <u>group problem solving</u> processes in communications.

THE IMPORTANCE OF AUDIENCE ANALYSIS

Intelligence products go to all kinds of users--other analysts in one's own and other agencies, national security analysts and policy analysts and planners throughout the defense policymaking community, members of Congress and their staff people, individuals concerned with military and foreign policy issues as decisionmakers (from the low level policymaker on the National Security Council all the way up to the White House and president, who wears many hats--including one marked Chief of National Security and Guardian of the Ultimate Key). A more diverse potential audience could not be imagined.

How to present and communicate finished intelligence depends very much on the specific audience. (Sometimes, the audience is one or a few people; sometimes, it is a lot of people; sometimes, quite frankly, it is no one--because some long-standing requirement simply demands that a particular product be produced.)

The type of document or product says a lot about the size, nature, and expectations of the audience in that particular case. Perhaps the most dramatic distinction is the one between most basic intelligence and certain I&W (indications and warning), current, and estimative intelligence products. The basic product essentially goes to experts, who are well grounded in the details and specifics of the country, area, or issue being dealt with. This is true of much current and I&W finished intelligence as well.

At the other end of the continuum, there are the products that get read by top level policymakers--sometimes the president himself. Certain fast breaking warning situations obviously fall into this category, as does current intelligence for a "hot" topic or part of the world. The third kind of product in this category is the occasional estimate. High priority National Intelligence Estimates--such as the annual one on Soviet strategic intentions and capabilities--get read by many consumers at all levels of the hierarchy. This is even more applicable to some Special National Intelligence Estimates or SNIEs (pronounced "sneeze"), which are produced on an ad hoc and usually special request basis and deal with very pressing problem areas. On the other hand, note that the very high visibility estimates are only the tip of the iceberg; there are many DIA, CIA, and other regularly published estimates that go only to experts and concern a variety of subjects--ranging from a country's projected military capability to the prospects for political instability in nation X.

High level policymakers are busy and are turned off by long documents. There is tremendous pressure in current intelligence to be brief and reduce twenty pages to a few lines (a challenging task, especially for the verbose and for those who are inexperienced in the fine art of precis writing, where you take a lengthy report or assessment and shave it to the bare minimum--

without losing the gist or essence of the product). Serious problems have surfaced with many standard estimative products. NIEs (which are community-wide estimates and are coordinated across the community, with provisions for dissenting footnotes) can run to several hundred pages. It is now commonplace for presidential staff aides and others who provide support to high level policymakers to prepare briefings and papers which bulletize and abstract the highlights of NIEs and similar estimates.

The key criterion in communication and presentation in terms of audience analysis, then, is <u>length</u>. Products that go to lower level audiences can be longer (but do not try the reader's patience--patience is not an infinite commodity). If you want busy policymakers or commanders to read what you produce and disseminate, however, keep it short! The shorter, the better. As a general rule of thumb, the longer the document, the higher the probability that it will be tossed onto the stack of "things to read," which, of course, no one ever gets around to.

There are certain very general rules and related considerations to remember about audience analysis. One especially important rule is the need for a short but accurate and well written abstract to front-end written products and the equally valuable practice of generating good summary charts and other presentational devices (including readable, concise lists of key bullets) in spoken intelligence. Bringing it all together for the reader or listener is a precondition for effective presentation and communication. Incidentally, psychological experiments furnish additional ammunition for this point; if you spell out the conclusion, people are more likely to agree with and remember it.

A second general consideration flows from the many studies of the nature of the relationship between the intelligence and policy communities. This can only be described as a symbiotic, classical love-hate marriage (of opposites). The typical analyst is immersed in the specifics of an analytical arena and uses detailed situational logic to describe, explain, predict, and otherwise do analysis (and relies on "theory" to a lesser extent). The typical policymaker, in contrast, utilizes sweeping grand theories (taught to them by or through the works of such luminaries as Henry Kissinger and the late Hans Morgenthau) and comparative analysis (especially in the form of analogies) and looks at things from the "macro" perspective or the big picture.

The political scientist Richard Betts has devoted a lot of attention to the gap between the intelligence and policy communities.[4] Communications can play a central role in bridging this gap. Keep the perspective and priorities of the consumer in mind; translate jargon into his "language" when and as necessary; remain conscious of the chasm.

The writings of Betts on this subject lead to a third point. Betts notes that the analyst often wants to pose the really key questions, clarify the analytical situation, and illuminate the central imponderables. Things are complex, says the analyst, and the decisionmaker had better be prepared to deal with this complexity ("after all, I know a lot more about this than he does"). The policymaker, on the other hand, prefers facts, not questions, overlooking the fact that there are my facts, your facts, the bare facts, and many other variants of this slippery creature. The harassed policymaker also wants definitive answers to very soft and unanswerable questions ("after all, I am an excellent analyst myself, and I do not need intelligence analysts to tell me how to do analysis; besides, I am busy and have to integrate all of this and look at things from the vantage point of the entire world; just give me that facts").

Betts recommends that analysts be allowed and even encouraged to ask the unanswered questions and otherwise needle the boss or the policymaker. This is all admirable, but it should be emphasized that the communications process comes into play here. The need to strike a balance between what the user needs and what he or she wants is central. How to get the message across is key here. It is fine to raise the vital but unanalyzed issues, identify the central uncertainties, and so forth, but how to couch and generally communicate this is the most important consideration.

A fifth point about audience analysis is to remember the classical definition of intelligence as <u>evaluated, policy-relevant information.</u> Intelligence is not "just the facts." Intelligence is assessed and policy-germane information. Generally, do not communicate information that is not relevant to today's or next month's policy concerns (especially if the product is in the current/I&W area and is going to high level people). Some would add a very important amendment to this clause of the audience analysis intelligence constitution. Policymakers will thank the analyst (in the long run) if he or she alerts them to problems no one is concerned about right now. The 1973 oil crisis is a classic example; there were people long before the 1973 Middle East war and the resulting Arab oil embargo who knew that oil was inevitably going to become a permanent crisis arena--but everyone else was too busy with immediate problems to pay any attention to them.

Finally, Socrates advised us to "know thyself." This is very good advice for intelligence analysts. In addition, know thy audience. This is easier said than done in most instances. Analysts do not get much--if any--feedback from the typical consumers of their products. Often, they will not even know who has read it or thrown it into the circular file. But every effort must be made to know the members of the audience--who they are, what their needs and preferences are, what they like and dislike about the products they receive. Intelligence is produced for users--and they are the audience of concern.

THE ART OF LISTENING

Listening is a very important part of the communications process. In fact, many studies in the communcations literature have concluded that listening is the single most essential element of the process and that it is an area in great need of improvement. A classic 1952 Harvard Business Review article observed that "... the biggest block to personal communication is man's ability to listen ..."[5] An article in the October 1983 issue of the journal Communication Education noted that "good oral communication ability," which includes good listening skills, was the highest ranked quality among corporate personnel managers when they were asked to identify what they looked for in hiring college seniors.[6]

Analysts often have very real problems listening; there is a big difference between nodding and really listening. Analysts tend to be opinionated people who care passionately (sometimes almost too passionately!) about what they analyze and have very firm beliefs and convictions. Put two or more analysts in a room, and the odds are that you will have a disagreement; put more than a couple of analysts into a room, and the odds are that you will have a big disagreement.

This becomes important from the perspective of listening as a prelude to preparing to communicate and present finished intelligence. Thus, one of the vantage points from which we can discuss the listening process is that of the analyst who is getting ready to disseminate conclusions and judgments. The other perspective is listening strategies that can be followed in terms of users; how can the user be induced to really hear what the analyst is saying?

The communications literature on listening has repeatedly documented the fact that employees often do not listen well because they think that they are already good at it. This finding has implications for both the analyst preparing to present finished intelligence and the analyst trying to shape the listening behavior of the members of the intended audience. Also, from a training viewpoint, considerable emphasis is placed on skills associated with "active listening" (giving feedback, rapport, empathy) as opposed to the more passive "informational listening" (such as, taking notes, remembering). Interestingly, the lack of training or knowledge about good listening is one of the central problems which prevent organizational members from listening effectively.

In preparing to present and communicate intelligence, the ability to really listen to one's colleagues and peers is absolutely critical. Brainstorming sessions--which will be discussed in the following section of this chapter--and other techniques can be employed here. Meetings, however, emerged as the biggest problem area in one study of organizational situations and listening.

Why is this so? Meetings are notoriously conducive to game playing, oneupmanship, and posturing. People often "communicate" in meetings from behind roles and other facades. When the tendency for people to assume that they are already good listeners is taken in account, there is clearly a recipe for a meeting that is a waste of time--at best.

Empathy turns out to be the single most important component of effective listening. Interestingly, empathy--which is positive sympathy with the other person or sympathy as the ability to identify with the perspective and needs of the other individual--is one of the traits of a good intelligence analyst. Analysis requires the ability to see and understand--the situation from the other side's vantage point. Meetings where empathy is in short supply--and posturing and game playing predominate--preclude effective listening.

How can it be guaranteed that the consumer really hears (or reads) the intended message? Here, respect for (and a genuine awareness of) the user's needs, preferences, and interests is the single most determinative factor. The gap between the intelligence and policy communities is inevitable because of different missions, bureaucratic realities and constraints, and socialization processes (this is very similar to the inescapable gap between the operators and intelligence officers within the services). However, this does not mean that intelligence cannot be communicated effectively. But always keep in mind that it is up to the analyst to accomplish this; it is not the job of the policymaker or commmander to change his or her style of work or mode of thinking.

How, then, do analysts induce good listening on the part of the users of their products? The one key answer is a constant process of requirements analysis. By this, we mean endless cycling through the process of determining why analysis is being done for the consumer. What are the needs of the users? How do they prefer to get finished intelligence? What are the aspects of the agency's or unit's standard operating procedures for intelligence production that turn off users or cause them to tune out?

Techniques and procedures for doing requirements analysis are many and varied in nature. One of the most effective is interviews with users--to determine what they like and why (and what they do not like). Interviews can be conducted via the telephone, in person, or through the mail. The interview schedule or questionnaire format can range from very structured questions with preestablished response categories to very open-ended questions; a combination of the two forms is usually the most effective. The major obstacle, of course, is simple access to appropriate users. On a day-to-day basis, feedback tends to be minimal or nonexistent unless analysts go to the trouble of contacting users to get their reactions. Also, remember that consumers tend to be busy people (or at least portray themselves that way) so the interview should be as brief as possible. But feedback--however it is secured--is essential; feedback, as the communication literature informs us, is the key to good listening. Feedback, by the way, will enhance the analyst's own ability to listen to users and respond to what they want.

In addition to knowing and understanding the user's perspective, there are some tried-and-true techniques for maximizing the probability that the consumer will hear what the analyst has to say. Clear presentations are crucial. Attractively packaged products and briefings facilitate listening tremendously. Nothing alienates an audience more quckly than dense tabular displays and unattractive graphics. Pictures are worth many thousands of words; how one depicts things in graphs, charts, and other pictorial forms helps to ensure that the message will be heard. Leave nothing to chance; to get the point across, underline it and illuminate it. Finally, an <u>organized</u> presentation is absolutely essential for guaranteeing that listeners really hear what they are being told. Intelligence presentations should be tightly organized and rigorously pretested via dry runs and practice.

HOW TO EXPLOIT BRAINSTORMING AND GROUP PROBLEM SOLVING PROCESSES

Intelligence production emanates from several distinct levels of analysis. Finished intelligence can come from an individual analyst, from a small group (an established working group or an ad hoc task force), from an organization (DIA, CIA, and other agency-wide products), or from an inter-organizational process (community-wide, coordinated products, such as National Intelligence Estimates).[7] All of these levels have different strengths and liabilities from the vantage point of yielding high quality intelligence products. Here, the concern is with the use of group-based approaches to communicate intelligence.[8]

Groups--primarily in the form of small working groups rather than large, institutionalized groups--are used throughout the intelligence community. The quality of judgments and conclusions reached by groups varies a great deal. Among the central determinants of the quality of group products are: how much relevant expertise the group has; how motivated the group is to optimize the quality of its output; how clearly the group understands the actual problem area to be addressed; and the effectiveness of the overall group dynamics (the process by which the group operates). Group process factors are especially important because they impact (either adversely or favorably) on the other three aspects of group performance.

As a mechanism for analysis in general and for planning and structuring the presentation and communication of intelligence specifically, group problem solving is not always better than individual problem solving. Especially important in making a choice between the two are the nature of the problem (for example, complex problems lend themselves to group problem solving, especially if interdisciplinary analysis is required) and the goal that is sought. Possible goals and objectives include a high quality solution, a highly accepted solution, a quickly reached solution, and satisfaction with the final analytical product. Note that group problem solving tends to be preferred if the goal is a highly accepted solution or effective communication. Both are obviously relevant to good presentation and communication to users. If an analytical group shows high acceptance of the solution, it is obviously more likely that consumers will react the same way. There is no substitute for the group interaction process when it comes to weeding out unacceptable approaches and settling on a solution that has no major holes or flaws (that is, assuming that the group process is not biased in any way).

There are four distinct assets of group problem solving. The first is that the sum is generally greater than the parts which make it up in the sense that a group generates a greater total of knowledge and information. Groups also produce a greater number of approaches to a problem, an advantage that is especially desirable from the perspective of developing optimum ways to present finished intelligence. A third positive feature of group problem solving is that it increases acceptance of the solution. A low quality solution that has good acceptance can be more effective than a higher quality solution that lacks acceptance; this, of course, has direct relevance to the issue of user acceptance of results. Fourth, the group process leads to better understanding of the decision which has to be carried out. Decisions made by an individual must be communicated to those who have to implement the decision; analogously, an intelligence judgment or estimate that comes from one person must often be presented and defended by many others. A full (and personally acquired) knowledge of goals, obstacles, alternatives, and factual information is essential to communication--both within the originating unit and to external users.

Group problem solving also suffers from certain liabilities. One is social pressure; conformity can be the result of such pressure, and this is particularly bad for problems requiring solutions based on facts. A second defect of group problem solving is that the members of the group often settle on the first solution that comes along where the positive comments clearly outnumber the negative reactions. This means that higher quality solutions not considered by that time will fall by the wayside. The leader of the group may dominate the process and shape the solution. This is obviously a danger with dictatorial leaders, and also emerges as a problem for leaderless groups, where dominant individuals tend to emerge. Finally, a decidedly secondary goal--winning the argument--may come to predominate. In this situation, the goal can become "who wins?" rather than "what is the best solution?"

Generally, group problem solving improves the communication of intelligence findings and products. However, there is one particularly negative group syndrome which arises on occasion that is very dangerous to both analysis generally and problem solving as a prelude to communicating intelligence to users. This is the groupthink syndrome. Groupthink, a term coined by the Yale psychologist Irving Janis, is based on the group dynamics principle that groups are more than the sum of the individual members and can take on a life of their own.[9] The group process can degenerate into a situation in which pressures to maintain group cohesion--the desire to keep the group happy and unified rather than the supposedly dominant goal of finding the best solution--drive the analytical process.

Janis studied groupthink, a label that has obvious and intentional resemblance to <u>1984</u> terms like newspeak, in a number of foreign policy crisis decisionmaking cases. The U.S. failure to foresee the Japanese attack on Pearl Harbor, the Bay of Pigs decision in 1961 to attack Cuba, and a number of other decision fiascoes share the characteristics of groupthink. When groupthink operates, the decision group believes in basic strategic assumptions that are wrong, but no one perceives this because they are obsessed with maintaining group cohesion and not rocking the boat. As a result, members with doubts censor themselves (and get censored by others in the group, especially the one or more people who assume the role of "mindguard") and the group screens out conflicting evidence. This went so far in the Bay of Pigs decision as to include a refusal to open the discussion to lower level analysts. For example, one of the basic assumptions in the planning for the attack was that the rural Cuban population would rise up and join with the anti-Castro invaders to overthrow Castro. However, lower level CIA analysts had information which showed that, at that particular time, 80 percent of Cuba's rural population supported the Castro regime. Hardly the foundation for a popular uprising!

Janis also looked at cases where groupthink was totally absent, where pressures for conformity to the group mind-set did not surface. The most obvious was the Cuban missile crisis in 1962. During that crisis, there were no pressures to converge on a premature and artificial consensus. In fact, the decision was explicitly made to keep the discussions open and inject additional viewpoints. President Kennedy stayed out of the initial sessions so that his presence would not compel members to decide on the basis of what they perceived that he wanted. The decisionmakers showed unusual empathy for the Soviet leadership, intentionally refraining from doing anything that would humiliate the Russians or back them into a corner. Recall that empathy is vital to effective and successful communication.

The principles of groupthink and the characteristics of decisions without groupthink have clear relevance to intelligence group problem solving. Guard against the natural tendency for group cohesion pressures to override the real reason for the group's existence--to fashion the most effective strategies for presenting and communicating analytical results to the policy community.

Brainstorming is a particular technique for group-based problem solving that is unusually good for preparing to communicate results. Brainstorming involves open-ended and unstructured group discussions about ways to approach and solve problems. Brainstorming is especially valuable for generating ideas (and not nearly as good for evaluating ideas).

The essence of brainstorming is the willingness to suspend judgment and generate ideas in a free-wheeling fashion. Group members should refrain from criticizing ideas when they are first offered--even if they sound preposterous (and remember, someone else's ridiculous idea may end up being right--or may point in the direction of the best solution). Game playing and posturing are incompatible with good brainstorming. So, for that matter, are ranks and deferring to formal leaders. If a group is plagued by personality clashes, formal deference to rank, politics, and authoritarian leadership, do not try brainstorming--because it will not work.

SUMMARY

This chapter has emphasized several areas of communications, especially in relation to the users or consumers of finished intelligence. The ability to communicate clearly, effectively, and with empathy is essential to the intelligence analyst. The hours of work, thought, and effort that go into production are meaningless if the results cannot be presented and communicated. Audience analysis is the first ingredient of successful communications. Know thy audience is a maxim that is ignored at one's own peril. Especially critical is awareness of the size and nature of the very real gap between the intelligence and policy communities. The type of consumer who is the target of a product or briefing is also relevant; the contrast between intelligence which goes to other experts and the kind which goes to a very high level policymaker is particularly striking. A second focus has been the art of listening. People are not born with the ability to listen; it is a developed talent. Listening is quite properly regarded as the single most important component of the communications process--and the most neglected. Active listening (giving feedback, rapport, empathy) is an especially neglected part of the art--and very central to communicating with and to consumers. One can get the user to listen--and get the desired message conveyed--only through continuous requirements analysis. Know thy user! Finally, this chapter has looked in some detail at group problem solving and its usefulness for intelligence communications. Groups have numerous assets and liabilities. Groupthink is a special danger to guard against. Generally, however, the use of brainstorming and other group problem solving techniques will significantly enhance the prospects for presenting finished intelligence effectively.

NOTES

1. It is very tempting to try to prove (confirm) a theory or hypothesis rather than disprove (or refute) it. Astrologers are notorious for ransacking the evidence base in search of supporting data (as opposed to the scientifically sound strategy of seeking to disconfirm or reject the hypothesis). More generally, people often attempt to establish the validity of their favored hypotheses or viewpoints because of ideological, intellectual, and other biases and because it is easy for one's ego to become involved. The philosopher of science Karl Popper is associated with the position that we should <u>invent</u> theories in a creative fashion (bold conjectures) but <u>test</u> theories rigorously, with the

deck stacked against the theory (careful refutations). See Karl Popper, Conjectures and Refutations: The Growth of Scientific Knowledge (New York: Harper and Row, 1963).

2. See, for example, Richard E. Nisbett and Lee Ross, Human Inference: Strategies and Shortcomings of Social Judgment (Englewood Cliffs, NJ: Prentice-Hall, 1980).

3. For an overview of artificial intelligence and its many applications, see Stephen J. Andriole and Gerald W. Hopple, Sourcebook on Artificial Intelligence (Princeton, NJ: Petrocelli Books, 1985).

4. See especially Richard K. Betts, "Intelligence for Policymaking," in Gerald W. Hopple, Stephen J. Andriole, and Amos Freedy (eds.), National Security Crisis Forecasting and Management (Boulder, CO: Westview, 1984), pp. 19-23. See also Betts, "Analysis, War, and Decision: Why Intelligence Failures are Inevitable," World Politics 31(October, 1978): 61-98.

5. Quoted in W. Charles Redding, Communication Within the Organization (West Lafayette, IN: Purdue University and The Industrial Communication Council, 1972), p. 33.

6. Gary T. Hunt and Louis P. Cusella, "A Field Study of Listening Needs in Organizations," Communication Education 32 (October 1983): 393-401.

7. Graham T. Allison, Essense of Decision: Explaining the Cuban Missile Crisis (Boston, MA: Little, Brown, 1971) covers analysis from the perspective of the individual, the group, and the bureaucratic context.

8. Among the many books and articles on different aspects of group problem solving, the best include: Darwin Cartwright and Alvin Zander (eds.), Group Dynamics: Research and Theory, 3rd ed. (New York: Harper and Row, 1968); A. P. Hare, Handbook of Small Group Research, 2nd ed. (New York: Free Press, 1976); and H. Brandstatter, et. al. (eds.), Group Decision Making (London: Academic Press, 1981).

9. Irving Janis, Groupthink: Psychological Studies of Policy Decisions and Fiascoes (Boston, MA: Houghton Mifflin, 1982).

Part 4

The Issues

14
Ethics and Intelligence

Malcolm Wallop

THE PROBLEM

Ethics, morality, right, and wrong. In recent years these words have been thrown at the intelligence profession like so many stones. People in the profession have generally reacted the way the guests of honor at a stoning usually act: with resignation or anger, or by averting their hands. At any rate, in the profession these words are often understood as wreckers, show-stoppers, hindrances--with good reason. Since the mid-1970s the profession has been awash with rules and procedures instituted in the name of ethics, the least breach of which can cost a man his career. These rules have become well-nigh the only focus of debate in the intelligence community (other than the budget, of course).

A past issue of Foreign Policy carries an article by Stansfield Turner entitled "Intelligence, The Right Rules" that is typical of a whole debate, the point of which is to discover just the right wording for restrictions so as to strike the right balance between intelligence and morality. This debate is based on the supposition that good intelligence is necessarily immoral, and that good morality abhors intelligence work.

This approach is nonsense. The failures of intelligence which have so endangered this country of late--the failure to understand the Soviet strategic buildup and the failure to see the Iranian revolution developing before our very eyes, the great failure of counterintelligence known as the Nosenko case, to name but a few--were not due to excessive attention to moral considerations or to excessive regard for the rights of Americans, or to the opposite thereof. They were simply the result of incompetent work. There is far too little talk in the intelligence profession about what actions the threats we face demand of us. The ethical considerations primarily relevant to such problems are the ones which normally relate to shoddy work.

My point here is that the problems of intelligence may not be reduced to questions of ethics. Ethics and intelligence are related, but they have been unnecessarily and perhaps wantonly confused. My larger point is that ethical darts should neither have been hurled at--nor should they be regarded by--the intelligence profession as things extraneous to good performance.

Indeed, the performance of any American intelligence professional and his zeal for his job can only be enhanced by understanding the moral environment in which he works. The paramount feature of that environment is the role of the United States as the foremost force for decency in a largely indecent world.

The intelligence officer's job is to assist the United States by learning the truth and communicating it accurately to his superiors. This is not to say that, merely because the United States is morally preferable to the Soviet Union, anything goes, but it is to say that someone working for a just cause is in a situation morally different from someone who is not.

Intelligence consists of four disparate disciplines: collection; counterintelligence; covert action; and analysis. I propose to discuss separately the ethical problems peculiar to the first three, leaving analysis as the passive function for another day. Then, I will offer a few reflections on the ethical considerations applicable to the profession as a whole.

COLLECTION

Those who argue against clandestine collection on moral grounds say that it requires Americans to offer inducements and assistance to foreigners to do things which are probably against their country's laws and which are therefore wrong. Both the clandestine source and the clandestine agent debase themselves as human beings. They thereby betray their fellow countrymen's trust and work for Americans, while pretending to their fellow countrymen that they are not. Sources and agents submit to seduction and bribery and become traitors. The "controlled" source, or agent, is someone so much in the financial or psychological hands of a foreign power that he should not be able to stand to look at himself in the mirror. By recruiting such people, the U.S. not only debases the lives of individuals but also distresses the political ecology of whole nations.

But the biggest losers are probably the Americans doing the recruiting--and our own country. Recruitment of sources and agents requires techniques not employed in normal human intercourse, such as giving various inducements, getting commitments on the basis of less-than-complete information or under false pretenses, bypassing normal authority, etc.

People who do such things day in and day out debase themselves and become dangerous to their own country. That is because not only do they earn their daily bread making traitors and wretches of others, they also acquire dangerous skills, dangerous habits, and a dangerous lack of scruples. They lose any sense of limits. Once they have lied to others, broken other people's laws, they must find it easier to deceive their own countrymen, to break their own country's law. Routine reduces resistance to repugnance.

Our clandestine officers are told, in effect, to live by a double standard, one for foreigners, one for Americans. But double standards are nearly impossible to keep.

That argument concludes that the logical path out of a double moral standard leads to amorality, and that American intelligence officers took that path. They did not often discuss the moral implications of what they were doing. They did not attempt to justify their actions to themselves or to their colleagues; they simply did what their superiors required. Thus they came to live in a moral vacuum and committed abuses.

The argument's only valid element, that the techniques of clandestine collection are morally difficult to handle, are obscured by errors of fact and logic. In fact, the intelligence officer's tools are anything but abnormal in human intercourse. Reporters, attorneys, salesmen, and legislators routinely elicit more information, more commitment, than they give. Persuading, seducing, buying, cajoling cooperation is the very stuff of social intercourse. Intelligence men are neither more nor less likely to do these things badly than people in any other pursuit.

Clandestine collection does indeed involve suborning betrayal of trust. Clandestine officers do get people to break both trusts and laws, but it does not follow that clandestine collection on its face is morally unacceptable. The information gathered at the cost of moral compromise may achieve great good or avoid great evil. But, more important, not all trusts, not all laws, have the same moral status. Whereas a man would be debased by, say, suborning a Swiss law against selling heroin to minors, one would be ennobled by violating the Soviet law which prohibits teaching the gospel to minors.

<u>We must agree that betrayal of a liberal democracy is morally different from betrayal of countries like the Soviet Union, not because we are Americans, but because it is demonstrable that the Soviet Union stands on a moral plane quite different from that of liberal democracy.</u> The Soviets themselves agree, although for their own reasons. Their schools teach the fundamental tenet of Marxist morality: "Good is whatever contributes to success of the proletariat in its secular struggle with the bourgeoisie."

For Marxists, there is no standard of good and evil applicable to <u>both</u> progressives and reactionaries. We, for our part, believe <u>that</u> all men are created equal and can therefore only reject these contentions by counterposing a <u>single</u> moral standard, applicable to all men and all nations. Clearly, nations and laws must and do fall into different categories on this scale. This, in turn, means that--even as common sense dictates--we cannot pretend that different "political ecologies" have the same right to remain undisturbed.

A source or an agent recruited to work against a bad regime on behalf of a good one stands a chance of being improved thereby. The history of war is replete with the cases of ordinary people who developed extraordinary qualities in response to the inordinate demands of clandestine life behind enemy lines. A recent account, William Stephenson's <u>A Man Called Intrepid</u>, shows how commitment to the Allied cause ennobled even the exercise of the ancient dishonorable art of the courtesan. William Hood's recent book on the Popov case makes the same point. This point, however, must apply with less force when the recruitment is affected through bribery, blackmail, or deception.

All the more reason, therefore, to revive the lost art of recruiting people by emphasizing the objectives which the United States seeks to accomplish. Nevertheless, there are some people who can only be moved by the lowest motives. It is not ethically impermissible to deal with such people on their own level. Since they are already corrupt, their corruption might as well be put to the service of good ends--so long as they are not deliberately made worse.

I suspect that most agents are sensitive enough to recognize when to exploit them. Unless these agents really are psychological basket cases, they are likely to do what comes naturally--take the case officer for a ride. I recall a marine who used to run recruited agents in Vietnam and was telling us how to do it. He began by saying that agents were pretty unsophisticated people--that he would motivate them to go into dangerous areas by inflating the importance of their mission, giving them a little money, and promising them more. Did he get good information? No, the dirty bastards would just go into the forest for a week or so and come back with fabricated stories. Would he disregard their reports and employ others? No, these were the only reports available so, although he didn't really trust them, he had to use them to satisfy the requirements levied upon him.

Well, I suggest these simple folk were more sophisticated than our Marine, who had apparently lost at once his moral and operational bearings.

The argument that he who corrupts others also corrupts himself is valid so far as it goes. I simply point out that clandestine collection need not involve depravation either of others or of one's self. I will deal with this more fully later.

COUNTERINTELLIGENCE

Let me now turn to counterintelligence and begin with the question of when it is proper to intrude into the privacy of innocent people.

If counterintelligence officers knew who and where the spies, agents of influence, and terrorists were, they alone would be surveilled and arguments about the propriety of surveillance and file-keeping would not exist. But the job of counterintelligence is precisely to pick out those who are spies or traitors from those who are not.

To identify the former, one must look at both. Thus the controversy is always about the surveillance of people who are not spies or terrorists.

Let us approach the controversy through an example: suppose that a terrorist armed with explosives was known to be hiding in an apartment complex of 1,000 units. By what rights does one tap the telephone or surveil the occupants of any one of those units? The answer depends entirely on one's approach. If one believes that whenever a government turns its attention toward an individual without his knowledge, especially if it observes him, listens to him, or compiles records on him, it burdens him by invading his privacy, and that such a burden should never be imposed except upon wrongdoers, then there is but one question. How do I know the individual whose telephone I will tap is a wrongdoer? Approaching the problem this way, one must decide not to affect the lives of the 999 innocents in the apartment. This, of course, leaves the terrorist free to affect those lives with his bomb.

On the other hand, if one believes that a government's right to surveillance depends on the purpose for which and the circumstances in which it is carried out, then one will conclude that despite the potential for abuse, the government intends to help and protect. If the assistance could be rendered with the target's knowledge, innocents might well agree to be surveilled. But circumstances such as those force the government into secrecy as the most effective way to protect the 999 innocents.

But purists will ask, what if the government, as it surveils X to find the terrorist, finds that X is not a terrorist but a bank robber, or a political opponent who happens to cheat on his wife? In the first instance he could be prosecuted on the basis of evidence obtained without "probable cause." In the second instance, the government could use the information to blackmail the subject or to ruin him.

In recent years, we in the United States have tried to safeguard individuals from abusive uses of government records: (1) we restrict the gathering of information; (2) we restrict the uses of government records; (3) we provide for authoritative review of what information has been gathered and how it has been used. We have tried to substitute formal _a priori_ rules for good judgment before the fact and responsible review after the fact. I don't think it is possible to do this. Let me give one illustration.

I have said that in order to distinguish spies and terrorists from those who are not, one must look primarily through the majority who are not. The question of how many innocent people must be involved does not really depend on the investigations. It depends on circumstances beyond their control. In the 1950s, for example, the FBI thoroughly penetrated the Communist Party, USA and the groups on the Attorney General's list. The U.S. Government openly considered these groups to be subversive.

People applying for sensitive government jobs were asked whether "you are now or have ever been a member" of any of them. Of course, people stayed away from them in droves. Even the American Civil Liberties Union banned communists from its activities. The main communist "fronts" like the National Lawyers Guild were on the Attorney General's list and were therefore useless as "fronts." A charge not far from the truth was that some cells of the Communist Party consisted entirely of FBI informants. At any rate, by 1960 there were probably very few people close to subversive activities who could be termed innocent. Strangely, it was precisely because the people subject to surveillance were so few and so far from the mainstream of national life that there was little fear in the mainstream that anyone might be mistaken for a spy, subversive, etc. or become the subjects of surveillance.

All of this changed in the early 1960s as the movement for securing equal rights grew to encompass factions which aimed at radical changes in American society--or even at its physical destruction. It is instructive to recall that, for example, the violent Student Nonviolent Coordinating Committee and the violent Weather Underground evolved from a mainstream group, the Student League for Industrial Democracy, under the impact of the civil rights movement. Attacks on policemen, riots, the burning of whole sections of Detroit, Los Angeles, and Newark, the sabotage of power lines, and the calls to "kill the establishment" were not instantly rejected by all sections of the mainstream.

Thousands of upper middle class liberals and their children, for a variety of reasons, identified themselves--usually vicariously--with the radicals. It became fashionable in certain circles to sympathize with the radicals' ends, if not with their methods, and to offer various forms of aid. High society fund raisers for the Black Panther Party were common. The number of innocents and semi-innocents involved with activities normally warranting surveillance grew. The growth, in these same social circles, of opposition to U.S. participation in the Vietnam War swelled the ranks of those willing to identify themselves--again normally vicariously--with radical forms of opposition to their country.

The passing of classified documents to newspapers, which once would have been cause for ostracism, made Dr. Daniel Ellsberg, a civilian employee of the Pentagon, into a hero to be emulated. Radicals who worked with foreign enemies of the United States were not instantly put beyond the pale--quite the contrary, they were occasionally idolized by the press. (Indeed, as late as 1978, the Senate Judiciary Committee's report on the Foreign Intelligence Surveillance Act explicitly and retroactively declared that electronic surveillance of those anti-Vietnam activists who met with foreign communists would have been prohibited by the act.)

How many similar people were going to do such things? In sum, in the 1960s there was not only an increase in the number of activities of natural interest to counterintelligence, but, more important, a disproportionate increase in the number of friends and auxiliaries around those targets.

Neither then nor now could there be an *a priori* rule for designating who deserves a closer look and who does not. The investigator must be free to make good judgments on balance and be prepared to answer for them with reason and with results.

Counterintelligence officers must also face more mundane ethical choices. They must judge whether the cherished positive intelligence operations of people who outrank them within their own service have been exposed to compromise. Only a rather firm devotion to the truth will enable a subordinate who values his career to tell a superior that he's been very wrong, that his pet project is going bad, or that the only information he has in a particular field should not be used because it was acquired by means that the superior failed to make sufficiently secure. And only an extraordinary devotion to the truth will keep a superior officer who hears such things from using his power to humiliate such a messenger.

In his book <u>Honorable Men</u>, William Colby showed how he gave in to the perennial bosses' temptation. He could not follow the complex arguments the counterintelligence staff was bringing him to question the sources of information he needed to answer questions posed to him by the National Security Council, so he simply swept away the counterintelligence staff.

Another kind of self discipline--this one more mental than moral--seems absolutely necessary in counterintelligence: the ability to suspend judgment when sufficient information is lacking.

Let me now turn to the problem of domestic counterintelligence and begin by discussing Operation Chaos, the investigation of the anti-war movement in the late 1960s and early 1970s. The CIA's role in Operation Chaos was an abuse of its legal powers. The Church Committee's reports, as well as David Wise's and Morton Halperin's books, attempt to proceed from the premise that a legal abuse must also be an abuse simply. Law is one thing; prudence is another. Judgments concerning legality are logically separable from ones concerning prudence. The premise is false. To argue that a government should not investigate those who put obstacles in the way of military efforts during war, in cooperation with the enemy, is fraught with difficulty.

There were, however, domestic covert actions which abused both law and propriety itself. The FBI's campaign against Martin Luther King was intended, in the word of FBI memos, to "discredit him," to "take him off his pedestal, reduce him completely in influence," so as to make it possible for people more to J. Edgar Hoover's liking to "assume the role of the leadership of the Negro people." Of course, nothing either explicit or implicit in the Constitution or laws of the United States permits a government agency to appoint itself as the guardian of an ethnic group's political leadership.

The FBI's domestic covert action, COINTELPRO, begun in 1956 and aimed at disrupting the Communist Party, was grounded in common sense. Moreover, had the American people been consulted about the program, they would have approved overwhelmingly. In March 1960, FBI Headquarters ordered field offices to prevent the Communist Party's infiltration of "legitimate mass organizations, such as parent-teacher associations, civil organizations and racial and religious groups."

But this protective function could hardly be accomplished without some involvement with these legitimate organizations--if only to see how far the infiltration had gone and to notify the legitimate leaders that communist infiltration was occurring. Of course, as we have said, some infiltration was occurring and, at the same time, American non-communist leftists were spontaneously adopting violent methods and Marxist ideology. The expansion of COINTELPRO to "rabble rousers," "agitators," and "key activists" proceeded apace. That meant, among other things, that the FBI would request and receive information on the tax status of selected individuals and either try to cut off their access to funds or instigate bothersome IRS procedures against them. Here the confusion began. The IRS exists to collect taxes, not to conduct political harassment.

In 1961, the scope of COINTELPRO was broadened to include the Ku Klux Klan and other "white hate" organizations. They became targets because President Johnson and Attorney General Kennedy wanted to protect the efforts of "civil rights" activists in the South. FBI Headquarters specified that the methods to be used should be the same as those used against the communists.

Beginning in 1967, after the riotous summer of 1966, COINTELPRO was expanded to cover black nationalist groups. The FBI was to prevent the formation of a nationwide movement capable of uniting a significant portion of America's blacks into a violent revolutionary force.

At this point, questions should have been asked. Intelligence officers, National Security Council staffers, etc. should have asked their superiors whether the COINTELPRO was not becoming a substitute for overt policies by national political leaders to internally weaken the strongest "black nationalist" groups and their leaders and to keep them away from legitimate liberals.

But the questions were not asked and COINTELPRO grew. Beginning in 1968, after the riots which disrupted the Democratic National Convention in Chicago and the evidence of organized disruption both of American campuses and of the American war effort, the FBI broadened COINTELPRO to include the "New Left."

This was an amorphous classification, including the fringes of revolutionary movements down to the left wing of American liberalism. Again, the purpose was to make it difficult for these groups to organize, and to separate them from the liberals. According to the Church Committee, in July 1968, the field offices were further prodded by FBI Headquarters to:

(1) prepare leaflets using "the most obnoxious pictures" of New Left leaders at various universities;
(2) instigate "personal conflicts or animosities" between New Left leaders;
(3) create the impression that leaders are "informants for the bureau or other law enforcement agencies" (the "snitch jacket" technique);
(4) send articles from student or "underground" newspapers which show "depravity" ("use of narcotics and free sex") of New Left leaders to university officials, donors, legislators, and parents;
(5) have members arrested on marijuana charges;

(6) send anonymous letters about a student's activities to parents, neighbors, and the parent's employers;
(7) send anonymous letters about New Left faculty members (signed "a concerned alumnus" or "a concerned taxpayer") to university officials, legislators, members of the board of regents, and the press;
(8) use "cooperative press contacts;"
(9) exploit the "hostility" between New Left and Old Left groups;
(10) disrupt New Left coffee houses near military bases, which are attempting to "influence members of the armed forces;"
(11) use cartoons, photographs, and anonymous letters to "ridicule" the New Left;
(12) use "misinformation" to "confuse and disrupt" New Left activities, such as by notifying members that events have been cancelled.

As part of COINTELPRO, the FBI developed lists of "key rabble rousers," "key activists," and "key black extremists." The purpose of listing these individuals was to bring the government's full weight to bear against them. Of course, these individuals were to be watched closely to see if they stepped outside the law. Just as important, FBI agents were to watch for non-legal opportunities to "get them." In the meanwhile, the nation's political leaders, by their public utterances and policies, fed these movements.

This is the basic question regarding COINTELPRO: of course, there are domestic as well as foreign enemies, but by what right does a democratic government take action against them? There can only be one rule: law supported by public opinion, and there can only be one exception to that rule. That was stated by Thomas Jefferson to defend himself against the charge that he had no constitutional authority to purchase the Louisiana Territory from France. He admitted he had gone beyond the law, but as soon as practicable, he laid before public opinion the results he had achieved thereby, argued that the results were worth the breach, and dared his opponents to try to impeach him or be quiet. But in COINTELPRO, the U.S. Government followed neither the democratic rule nor the democratic exception. In the case of COINTELPRO, the U.S. Government did not merely surveil, did not merely "throw the book" at its least favorite people. It operated beyond "the book" of laws, did not achieve the intended results, and did not lay its case before public opinion. This was not only an error, but a crime and an error.

COVERT ACTION

Is it right to affect other nations' affairs by secret means? Let's begin by noting that apart from a greater degree of secrecy, the means of covert action do not appear to be different either substantively or morally from those of overt political activity. Usually, neither international law nor political theory treats the political acts in question differently when they are done with a greater degree of secrecy than when they are done with a lesser degree of secrecy. Military action is violent, regardless of whether its source is acknowledged. In political theory, acknowledgement of the source of a military act by itself does not justify an unjust one, nor does the opposite condemn a just one. A politician who acts at the behest of foreigners does so regardless of how many people notice. Political theory is more concerned with the motives and the results of both the leader and the led than it is with whether they avow their relationship.

International law is silent on the entire matter. The laws of various countries differ. A state can try to influence public opinion in another overtly, as well as covertly, and may use both overt and covert means to build up or tear down the influence of certain individuals and factions in another state. Neither the efficacy nor the moral worth of such actions depends primarily on the degree of secrecy with which they are undertaken.

Secrecy and deception, in some measure, appear to be constituent parts of overt political activity. What overt political activity--foreign or domestic--does not at one time or another include the advice that "I think it would be better if they heard this from you rather from us?" (or vice-versa). It seems, then, that the appropriateness of political action, direct or indirect, violent or nonviolent, more or less covert, is to be judged by a single standard: How well does it serve policy, bearing in mind that no policy is well served if pursued by means not proportionate to the good the policy seeks to achieve.

It must be reemphasized that interference in other nations' affairs can be quite overt. OPEC's overt raising of oil prices has changed much in the world. In 1979, Iran put itself in a position to affect the outcome of the American presidential election of 1980 by taking 52 American hostages. These overt acts were not without covert aspects.

In some well-known matters the mixture of overtness and covertness is more nearly even. The Soviet Union, in the past, has told American businessmen that growth in trade, something in which the businessmen are quite interested, would depend upon the U.S. Government's renouncing the principle of the Jackson-Vanik Amendment. The Soviets clearly expect these businessmen to influence debates inside the U.S. in ways favorable to Soviet interests but not to trumpet the fact that they stand to gain by their alignment with Soviet policy. Therefore, if the objective of foreign policy is to change decisions which foreign states would otherwise make, then it makes no sense to disapprove of some methods precisely on the ground that they interfere in other states' internal affairs. Let us look further.

Historically, there has existed a proportional relationship between the ends which states have sought to achieve and the means by which they have pursued them. Simple negotiations with regard to commercial matters of marginal interest do not normally call forth attempts to bypass the other side's official negotiators, much less to alter the political system which the negotiators represent. On the other hand, when states believe that either their highest interest or their most cherished beliefs (or both) are at stake, it would be surprising if they limited themselves to official contacts. But since states allow only their own citizens to take part in their own political process, adversaries in these circumstances can only take part in other nations' affairs covertly.

The proximate purposes of foreign policy, whether pursued covertly or not, are the same: to affect the other side's decisions. But whereas overt acts speak to the other side's body politic, covert ones are meant to exercise influence from within the other side's body politic.

The argument has sometimes been made that such interference is inappropriate for democracies. But simply because a nation is a democracy, it may not disregard with impunity the requirements for survival. Democracies which fail to use the means required to prevail over those who intend their destruction simply perish.

Yet the argument has valid aspects: it is inappropriate for democracies, especially in our times, to try to subvert other democracies, because in such governments power resides in popular opinion, and because modern liberal democracies do not restrict what citizens can hear. If the political leaders of one democracy wish to interfere in another's politics, they have but to do abroad what they do at home.

It may be objected that because a nation's electorate would not take kindly to foreign advice, a foreigner seeking to interfere would do so most effectively by supporting local agents whom their fellow citizens would falsely believe were acting on their own. Of course, when such acts occur, they are subversive.

The second problem concerns loyalty to the foreign assets one employs in covert activities. This has troubled me greatly. In the postwar period, and especially since 1961, this country has not undertaken covert activities with the purpose of prevailing--of actually succeeding in turning a foreign situation around.

But we have recruited people to do the dirty work, to expose themselves to danger, who would not have cooperated with us unless they had been led to believe that we were going to go "all the way" to liberate their countries. As a result, the salient feature of U.S. covert action has been the betrayal of its foreign assets. Ukrainians and Belorussians, East Europeans, Chinese, Kurds, Vietnamese, and Laotians, among others, have been recruited, armed, sent to infiltrate or fight U.S. enemies, and abandoned to die.

Officials of the CIA, when reminded of this, effect a tough mien and declare that, in the real world, betrayal is often necessary. But this is retail machiavellianism and wholesale naivete. Surely there is a difference between the occasional betrayal which purposeful nations commit on the way to success and which can be justified after the fact by pointing to the greater good accomplished, and the routine betrayal which the improvident and weak-willed commit willy-nilly as they stumble from defeat to defeat.

CONCLUSION

You will have noticed that many of the ethical problems I have described are not peculiar to intelligence. A moment's reflection is enough to realize that intelligence is but one of many tasks in society which equip their practitioners with dangerous combinations of skills and chances to misuse them. The training and responsibilities of a Certified Public Accountant make him society's guardian against financial swindles. Alas, they also make him better able to perpetrate such swindles than anyone else, and constantly subject him to the trial of huge sums passing through his hands and under his pencil.

Some succumb. Physicians are entrusted with dangerous drugs, with the right to cut into people's bodies, and with immunity from criminal prosecution for deaths which occur in their job. The people entrusted to the care of a physician are usually in precarious health. They are either burdens which someone might like to shirk, or charges for which someone is willing to continue to pay. The physician is tempted to make a profit either by helping families and society rid themselves of burdens, or by collecting money on the mere pretense of delivering care because of government payments.

In the Soviet Union, psychiatry has allowed its inherent tendency to be a tool for making individuals conform to society to grow in the service of totalitarianism.

Finally, every lawyer knows the temptation of sophistry--to make the worst cause appear the better. Yet, proposals to do away with lawyering are usually rejected on the ground that the adversary system can help to discover where justice lies. There are also no serious proposals to do away with M.D.'s and CPA's.

The prime example of a necessary social function which is inherently dangerous to society is government itself. Briefly put, men who are empowered to keep peace, suppress wrongdoing, and protect liberty are _ipso facto_ able to sow terror, enthrone wrongdoing, and destroy liberty. How may society guard itself from its guardians? This question was investigated definitively--at least on the level of principle--in Plato's _Republic_. The essence of Plato's argument, which has become our civilization's fundamental answer to this question, is that one cannot do away with dangerous occupations. One can no more remove from the guardians the sword, the opportunity to lie, than one can take knives and dangerous drugs away from physicians. Such easy solutions simply destroy arts without which individual and collective bodies perish.

The only real solution is to wed the practitioners of dangerous arts to the correct purposes of those arts. This is difficult to do, both intellectually and in practice. Yet, the Hippocratic oath has kept most Western physicians from becoming monsters or mere businessmen, while most professionals have attempted with varying degrees of success to follow a similar path.

The Hippocratic oath departs from the fact that the only proper end of medicine is the health of the individual patient. Even the most liberal interpretation of this concept disqualifies from the category of medicine actions taken for the patient's mere comfort, or pleasure, or in the interest of anyone but the patient. The art's <u>end</u>, individual health, governs its <u>means</u>.

Even the art of government has been regulated to some extent by the perception that its end is the "common good." The enormous variety of interpretations to which this term is subject, nevertheless, has not prevented even uneducated Westerners from adopting it as a standard to judge governments according to Aristotle's precise distinction: good governments rule in the interest of all the people; bad ones rule in the interest of the rulers. That is but the very beginning of wisdom on government. A whole political science follows from it, the purpose of which is to tell better governments from worse ones. By no means is this political science foolproof or malice-proof. Yet neither ignorance nor malice has been able to erase it as a standard by which to judge which actions are and which are not conducive to good government.

There is no reason to abandon this way of doing things and to adopt or eschew means for action on purely pragmatic or on purely moralistic grounds. Experience has taught us that one does not improve government by removing from it powers necessary and proper for the fulfillment of its tasks. Rather, one enumerates those tasks more closely, and seeks to understand them more fully, and one sees to it that governors spend their energies fully on those tasks.

This teaching applies to intelligence as it does to the armed forces, or indeed to diplomats and civil servants. It is not to be confused with the ethically untenable proposition that anything may justly be done if it is reasonably understood to advance the interest of the United States. Clearly, the price one pays ought to be proportionate to the benefit achieved. The point is quite another: <u>It is possible for an individual habitually to deceive foreigners and yet be truthful to his own people, just as it is possible for him to habitually break others' laws and respect his own, without following a double standard.</u>

Amorality not only corrupts our intelligence men and indeed our diplomats; it also deprives them of the energy and self-confidence which they need to operate. It just so happens that, as in the days of the founding, this nation stands nearly alone in the world as an imperfect, but nonetheless lively representative of the proposition that "all men are created equal." Those who serve this nation in foreign affairs have every right and every duty to believe that they are doing a service to anyone whom they convince to help this country advance the cause of liberty in the world.

Discerning the situations where morally questionable means may be employed is a difficult task for both mind and characters. But most good and necessary things are hard.

15
Law and Intelligence

Morton H. Halperin

The U.S. intelligence community now functions under laws and regulations which limit what it can do and which mandate a set of procedures for carrying out various functions. The current framework is unusual if not unique. In most countries, including democratic nations with a tradition of the rule of law, intelligence agencies operate outside the normal systems of legal and political control and in almost total secrecy. Indeed, the United States for most of the period since World War II operated with a similar system.

Prior to World War II, the United States did not have a structure of permanent intelligence organizations. The military services carried on intelligence activities related to combat requirements and the FBI conducted some investigations that would now be considered "intelligence activity," but there was no central intelligence unit and no organized intelligence community. Various intelligence units came into existence during the war, including the Office of Strategic Services (OSS). These units, functioning at a time of declared war, operated essentially outside the formal legal structure. After the war a series of intelligence agencies were set up, but little attention was paid to their relation to the laws of the land. In fact, it was apparently assumed that if intelligence agencies were to operate effectively, they would have to be outside the limits laid down in the Constitution and the laws as they applied to the overt elements of the government. Quite a few activities of the newly formed intelligence agencies illustrate this view of how the intelligence community needed to operate and reveal the widespread support for this perspective within the executive and legislative branches of the government.

Typical is the effort of the National Security Agency to persuade U.S. owned and operated international cable companies to provide the agency with copies of cables being sent to and from the United States if such materials were of potential interest to the intelligence community. There was widespread support in the government for this effort--despite a law which made it a crime for the companies to divulge the contents of the cables to anyone but the intended recipients. When the cable companies balked at responding favorably to a request which seemed to require them to break the law, they were given a meeting with President Harry Truman, who asked them to cooperate and assured them that they would not be prosecuted for breaking the law or otherwise be liable. The companies then agreed to provide the requested cables and the program continued to the mid-1970s, when the Attorney General sent NSA a memorandum suggesting that the program might be illegal.[1]

Contrary to normal procedures, Congress played almost no role in establishing the intelligence agencies or defining their permissible scope of activity. The Central Intelligence Agency (CIA) was established pursuant to an act of Congress. During the debate about establishing the CIA, some attention was given to the danger that the agency would become a "gestapo" which would spy on U.S. citizens. The agency was specifically prohibited from performing "internal security" functions, but no other restrictions were specified and that restriction was interpreted so as not to preclude CIA clandestine activity in the United States. The CIA, in fact, operated on the basis of a series of presidential and Director of Central Intelligence directives; the very existence of these directives was kept secret until the mid-1970s.[2]

Most other intelligence agencies were established by presidential directive or by order of a cabinet officer. Often, the directive was secret and even the agency's existence was not publicly revealed. The scope of the activities of the agencies was secret, and they operated with few if any rules designed to guarantee compliance with U.S. laws or respect for constitutional rights.

Officials outside of the intelligence community played almost no role in defining the rules of conduct for the intelligence agencies or supervising their behavior to determine its appropriateness. The CIA, for example, negotiated an agreement with the Department of Justice which exempted it from the law which requires all agencies to call to the attention of the Attorney General acts by their employees which may constitute violations of law.[3] There was no mechanism for the Justice Department to examine intelligence directives or the actual behavior of intelligence officers to determine if it were lawful. Congress played almost no role; oversight and budget approval were the responsibility of a small informal group in each house. These groups saw their role as one of providing the needed funds and asking as few questions as possible.

This system remained essentially in place until the intelligence investigations which were part of the more general, Watergate-related set of inquiries into the activities of the executive branch. The wedges which opened the curtain on the heretofore secret activities of the intelligence community included the accusations of CIA involvement in the Watergate break-in or its cover-up, controversy surrounding the CIA role in the overthrow of the Allende government in Chile, references to COINTELPRO in documents stolen from an FBI field office, the death of longtime FBI director J. Edgar Hoover, and a New York Times story reporting on extensive CIA surveillance of U.S. citizens.

These revelations led to the appointment of a presidential commission on CIA domestic activity and then to full scale investigations of the intelligence community by special committees of both the House and Senate--as well as a number of more narrowly focused investigations and numerous press leaks.[4] A number of abuses by intelligence community agencies came to light as a result of these investigations. Both at the time and in retrospect, there was considerable controversy about the degree to which the intelligence agencies engaged in inappropriate conduct.

The unchallenged record makes it clear that the intelligence agencies did engage in a number of activities which clearly violated the Constitution and the laws of the land. Perhaps the most serious threat to liberty was the FBI COINTELPRO since it was aimed not simply at illegal surveillance, but also at the manipulation and disruption of what the Bureau knew to be lawful political activity. In fact, COINTELPRO was instituted by J. Edgar Hoover as a result of a series of Supreme Court decisions which established the right of political dissent and prevented the government from indicting and convicting people because of their political beliefs or activities. Hoover decided that certain individuals--whom he viewed as "subversive"--were now beyond the reach of the law and that he had to take the law into his own hands by having the Bureau move secretly against them. Thus began a program involving efforts to use a variety of means to disrupt lawful political activity, including false threats of violence, fake letters aimed at disrupting marriages, and a host of other techniques (some of which seemed to be aimed at promoting violence among targeted groups or between them and violence-prone gangs). The targets of COINTELPRO included the anti-Vietnam War movement, the civil rights movement, and the black nationalist movement as well as the Communist Party (USA), the initial target.[5]

Another intelligence program which came to light in the mid-1970s was the CIA's operation CHAOS, a large scale program of surveillance of the anti-war and black nationalist movements. The program was instigated in response to pressure from Presidents Johnson and Nixon, who sought proof of foreign communist control and manipulation of the anti-war movement. However, the program, which included operations in the United States and the extensive gathering of information relating to lawful political activity, uncovered no evidence of foreign control of the anti-war movement.[6] Another CIA program involved the systematic opening of mail coming into and out of the United States, primarily mail to and from the Soviet Union. Many letters from private Americans, including political figures, were opened and copied.[7] The Rockefeller Commission, established by President Gerald Ford, described a number of other domestic activities of the CIA which the commission members, including Ronald Reagan, viewed as improper.[8]

Other intelligence agencies also carried on improper programs. NSA, in addition to reviewing cables provided by U.S.

cable companies, established watch lists at the request of the CIA, the FBI, and other intelligence agencies and provided copies of cables sent to and from the Americans included on the lists.[9] The Army conducted a large scale program of surveillance of domestic dissent.[10] The Internal Revenue Service directed audits of political opponents of the regime.[11]

After viewing all of these activities and many others, the Senate Intelligence Committee (the Church Committee) summed up its conclusions as follows:

> Too many people have been spied upon by too many Government agencies and too much information has been collected. The Government has often undertaken the secret surveillance of citizens on the basis of their political beliefs, even when those beliefs posed no threat of violence or illegal acts on behalf of a hostile foreign power. The Government, operating primarily through secret informants, but also using other intrusive techniques such as wiretaps, microphone "bugs," surreptitious mail opening, and break-ins, has swept in vast amounts of information about the personal lives, views, and associations of American citizens. Investigations of groups deemed potentially dangerous--and even of groups suspected of associating with potentially dangerous organizations--have continued for decades, despite the fact that those groups did not engage in unlawful activity. Groups and individuals have been harassed and disrupted because of their political views and their lifestyles. Investigations have been based upon vague standards whose breadth made excessive collection inevitable. Unsavory and vicious tactics have been employed --including anonymous attempts to break up marriages, disrupt meetings, ostracize persons from their professions, and provoke target groups into rivalries that might result in deaths. Intelligence agencies have served the political and personal objectives of presidents and other high officials. While the agencies often committed excesses in response to pressure from high officials in the Executive branch and Congress, they also occasionally initiated improper activities and then concealed them from officials whom they had a duty to inform.
>
> Government officials--including those whose principal duty is to enforce the law--have violated or ignored the law over long periods of time and have advocated and defended their right to break the law.[12]

Out of these investigations and the revelations of wrong-doing came a consensus on the need for intelligence agencies to operate in a different way. First and most important, there was agreement that intelligence agencies must operate within the law, that they were to be subject to the Constitution and to the laws of the land. Any necessary exceptions were to be clearly articulated, embodied in clear rules issued by those with authority to do so, and subject to judicial testing of their constitutionality.

It was also agreed that clear and precise rules needed to be promulgated specifying the authority of the intelligence agencies, particularly with regard to operations within the United States, as well as the surveillance of Americans at home and abroad. To the degree that it could be done without jeopardizing investigations, it was agreed that the rules should be made public.

There was consensus also on the need for mechanisms to insure against future abuses. These were to include an active role for newly created congressional intelligence committees, a role for the Department of Justice and the Attorney General in approving general guidelines as well as some specific activities, and internal review mechanisms using the inspector general and general counsel of each agency.

There remained considerable areas of disagreement: about whether the rules under which the agencies operated should be embodied in legislative charters or presidential and agency directives, about the content of the rules, about the degree to which they should be made public, and about the appropriate roles of the oversight bodies in the Congress and the executive branch.

Nonetheless, the new consensus has led to the creation of a substantial body of intelligence law which is meant to guide the conduct of intelligence agencies. With this background, the remainder of this chapter will describe the rules as they existed in the summer of 1984.

THE CURRENT LAWS AND PROCEDURES

It is no simple matter to describe the current laws as they relate to the intelligence agencies of the government. For one thing, the rules are not all found in one place. Some are in the Constitution as interpreted by the courts. Others are in statutes enacted by the Congress--some referring specifically to intelligence agencies and others which are more general but are interpreted so as to affect the conduct of intelligence agency officials. Other rules are embodied in executive orders issued publicly by the president. Some are to be found in less formal presidential directives, some secret and some public. Finally, some rules are in directives issued by the Director of Central Intelligence, the Attorney General, and heads of agencies. Some of these rules are meant to implement presidential or Attorney General directives; others are completely or partly classified. In the past there were some directives whose existence was not publicly acknowledged or even known and there is no way to be sure that such directives do not now exist or, if they do, to know how they modify or expand the rules laid out in other regulations.

The rules which exist are designed to affect various kinds of intelligence activities. The most extensive rules are directed at the surveillance of Americans. These rules, as will be described more fully below, vary depending on which agency is carrying out the operation, whether the surveillance is taking place in the United States or abroad, which surveillance technique is being used and how intrusive it is judged to be, and the reason why the surveillance is being conducted. Other rules relate to the conduct of covert operations and to requirements for reporting and oversight both within the executive branch and to the Congress. There are also rules relating to the disclosure of information--both describing what must be released and establishing penalties for unauthorized disclosure.

SURVEILLANCE OF AMERICANS

The most detailed and extensive rules relate to the surveillance of Americans. This is in part because this was the area of the greatest abuse. It is also because of the perception that intelligence agencies should focus their attention on foreigners and particularly on foreign governments in gathering information. Most people believe that the government should leave them alone unless they are suspected of engaging in illegal activity. If intelligence agencies are to conduct surveillance of U.S. citizens, they should do so according to carefully prescribed rules which strike a balance between the need for information which can only be secured from Americans and the right and desire of Americans to be left alone.

In developing the rules which affect such surveillance, intelligence agency officials divide their requirements into three categories related to the status of the person brought under surveillance. The first category relates to counterintelligence, i.e., to the effort to learn about the activities of hostile foreign powers and their intelligence services. Americans who are believed to be working for or with such foreign powers are subject to surveillance not only for counterintelligence purposes but also to learn what they know about the plans, activities, and capabilities of foreign governments' positive foreign intelligence.

The second category of surveillance relates to the targeting of Americans who are not suspected of having a relationship with a hostile foreign power, but who are simply believed to be in possession of positive foreign intelligence information. As will be described below, the authority to conduct surveillance of such "innocent" Americans is much more circumscribed.

Finally, there is a residual category of surveillance relating to finding out about an American in order to determine if he or she might be approached to provide operational assistance to an intelligence agency.

To determine the rules which regulate any action by an intelligence agency designed to gather information from an American, one must specify which agency is conducting the surveillance, where the surveillance will take place (i.e., in the U.S. or abroad), which techniques are to be used, what the status of the targeted individual is, and with what degree of certainty that view of his or her status has been established. With all of that information one can determine whether the law permits the surveillance, whose approval is needed in advance and who must be notified, and what can be done with the information.

In describing the sources for these rules, we begin with the Constitution of the United States. Only two provisions of the Constitution appear to be directly relevant to these questions. These are the First and Fourth amendments, which read as follows:

First Amendment
Congress shall make no law respecting an establishment of religion, or prohibiting the free exercies thereof; or abridging the freedom of speech, or of the press; or the right of the people peaceably to assemble, and to petition the Government for redress of grievances.

Fourth Amendment
The right of the people to be secure in their person, houses, papers, and effects, against unreasonable searches and seizures, shall not be violated, and no Warrants shall issue, but upon probable cause, supported by Oath or affirmation, and particularly describing the place to be searched, and the persons or things to be seized.

The Fourth Amendment affects the ability of the government to enter homes or other premises as well as to examine packages of various kinds whether carried by a person or sent, for example, through the mails. In the late 1960s the Supreme Court held that wiretaps and other forms of electronic surveillance were also covered by the Fourth Amendment because it protected people and not places and provided protection where there was a reasonable expectation of privacy.[13]

How the Fourth Amendment relates to surveillances for national security purposes has been a matter of some dispute. Until the late 1960s the courts appeared to assume that the Fourth Amendment applied to national security situations in the same way that it applied in all other cases. Except in what are called "exigent" circumstances, a warrant from a judge was required and that warrant would only be given if there were probable cause to believe that the target had engaged in illegal activity.[14] When the Supreme Court held that the Fourth Amendment applied to wiretaps, it left open the possibility that a warrant might not be required in "national security" cases. Later, it restricted the scope of the possible exception to situations where the target of the surveillance was suspected of being an agent of a foreign power and indicated that, in such cases, it might not be necessary to have probable cause of a crime to justify an intelligence surveillance whether or not a warrant was required.[15] The Supreme Court has never decided whether there was a "national security" exception to the warrant requirement, but most lower federal courts which have considered the matter have concluded that there was such an exception.[16]

The impact of the First Amendment is much less precise. The Supreme Court has frequently interpreted the First Amendment to provide for a right of secret political association.[17] This means that the government may not conduct a program for the purpose of learning about the lawful political activity of Americans. It can, however, conduct surveillance which results in its learning about such activity provided it has another compelling purpose (such as the gathering of important intelligence information) and provided that the intrusion is the least necessary to accomplish the purpose.[18]

Despite the recommendation of the Church Committee and the parallel Pike Committee in the House of Representatives that Congress enact comprehensive legislation laying out the rules for conducting the surveillance of Americans, Congress has, in fact, enacted very few such statutes. The only statutes which directly regulate the surveillance activities of the intelligence agencies are the National Security Act of 1947[19] and the Foreign Intelligence Surveillance Act of 1978 (FISA).[20] The former is extremely cryptic, applies only to the CIA, and states that the CIA shall have "no police, subpoena, law enforcement powers, or internal security functions."[21] While some members of Congress may have understood this phrase to prohibit any CIA activity in the United States, it has in practice been interpreted to prohibit only law enforcement activity.

In contrast, FISA regulates with great precision the procedures for conducting electronic surveillance within the United States. With a few exceptions in situations where the likelihood of overhearing Americans is very low, the law requires a court order before electronic surveillance can be conducted or before NSA can place an American on a watch list. The statute specifies the circumstances under which Americans suspected of being agents of a foreign power engaged in illegal activity can be the subject of surveillance. It also requires limits on the distribution of information obtained from or about Americans.[22]

Because of the limited guidance provided by the Constitution and the virtual absence of relevant legislation, most of the current rules relating to surveillance of Americans are spelled out in an Executive Order on U.S. Intelligence Activity. The order in effect as of July 1984 was Executive Order 12333, issued by President Ronald Reagan in 1981.[23] That order replaced a Carter Administration Order, which in turn replaced the first such order, which had been issued by President Ford.[24] The order provides basic rules and principles for the conduct of surveillance of Americans as well as delimiting the basic functions of each intelligence agency.

It is not possible to describe all of the provisions of the Executive Order as they relate to each activity of each agency. Only some of the major issues and limitations established by the Order are discussed.

The Executive Order, in part 2 (set out in full below), establishes a series of restrictions on the collection, retention, and dissemination of information concerning U.S. citizens and permanent resident aliens (called together "United States persons"). It directs that in all investigations the "least intrusive collection techniques" be used in activities conducted in the United States or directed against Americans abroad. The Order distinguishes between "Fourth Amendment" techniques, other intrusive techniques, and more routine methods of investigation.

Conduct of Intelligence Activities

2.1 Need. Accurate and timely information about the capabilities, intentions and activities of foreign powers, organizations, or persons and their agents is essential to informed decisionmaking in the areas of national defense and foreign relations. Collection of such information is a priority objective and will be pursued in a vigorous, innovative and responsible manner that is consistent with the Constitution and applicable law and respectful of the principles upon which the United States was founded.

2.2 Purpose. This Order is intended to enhance human and technical collection techniques, especially those undertaken abroad, and the acquisition of significant foreign intelligence, as well as the detection and countering of international terrorist activities and espionage conducted by foreign powers. Set forth below are certain general principles that, in addition to and consistent with applicable laws, are intended to achieve the proper balance between the acquisition of essential information and protection of individual interests. Nothing in this Order shall be construed to apply to or interfere with any authorized civil or criminal law enforcement responsibility of any department or agency.

2.3 Collection of Information. Agencies within the Intelligence Community are authorized to collect, retain or disseminate information concerning United States persons only in accordance with procedures established by the head of the agency concerned and approved by the Attorney General, consistent with the authorities provided by Part 1 of this Order. Those procedures shall permit collection, retention and dissemination of the following types of information:

(a) Information that is publicly available or collected with the consent of the person concerned;

(b) Information constituting foreign intelligence or counterintelligence, including such information concerning corporations or other commercial organizations. Collection within the United States of foreign intelligence not otherwise obtainable shall be undertaken by the FBI or, when significant foreign intelligence is sought, by other authorized agencies of the Intelligence Community, provided that no foreign intelligence collection by such agencies may be undertaken for the purpose of acquiring information concerning the domestic activities of United States persons;

(c) Information obtained in the course of a lawful foreign intelligence, counterintelligence, international narcotics or international terrorism investigation;

(d) Information needed to protect the safety of any persons or organizations, including those who are targets, victims or hostages of international terrorist organizations;

(e) Information needed to protect foreign intelligence or counterintelligence sources or methods from unauthorized disclosure. Collection within the United States shall be undertaken by the FBI except that other agencies of the Intelligence Community may also collect such information concerning present or former employees, present or former intelligence agency contractors or their present or former employees, or applicants for any such employment or contracting;

(f) Information concerning persons who are reasonably believed to be potential sources or contacts for the purpose of determining their suitability or credibility;

(g) Information arising out of a lawful personnel, physical or communications security investigation;

(h) Information acquired by overhead reconnaissance not directed at specific United States persons;

(i) Incidentally obtained information that may indicate involvement in activities that may violate federal, state, local or foreign laws; and

(j) Information necessary for administrative purposes.

In addition, agencies within the Intelligence Community may disseminate information, other than information derived from signals intelligence, to each appropriate agency within the Intelligence Community for purposes of allowing the recipient agency to determine whether the information is relevant to its responsibilities and can be retained by it.

2.4 Collection Techniques. Agencies within the Intelligence Community shall use the least intrusive collection techniques feasible within the United States or directed against United States persons abroad. Agencies are not authorized to use such techniques as electronic surveillance, unconsented physical search, mail surveillance, physical surveillance, or monitoring devices unless they are in accordance with procedures established by the head of the agency concerned and approved by the Attorney General. Such procedures shall protect constitutional and other legal rights and limit use of such information to lawful governmental purposes. These procedures shall not authorize:

(a) The CIA to engage in electronic surveillance within the United States except for the purpose of training, testing, or conducting countermeasures to hostile electronic surveillance;

(b) Unconsented physical searches in the United States by agencies other than the FBI, except for:

(1) Searches by counterintelligence elements of the military services directed against military personnel within the United States or abroad for intelligence purposes, when authorized by a military commander empowered to approve physical searches for law enforcement purposes, based upon a finding of probable cause to believe that such persons are acting as agents of foreign powers; and

(2) Searches by CIA of personal property of non-United States persons lawfully in its possession.

(c) Physical surveillance of a United States person in the United States by agencies other than the FBI, except for;

(1) Physical surveillance of present or former employees, present or former intelligence agency contractors or their present or former employees, or applicants for any such employment or contracting; and

(2) Physical surveillance of a military person employed by a nonintelligence element of a military service.

(d) Physical surveillance of a United States person abroad to collect foreign intelligence, except to obtain significant information that cannot reasonably be acquired by other means.

2.5 Attorney General Approval. The Attorney General hereby is delegated the power to approve the use for intelligence purposes, within the United States or against a United States person abroad, of any technique for which a warrant would be required if undertaken for law enforcement purposes, provided that such techniques shall not be undertaken unless the Attorney General has determined in each case that there is probable cause to believe that the technique is directed against a foreign power or an agent of a foreign power. Electronic surveillance, as defined in the Foreign Intelligence Surveillance Act of 1978, shall be conducted in accordance with that Act, as well as this Order.

2.6 Assistance to Law Enforcement Authorities. Agencies within the Intelligence Community are authorized to:

(a) Cooperate with appropriate law enforcement agencies for the purpose of protecting the employees, information, property and facilities of any agency within the Intelligence Community;

(b) Unless otherwise precluded by law or this Order, participate in law enforcement activities to investigate or prevent clandestine intelligence activities by foreign powers, or international terrorist or narcotics activities;

(c) Provide specialized equipment, technical knowledge, or assistance of expert personnel for use by any department or agency, or, when lives are endangered, to support local law enforcement agencies. Provision of assistance by expert personnel shall be approved in each case by the General Counsel of the providing agency; and

(d) Render any other assistance and cooperation to law enforcement authorities not precluded by applicable law.

2.7 Contracting. Agencies within the Intelligence Community are authorized to enter into contracts or arrangements for the provision of goods or services with private companies or institutions in the United States and need not reveal the sponsorship of such contracts or arrangements for authorized intelligence purposes. Contracts or arrangements with academic institutions may be undertaken only with the consent of appropriate officials of the institution.

2.8 Consistency With Other Laws. Nothing in this Order shall be construed to authorize any activity in violation of the Constitution or statutes of the United States.

2.9 Undisclosed Participation in Organizations Within the United States. No one acting on behalf of agencies within the Intelligence Community may join or otherwise participate in any organization in the United States on behalf of any agency within the Intelligence Community without disclosing his intelligence affiliation to appropriate officials of the organization, except in accordance with procedures established by the head of the agency concerned and approved by the Attorney General. Such participation shall be authorized only if it is essential to achieving lawful purposes as determined by the agency head or designee. No such participation may be undertaken for the purpose of influencing the activity of the organization or its members except in cases where;

(a) The participation is undertaken on behalf of the FBI in the course of a lawful investigation; or

(b) The organization concerned is composed primarily of individuals who are not United States persons and is reasonably believed to be acting on behalf of a foreign power.

2.10 Human Experimentation. No agency within the Intelligence Community shall sponsor, contract for or conduct research on human subjects except in accordance with guidelines issued by the Department of Health and Human Services. The subject's informed consent shall be documented as required by those guidelines.

2.11 Prohibition on Assassination. No person employed by or acting on behalf of the United States Government shall engage in, or conspire to engage in, assassination.

2.12 Indirect Participation. No agency of the Intelligence Community shall participate in or request any person to undertake activities forbidden by this Order.

(Compilation, pp. 316-319)

Perhaps the most controversial provision in the Order relates to physical searches which would require a warrant if conducted for law enforcement purposes. Congressional legislation requires a warrant for electronic surveillance in the United States, but it has not imposed any limits on electronic surveillance directed at Americans abroad or on physical searches in the United States. Thus the right of intelligence agencies to enter the homes and offices of Americans or to inspect sealed packages is controlled by the Fourth Amendment itself and by the provisions of the Executive Order and agency implementing directives. The section of the Order dealing with this issue reads as follows:

2.5 Attorney General Approval. The Attorney General hereby is delegated the power to approve the use for intelligence purposes, within the United States or against a United States person abroad, of any technique for which a warrant would be required if undertaken for law enforcement purposes, provided that such techniques shall not be undertaken unless the Attorney General has determined in each case that there is probable cause to believe that the technique is directed against a foreign power or an agent of a foreign power.[25]

The phrase "agent of a foreign power" is not defined in the order or in any of the public agency implementing directives, although there have been some suggestions that the definition included in the Foreign Intelligence Surveillance Act has been applied. What this means is that an agency which wants to inspect papers in the home of an American whom it believes to be operating under the direction and control of a foreign power and engaged in clandestine intelligence activity can apply to the Attorney

General to authorize the FBI to conduct the search. If the Attorney General finds that the target is an "agent of a foreign power," he may authorize the search. The FBI would then surreptitiously enter the designated home or office and copy the material covered by the Attorney General authorization. In contrast to normal search warrant procedures, the agents would not knock and announce their purpose before entering the premises nor would they leave behind a notice of what they had copied or seized. It is not known how often such searches are in fact conducted, but some believe that any such searches would violate the Fourth Amendment. The limited judicial guidance which is available is not consistent.[26]

The Executive Order also puts special limits on the right of intelligence agencies to engage in what is called "undisclosed participation in organizations within the United States."[27] Because of the acknowledged right of secret political association, the Order provides that such participation may take place only when it is "essential to achieving lawful purposes" and sets out various requirements for high level approval and limits on the circumstances in which various agencies can use the technique. It also establishes special limits on activity which is designed to influence the activity of the organization--a technique which some believe should never be permitted.

With regard to other techniques, the Order basically leaves the control of FBI activity to the Attorney General, who has issued a directive to the Bureau on "counter-intelligence." Much of this directive is classified. The Order puts various other restrictions on other agencies. For example, it prohibits CIA electronic or physical surveillance in the United States (with certain exceptions). The precise implications of these limitations are difficult to determine without access to the various agency implementing directives. Many of these are classified either in full or in part; even to the degree that they are not classified, they are not published elsewhere.[28] Thus, it is not possible to specify precisely the specific limits on the authority of each intelligence agency to conduct surveillance of Americans.

COVERT OPERATIONS

The Congress has never explicitly authorized covert operations by the CIA. At the same time, it continues to authorize and appropriate funds for such operations in the annual Intelligence Authorization Act and in the Department of Defense Appropriations bill.

What Congress has done is to require the President to make certain findings and to report these to the Congress if he chooses to undertake a specific covert operation. Beginning in 1975 Congress has required that the President personally find that an operation was "important to the national security of the United States" before it could be undertaken. This requirement was originally embodied in the so-called Hughes-Ryan amendment to the

Foreign Assistance Act, which also required that the appropriate committees of the Congress, including the Foreign Affairs and Foreign Relations Committees, be fully informed.[29]

In 1980 Congress revised the system for its oversight of covert operations as part of a set of procedures for general congressional review of intelligence community activity.[30] That legislation, originally introduced as the Intelligence Oversight Act and then passed as part of the 1981 Intelligence Authorization Act and codified as Title 5 of the National Security Act of 1947, requires that the House and Senate Intelligence Committees be kept "fully and currently informed" on all intelligence activity. The statute limits reporting to the two intelligence committees, but those committees are responsible for reporting such operations to other committees if their responsibilities are affected. In general, notice of such operations must be provided in advance.

The legislation does not put any specific limits on the conduct of covert operations. Congress considered such limits in the context of comprehensive charter legislation for the intelligence agencies, but no consensus emerged on appropriate limits. The only public limits on such operations are in the Executive Order on Intelligence. These restrictions, which apply to what the Order refers to as "special activities," are: (1) a prohibition on assassinations; (2) a prohibition on the conduct of covert operations by any agency other than the CIA unless the president determines "that another agency is more likely to achieve a particular objective;" and (3) a prohibition on activities "intended to influence United States political processes, public opinion, policies, or media." The requirement in earlier executive orders that covert operations be conducted only abroad was eliminated in the Reagan Order.[31]

Congress has also enacted legislation relating to specific covert operations. The Clark Amendment prohibits support for military or paramilitary operations in Angola.[32] The Boland Amendment prohibited aid for the purpose of overthrowing the government of Nicaragua and was followed by an amendment limiting the funding available for the covert operation directed at the government of Nicaragua.[33]

RESTRICTIONS ON THE DISSEMINATION OF INFORMATION

Congress has enacted a series of statutes which regulate when information must be made public and which also establishes penalties for the unauthorized disclosure of information. The Executive branch has supplemented these by an Executive Order on classification and by prepublication review requirements embodied in agency regulations and agreements.

The basic standards for determining what information can be kept secret is embodied in the Executive Order on Classification. The current order 12356, issued by President Reagan, provides that information shall be classified at least "Confidential" if its disclosure "reasonably could be expected to cause damage to the national security." To be eligible for classification, the information must be within one of a series of listed categories. The categories of direct relevance to intelligence include intelligence activities (including special activities), or intelligence sources or methods, cryptology, and confidential sources. The order also provides that disclosure of "the identity of a confidential foreign source, or intelligence source or methods is presumed to cause damage to the national security."[34]

If a request is made under the Freedom of Information Act (FOIA) to an agency of the government for information, the material must be released unless it is properly classified pursuant to the executive order on classification, if it fits within one of the other enumerated exemptions such as that for law enforcement or personal privacy, or if a specific statute authorizes the withholding of the information.[35] Among the statutes which apply to intelligence information is the provision of the National Security Act of 1947 which requires the protection of intelligence sources and methods,[36] the provision of the CIA Act of 1949 permitting the withholding of information describing the organization, functions, or names of CIA personnel,[37] and the statute authorizing the withholding of information relating to the activities of NSA.[38]

There is no statute which makes it a crime to reveal classified information *per se*, but several statutes and directives prescribe penalties for unauthorized disclosure of specific forms of intelligence information. Various criminal statutes penalize disclosure of defense information, including intelligence information, to agents of foreign powers.[39]

There is considerable debate and uncertainty about whether these general "espionage" statutes can be applied to disclosure of information by government officials to the press.[40] However, there are several specific statutes which clearly do apply to such disclosures or "leaks." These include statutes relating to communications intelligence, codes, atomic energy, and the identities of covert intelligence agents.[41] Congress has also enacted a statute which establishes procedures for the introduction of classified information in a criminal trial.[42]

By agency regulation and agreements signed by career officials of the CIA and NSA, they are obliged to submit for prepublication clearance any text which relates to intelligence matters and which is based on what they learned while in the government. The Supreme Court has upheld the validity of such requirements even as applied to former government officials and to the imposition of financial penalties for the failure to submit manuscripts even if they contain no classified information.[43] Employees of other agencies are often required to sign limited prepublication review agreements related to the clearance of intelligence information based on access to compartmentalized information. An effort to apply the requirement for prepublication review to all of those who have access to Special Compartmentalized Information was made by the Reagan Administration, but then withdrawn in the face of substantial congressional and other opposition.

NOTES

1. Select Committee to Study Governmental Operations With Respect to Intelligence Activities, U.S. Senate, 94th Cong., 2d Sess., 1976 (Hereafter cited as "Church Committee") Final Report, Book III, pp. 765-77.

2. The Current National Security Council Intelligence Directives (NSCIDs) and Director of Central Intelligence Directives are classified. Many earlier versions have been declassified and released in response to requests made under the Freedom of Information Act. Those that have been released are available in and from the Library of the Center for National Security Studies (CNSS) in Washington, D.C.

3. Report to the President by the Commission on CIA Activities Within the United States, June 1975 (Hereafter cited as "Rockefeller Commission"), p. 14.

4. Church Committee; Rockefeller Commission; House Select Committee on Intelligence, 94th Cong., 2d Sess., 1976 (Hereafter cited as "Pike Committee"). See generally Morton H. Halperin, et. al., The Lawless State (New York: Penguin Books, 1976).

5. Church Committee, Final Report, Book III, pp. 1-78.

6. Ibid., pp. 679-732; Rockefeller Commission, pp. 130-150.

7. Church Committee, pp. 559-678; Rockefeller Commission, pp. 101-115.

8. Ibid.

9. Church Committee, Book III, pp. 735-764.

10. Ibid., pp. 785-834.

11. Ibid., pp. 835-920.

12. Ibid., Book II, p. 5.

13. Berger v. N.Y., 388 U.S. 41 (1967); Katz v. U.S., 389 U.S. 347 (1967).

14. Abel v. U.S., 362 U.S. 920 (1952). See U.S. v. Ehrlichman, 376 F. Supp 29 (D.D.C. 1974), aff'd 546 F. 2d 1910 (D.C.Cir. 1976).

15. U.S. v. U.S. District Court, 407 U.S. 297 (1972).

16. See, e.g., U.S. v. Butenko, 494 F. 2d 593 (3rd Cir. 1974); cert. denied, 419 U.S. 881 (1974), U.S. v. Truong, 629 F. 2d 908

(4th Cir. 1980). See also: Zweibon v. Mitchell, 516 F. 2d 594 (D.C. Cir. 1975) (plurality dicta).

17. Buckley v. Valeo, 424 U.S. 2 (1976); NAACP v. Button, 371 U.S. 415 (1963). See generally cases cited in Norman Dorsen, et. al., Emerson, Haber and Dorsen's Political and Civil Rights in the United States, 4th ed. (Boston: Little Brown, 1976), pp. 933-34.

18. See, e.g., NAACP v. Button, 371 U.S. 415 (1963); Bates v. Little Rock, 361 U.S. 516 (1960); Shelton v. Tucker, 364 U.S. 479 (1960).

19. National Security Act of 1974, 50 U.S.C. 401, reprinted in Compilation of Intelligence Laws and Related Laws and Executive Orders of Interest to the National Intelligence Community, prepared for the use of the Permanent Select Committee on Intelligence of the House of Representatives, 98th Cong., 1st Sess., April 1983 (Hereafter cited as Compilation), pp. 1-16.

20. Foreign Intelligence Surveillance Act of 1978, P.L. 95-511 (1978), 92 Stat 1783, 50 U.S.C. 1801 et. seq., reprinted in Compilation, pp. 71-86.

21. 50 U.S.C. 403(d) (3), Compilation, p. 7.

22. Ibid.

23. Executive Order No. 12333, United States Intelligence Activities, Dec. 4, 1981, 46 F.R. 59941, reprinted in Compilation, pp. 308-321.

24. Executive Order No. 11905, United States Foreign Intelligence Activities, Feb. 19, 1976; Executive Order No. 12036, United States Intelligence Activities, Jan. 26, 1978.

25. Compilation, p. 318.

26. Compare U.S. v. Truong, 629 F. 2d 908 (4th Cir. 1980) with U.S. v. Ehrlichman, 546 F. 2d 1910 (D.C.Cir. 1976) (concurring opinion).

27. Sect. 2.9, Compilation, p. 319.

28. Those that have been released are available in the library of CNSS; see fn 2.

29. 32 U.S.C. 244, Compilation, p. 178.

30. 50 U.S.C. 413, Compilation, pp. 177-178.

31. Sections 2.11; 1.8(e); 3.4(h), Compilation, pp. 308-21.

32. 22 U.S.C. 2293 note Compilation, p. 233; P.L. 98-212, (1983) Sec. 755.

33. P.L. 93-377 (1982), Sec. 793, Compilation, p. 233; P.L. 98-212, (1983) Sec. 775.

34. Executive Order No. 12356, National Security Information, April 1, 1982; 47 F.R. 14874, Compilation, pp. 323-337.

35. 5 U.S.C. 552(b), Compilation, pp. 323-337.

36. 50 U.S.C. 403(b)(3), Compilation, p. 7.

37. 50 U.S.C. 403g, Compilation, p. 23.

38. P.L. 86-36, 50 U.S.C. 402 note, Compilation, pp. 59-66.

39. 50 U.S.C. 782, 18 U.S.C. 793-798.

40. Morton H. Halperin and Daniel Hoffman, Freedom v. National Security (NY: Chelsea House, 1973), pp. 236-248.

41. 18 U.S.C. 798; 18 U.S.C. 952, 42 U.S.C. 2014, et. seq.; Intelligence Identities Protection Act, P.L. 96-456 (1980); 94 Stat 2025, 18 U.S.C. app., Compilation, pp. 87-92.

42. Classified Information Procedures Act, P.L. 96-456 (1980); 94 Stat 2025, 18 U.S.C. app., Compilation, pp. 87-92.

43. Snepp v. U.S., 444 U.S. 507 (1980).

16
The Intelligence Community and the News Media

George H. Quester

The relationship of the U.S. news media and the intelligence community is beset with inherent contradictions. The two might often be seen as natural allies since each is intent on uncovering information in a world where many regimes have become increasingly good at concealing information. As natural duplicates in the delivery of the same product, the two could also be seen as competitors and rivals. And finally, as the uncovering of information often paradoxically depends upon some prior concealment of information, the two can be seen as natural enemies, inherently working to frustrate the other's activities.

THE SEARCH FOR INFORMATION: COOPERATION, COMPETITION, AND CONFLICT

Many Americans might assume initially that intelligence and press activities are entirely different. The first is carried on by the state, the second (in our society) by agencies entirely independent of the state. The First Amendment to the United States Constitution stipulates that the press is to be free of interference by Congress or the Executive Branch, the single industry in our society most specifically exempted from governmental regulation. The exemption is very much in accord with the norms of popular attitudes. The intelligence community, conversely, is now supposed to be under greater presidential and congressional oversight, with the public feeling that this is most proper and essential.

Yet the harsh fact is that most other nations are not as open as the United States. (Indeed, it can be argued that there is no nation in the world as open as the United States, in the details of its governmental dealings that can be obtained by one and all.) Since other countries are not going to pass duplicates of our own Freedom of Information Act, Americans will generally want to have the combination of nongovernmental media and governmental intelligence operatives doing all they can to free up some of the information. And since information builds on information, what the press unearths will nourish the intelligence community, just as what the intelligence community unearths will nourish the press.

To produce versions of the same product is to be engaged in a somewhat cooperative venture, but it is also a competitive venture, involving a race to serve the "customers." One sees this most graphically in the morning "intelligence briefing" at various Defense or State Department operations, where the "Secret" or "Top Secret" news is often slightly behind, in timing and in specificity of detail, what one has just obtained from the New York Times or Washington Post or from the television network newscasts of the morning. However common the effort in the unearthing of information, the media perceive themselves to be in prideful competition with the intelligence community on who can get the story first, who can get it best, and who can reach the public with it first. And the intelligence briefer is beset with a similar pride, feeling not a little abashed if his "classified" version of what is happening has less detail than what any American can get from a newspaper or the news on television.

Such competition is generally healthy, of course, just as competition is largely healthy with respect to all the other commodities we cherish. Exceptions to the desirability of competition arise only when there are significant economies of scale for a particular product, such that a monopoly operation could achieve greater efficiencies and could deliver a better product to the consumer. There will be times when, if they work together, the press and the intelligence community might be able to offer more complete information to the U.S. government and public. Yet the problems of regulation and incentives here would be stupendous since the information-gathering area is probably the last sector Americans would ever wish to treat as a "natural monopoly," characterized by extensive coordination or cartelization.

When do the press media and the intelligence community become natural adversaries? To gain information--in a hostile world filled with governments intent on concealing and suppressing information--one must conceal a little information of one's own. Above all, one must conceal the identity of information-gathering agents and the details of information-gathering techniques; otherwise, they would quickly be neutralized and rendered worthless.[1] If a foreign government knows which one of its lower officials is a U.S. spy, it can quickly execute that spy, conceal important information from him, or even feed him false information. And the same holds true, of course, for our technological capacities in code-breaking or electronic intelligence. If we were to paraphrase Woodrow Wilson's idealistic phrase to something like "open information, openly arrived at," we would have nothing more than a contradiction in terms. An adversary intent on hiding information could exploit our own openness of search methods to reinforce his own techniques of concealment.

The analog for the press comes in the confidentiality of sources as courts are increasingly (if at times unevenly) according reporters the privilege of concealing their sources of information.[2] If the reporter had to open up the identity of his sources about police corruption, the police could easily conceal such corruption in the future. The press thus also needs secrecy in order to beat down secrecy.

Yet if the press is intent on finding information about all of the world, it will at times uncover details about how the intelligence community gathers information. What is the product for one compromises an input for a similar product of the other. And a compromise in reverse would occur if the intelligence media uncovered more about the sources and methods of the press.

The press will thus tend to be strong supporters of arrangements such as the Freedom of Information Act, while the intelligence community will oppose such an opening of government files, and, at the very least, demand an exemption for itself. The prosecuting attorneys of state governments and the federal government will conversely be generally trying to cut back press prerogatives on confidentiality of sources, with the media resolutely defending and asserting this prerogative.

As a slight digression, we might comment also on the roles of a sibling of the press and electronic media: the academic information gathering and research activities of our universities. Some of the same complications with the intelligence community exist here. We again are in a cooperative venture in information gathering (one should remember how many U.S. academics did World War II duty with the OSS, and how many have worked since for succeeding intelligence agencies), a slightly competitive pattern (who can publish the best books on the Soviet Union, those working for the CIA, or those entirely independent of the Agency?), and then an outright adversary relationship (as one man's ability to gather information is upset by the information gathered by another).

The attitudes of academics are hardly totally synchronous with those of the press media, however. Academics often use "journalistic" as a derogatory phrase, regarding their media brothers as too inclined to sensationalism and entertainment, or too closely tied to the events of the moment and not reflective enough about the greater relationship involved. And if we wished to categorize the various actors as "left or right" ("right" here meaning most in sympathy with our government in its foreign policy confrontation with the Soviet Union), the press media might often be to "the right" of the academics. There was even a time when the press was enlistable by a President who was pleading for restraints on news coverage because of the national interest, a plea that could not have been addressed to university professors on the contents of their lectures and books.

This difference emerges in part because the media are inclined to see liberal press freedoms as something penultimately important, to be defended around the world, amid accusations by leftists and other advocates of a "New International Information Order" that the press is just another capitalistic business, urgently in need of regulation or state takeover.[3] Some university professors thus verbally question the importance of "bourgeois civil liberties," while enjoying such liberties of freedom of speech and press themselves. They explain away moves in India or Mozambique or Nicaragua to suppress press dissent, arguing that considerations of poverty and nutrition and material equality and economic democracy must come ahead of any such useless appendages of political democracy. The same radicals who would never feel filled in on the day's news unless they had read the New York Times might question whether the press can ever be "free," invoking arguments about "paradigms" and the importance of material arrangements of capital and labor. Somewhat more under the gun, the press is far less willing to endorse such doubts about the importance of freedom of the press, or doubts about the liberal pursuit of information.

Yet the difference should not be exaggerated here. Most academics would indeed join most spokesmen for the news media in continuously endorsing the importance of the free pursuit of information. Thus, they might welcome some of the intelligence activities which bring such information back out of the Soviet Union, but would deplore whatever secrecy is involved in the process, as well as any cloak of secrecy the U.S. government might wrap around itself.

JUSTIFICATION FOR SECRECY?

What justifies secrecy within the foreign policy operations of a country like the United States? As noted, the press and the academic world tend to lobby for very narrow categories of what can be kept secret, ridiculing government explanations for extending such classification to wider ranges of information.[4]

If the Soviets already know something, what would be the point of keeping it classified within our own government? While "military secrets," facts the adversary would not know, facts which might affect the outcome of battles or of political crises, are usually conceded by the press, everything else (i.e., what the Soviets already would know) is seen as being pointlessly guarded if there is any attempt by the U.S. Government to keep the media and public from it.

Yet the points we made before about the confidentiality of sources of information apply here just as well. The reason we might have to classify an analysis of Soviet grain production as "secret" might simply be the method by which we obtained the information. If Moscow knew how much we knew about their grain or oil or tank production, it might be able to decipher how we came to know, and then preclude our learning and knowing such facts in the future.

The justifications for secrecy must thus go beyond the category of things the Russians (or any other adversary) do not know. Equally plausible would be: things the Russians do not know we know, in order to protect our sources, and to protect whatever surprise we could carry off because we know; things the Russians do not know we know they know; and things the Russians do not know we know they know we know.

After a short number of iterations, such an exercise becomes impossibly mind-numbing, suggestive of comedy and ridicule, parallel to a scene from Peter Ustinov's film <u>Romanov and Juliet</u>. Yet the point remains that the source of information can be endangered when a government admits to having information. Similarly endangered is whatever strategic advantage could have been extracted from a situation where we know more than Moscow knew we knew.

This is hardly a blanket endorsement of secrecy. Much of the political and military reality of the nuclear age requires cooperation as much as competition, so that the two superpowers must actually welcome being spied upon, being subjected to "verification by national technical means." Even what used to be regarded as a "military secret" might thus now better be shared with an adversary, lest he go into a panic by assuming that we have more missiles than we actually have. If the U.S. press gets past whatever secrecy barriers our government might erect on some of these questions, the national interest may be well served. The problem of symmetry comes on whether the U.S. press can do as good a job of getting past Soviet barriers of secrecy, or whether the intelligence community will have to do the bulk of the work here. Here a critical factor would be whether a compromise of secrecy about such intelligence agencies might not compromise their ability to monitor the Soviet Union on the bigger issues of arms control.

A skeptic about the totality of secrecy within the U.S. government would question whether these more complicated arguments ever justify more than a small fraction of all the documents that are classified. The remainder are interpreted to be a monument to someone's compulsive love of secrecy, or else the self-protecting machinations of bureaucrats or elected officials intent on retaining their offices. Abusing the principle of secrecy intended to deny information to an enemy, those incumbents presumably use such secrecy to deny their own public the information which would reflect badly on their performance.

Such skepticism is certainly in order. Yet we cannot then convert it into a blanket opposition to all secrecy. We indeed live in a very strange world since nuclear weapons were invented. What used to be objectionable as Soviet espionage could now sometimes be welcomed as verification. Yet the sorting of bad and good kinds of espionage, or bad and good kinds of secrecy, is still not particularly easy. It is self-serving for the press and the academic community to suggest that all kinds of secrecy, beyond the most basic, are somehow silly.

A PARALLEL PROBLEM: WINNING AN AUDIENCE

Since such inherent similarities exist between the media and the intelligence community, in their information-gathering roles, it is no surprise that we can find a number of problems which they hold in common.

One such elementary problem comes in winning the attention of an audience. Newspapers need to sell copies, and television news programs need to win audiences. Intelligence briefers similarly need to win the attention of government officials and military commanders. A warning of an upcoming attack which is not heeded is of very little value, as illustrated in the warnings of Hitler's 1941 attack which were ignored by Stalin,[5] or the unheeded predictions of the Tet and the Yom Kippur attacks.

Each reporter will thus be tempted to add human interest and to hedge against error. Even the least sensationalistic of the press will be steered by the entertainment factor, by the audience's choice of whether to pay attention or not, and so will intelligence briefers. The intelligence briefer will also try to err on the pessimistic side--on the fail-safe theory that fewer people will mind if he is wrong, and more people will congratulate him for his prescience if his pessimism turns out to be correct. This bias is also evident in many academic analyses of the international scene. For example, consider the many predictions of future rates of nuclear weapons proliferation; virtually all of them err on the pessimistic side. Weather forecasters are also inclined to such misleading pessimism, in large part because the public demands this of them.

A PARALLEL PROBLEM: OVERCOMING BIAS

A second problem is that the intelligence community and the news media are burdened by biases in their gathering of information. These are biases which analysts may try to override. However, they are not easily compensated for, even by the most strenuous and self-conscious efforts. "How does one avoid being surprised?" This has been the central fixation of U.S. intelligence operatives ever since Pearl Harbor, with such later surprises as the Tet Offensive and the Yom Kippur War adding new case material to be pored over. The pessimist might regard surprise as inevitable. As one tries to "anticipate the unanticipated," the natural response will be to concentrate on what is expected, and thus remain vulnerable to surprise.[6]

The task is not hopeless, although it is inherently quite difficult. One can deputize "devil's advocate" staffers to make the most of the case for the unexpected, to determine what consensus seems to be developing, and then to intervene to keep other possibilities alive. The difficulty with this role is that it may all too quickly become type-cast, so that whatever the devil's advocate says comes to be regarded as procedurally predictable, "the opposite of what everyone else was thinking," the opposite of the likely truth. Thus, this advice is not heeded.[7]

If the particular American problem here is having too great a tendency toward common sense, toward "groupthink" consensus, then this is a problem which could therefore affect the media just as much as it does the intelligence community or the inner circles of government.[8] How does the press guard against habitually coming to the same conclusions about the events of the day? How does it work to avoid being surprised, alerting its readers to what they would not have anticipated themselves?

One could then extract some lessons from the media which might help to solve this problem within the intelligence community, even if the solutions are difficult to implement. The press relentlessly searches for the opposite of what was expected, in large part because it is in competition with rival newspapers, or in a competition between the printed press and television. Rather than tagging one of the sources the "devil's advocate," every reporter is told to search not only for the truth, but also to find truth that no one else has found.

Our analog within an intelligence community might thus explain and justify the existence of seemingly redundant and competing intelligence agencies. What looks like needless duplication might then amount to a "pluralistic approach," delivering more possible interpretations of events, and more options, to the decisionmaker.

Yet competition, as in the evening sessions of television's "action news," does not always produce diversity; the competing dispensers of information may all steer too much toward what they assume the bulk of their listeners want to hear. What if CIA, DIA, and the other intelligence agencies all began competing in telling the President what everyone thinks he wants to hear?

Thus we can easily become bogged down in an epistemological discussion of how to avoid being overloaded by bias, of "how do we break out of our paradigms." The clearest solution, <u>when</u> we can find it, is to go to some new technological breakthroughs in gathering and sifting information. An agent in place, a new mode of radar surveillance, or a new and reliable breakthrough in code-breaking can change our view of what is happening in a clear and unmistakable way. By comparison, all of our efforts to correct for bias by some kind of psychological self-cross-examination may run afoul of the limits of human ingenuity in introspection.

A PARALLEL PROBLEM: ABUSES OF SECRECY

Another problem which suggests parallels between the intelligence community and press emerges from the modicum of secrecy which each may need to execute its information-gathering function and from the possible abuses of this secrecy. For the intelligence agency, the continuing temptation is to go beyond gathering information about reality, to begin attempting to alter reality. The secrecy needed for effective espionage can also be harnessed for sabotage. The covers needed to watch foreign revolutions can be used to foster revolutions favorable to our side.

Is there an equivalent for this on the side of the press media, in some kind of political Heisenberg Uncertainty Principle by which we change reality by the very process of looking at it (strictly speaking, by the process of sending press representatives to look at it)? Some suggestive possibilities of distortion and abuse arise here, when the arrival of a television camera crew leads rioters to become more riotous, or when civil rights demonstrators or anti-civil rights Klansmen wait for the media to arrive before beginning to violate the law. The abuses become worse when the media representatives egg the rioters on, inciting them to live up to their potential, lest the story fail to be interesting enough to make the evening news. Watchers of U.S. television reporting of the demonstrations outside the United States Embassy in Teheran could have concluded that these riots were continuous, reflecting the crowd's endorsement of the seizure and holding of the hostages inside, and reflecting a deeper Iranian anger at the United States. Yet the facts were that such demonstrations were activated by the Iranians only for the minutes the television cameras were in operation.

Virtually every discussion of contemporary terrorism, particularly the seizure of international airliners, notes how the press and the electronic media have become an indispensable link to the political goals the terrorists wish to achieve.[9] The press, by covering the news, changes the news, i.e., causes some of the news to happen.

Instances when the press actively foments such new and disruptive versions of the news are relatively rare. Yet there clearly are cases when the press knows that it can have a disruptive impact merely by its presence. Nonetheless, it elects to be present, hungering for interesting and exciting news for the immediate moment or fearing the acceptance of precedent by which it might be shut out of news in the future.

The press must be assured of its right to talk to people in the area of a crime without having its notes subpoenaed by the local district attorney. Yet the privileged communications that then occur may not always be governed by the most perfect of ethics.

There are still some very important differences. The press is not accused of having engaged in outright violence behind whatever secrecies it is entitled to, while intelligence agents have handled firearms enough times. The press has not yet violently overthrown any governments, while the U.S. intelligence community is accused of having done this in the past. Yet media representatives are usually close by when violence occurs. It would be foolish to claim that the press has always behaved so as to reduce such violence, or even to have no impact on such violence.

Some of the same ethical burdens also affect the choices made by academics. To repeat our general point, one does not operate most efficiently at collecting information unless one withholds some of the information. One must protect one's sources against the KGB, the Mafia, or the local District Attorney, or simply against the prurient curiosity of campus colleagues. Many of the on-campus ethical issues with regard to "human subjects" are related to the protection of privacy and confidentiality, as one man's research-data-input could be another's tool to ridicule or blackmail.

This opens yet another category of secrecy and confidentiality. The same campuses which, in a "spirit of openness," forbid their professors from working on classified government projects, may still require that the personal details of other human beings' private lives be kept safely away from public gaze (that is, that this information be, in effect, "classified"). Issues of proprietary interest (for example, when patentable physical discoveries are made in university engineering laboratories) compound the conflicting layers of information-sharing and information-withholding. In its most basic form, such concern for possible commercial trade secrets is not so different from the competition among servers of customers we noted earlier (the competition between the New York Times and Washington Post, or between the New York Times and the morning intelligence briefing). "Truth is truth," but whoever can get the truth to a customer first may wish to keep it from leaking prematurely through a rival supplier.

As an illustration of how the cross-cutting issues of information-sharing and secrecy can entangle each other, a university seminar on cryptanalysis and code-breaking techniques has now become extraordinarily sensitive, with the U.S. government pressing for the exclusion of representatives from any potentially hostile country and more generally urging that such seminars not even be held.

Again, this is not meant to read like a ringing endorsement of secrecy. The author is one of those convinced that we have too much secrecy in the U.S. government, fostered by people who make a fetish of hiding information, and by others who are always too cautious to decide that such secrecy is unnecessary. Yet some kinds of secrecy are necessary--not only secrecy to protect government plans, but also to protect the sources of information we have about other governments' plans, and to protect the sources of data for the press and for university researchers, and to protect the proprietary rights of producers of information.[10]

To illustrate the point rather graphically, we have a thriving "commerical espionage" industry within the United States, as entrepreneurs try to obtain advance warning of their competitor's plans and styling changes, and as manufacturers attempt to obtain each other's closely-held formulas and trade secrets. Which is more inconsistent with the liberal spirit we desire for our universities, press, and politicians: the secrecy or attempts to penetrate it? Perhaps both commercial secrecy and commercial espionage would strike us as unsavory; we would not like to live next door to the specialists of either end of this competition. Yet this might simply involve a grand evasion, as what is inevitable and necessary goes undiscussed just because it tends to spoil the image we had of our society.

A PARALLEL PROBLEM: IMAGES OF PREDOMINANCE

Another problem shared by both the U.S. news media and intelligence community is that both are regularly accused of being too salient and too powerful. The comparison here is a little uneven; the CIA's claim to world predominance in intelligence work might easily be challenged by the KGB, while the leadership of the United States press and film industry, in what is sometimes labelled "media imperialism" or "cultural imperialism," is really unchallenged. We may have to fear Soviet secret government agencies more than anyone else's, but who would ever read <u>Pravda</u> if they had access to the <u>New York Times</u>, or watch a Soviet television program if they could watch a Hollywood product instead?

It will thus be impossible to settle a debate in India or Italy or Singapore over whether the Soviet or the American intelligence community is the more powerful. This is due in part to the subjective feelings of all the people commenting on the issue, and in larger part to the fact that intelligence operations are carried on under the cover of secrecy.

By contrast, the struggle for the newsstand, cinema, or television screen in such places is much more open. If there is anything secret about the greater appeal of Western news or entertainment services, it gets burrowed down in arguments about subliminal advertising techniques, or about "paradigms," as the United States is allegedly using the methods of Hollywood and Madison Avenue to sell neutral bystanders products they do not need and opinions that are not genuinely theirs.[11]

Just as the U.S. media oppose and criticize any censorship and secrecy within the United States (thus typically putting them into a "left" opposition role vis-a-vis the intelligence community), they oppose all such censorship and government control in the outside world (this time assuming a "rightist" role by advocating and exercising U.S. pluralism). As noted earlier, despite whatever views they may have about the wrongs and rights of U.S. foreign policy, it is altogether remarkable how resolutely most of the media and its reporters will "rally round the flag" when they are confronted with foreign "New International Information Order" proposals to control the free flow of press information (proposals allegedly designed to weed out the secret advantages conferred by the industrial and technical skills of the U.S. communications industry).

At times, therefore, the interests of the U.S. intelligence community and U.S. media become remarkably the same. Each favors the "right to listen" for audiences everywhere, opposing jamming and censorship. Each favors its own "right to listen," including the right of reporters to travel around the world, the right to listen to the radio broadcasts of the closed societies to see what can be extracted from scarce information, and the right of space-based electronic and visual sensors to look down to obtain data about the countries on the globe below.

The responses of the two U.S. communities to charges of excessive preeminence in the world might also be parallel, although the underlying rationales would be quite different. Confronted by KGB activities which at times are quite awesome, the U.S. intelligence community might not feel much need these days to be apologetic about any alleged U.S. preeminence in such clandestine gathering of information (and whatever clandestine auxiliary activities come along with it). Confronting no real challenger on the world scene, the U.S. media would not feel apologetic either. They feel that they have won this preeminence simply be delivering a better product, more entertaining where entertainment is the aim, and, where information is the aim, far more reliable than what emerges from much of the world's government-controlled news services.

THE NOVELTY OF THE PROBLEM

The United States is an old hand at maintaining a free press, dating back to the court decisions in the trial of John Peter Zenger, or at least to the addition of the First Amendment to the Constitution. By contrast, it is a novice at maintaining an intelligence community and in enshrining the kinds of government secrecy that are necessary for intelligence penetration of other states' secrecy. The earliest laws on espionage and government secrecy were passed only in 1911 and 1917, emulating the practices of Europe as it prepared for and then fought World War I.[12]

The U.S. aversion to secrecy and to secretive penetrations of other nations' secrecy persisted after World War I, expressed very memorably in Secretary of State Henry L. Stimson's indignant comment cancelling the U.S. efforts at reading foreign codes during the 1920s: "Gentlemen don't read each other's mail."[13] Advocates of "political realism" in the design of U.S. foreign policy accuse Americans of being excessively idealistic and naive about all of these matters. The phrase "open covenants, openly arrived at" misses the fact that secrecy can be crucial to the success of negotiation and other forms of policy, in a world where war and international conflict have not been stamped out by some form of world government.

The sheer novelty of our experience in an active role in world politics may thus explain not just the perspectives of Wilson and Stimson, but most U.S. actions and reactions. We may at some point reach a consensus about information and secrecy, about the role of the press and the intelligence community, as we become a mature participant in international politics. However, the years prior to and through World War II, and then through most of the Cold War and the Vietnam War, reflect major sways and reactions of U.S. attitudes.

The press might once have been appalled at any idea of censorship, even as part of a war effort. When the executive branch proposed government control over the media after the United States entered World War I, this was one "Win the War" proposal which Congress rejected, resoundingly testifying to the importance Americans still attached to the concept of freedom of the press.

The press has been rather more inclined to censor itself, to manage the news in accord with requests and pleas (not orders) from the President of the United States. They were quite willing to cooperate with requests from President Roosevelt after the shock of Pearl Harbor, and with presidents like Truman, Eisenhower, and Kennedy in the support of U.S. national interests in the Cold War.

When the Kennedy administration afterward spoke glowingly of having "managed the news" in the crisis over Soviet missiles in Cuba, the press showed some restlessness about the risks of being used and abused.[14] If it had contributed to the avoidance of a World War III and to the preservation of U.S. interests and freedom around the world, it had in the same cooperative moves perhaps been compromised as an objective and unfettered source of truth.

The liberal nightmare in the United States has always been that an active military and diplomatic defense of U.S. freedoms will lead to the erosion and compromise of such freedoms from within. When geographical isolation allowed the United States to dispense with large navies or armies, it also allowed for dispensing with anti-espionage laws or management of the news. To have to resist foreign powers now by the more normal means of international power politics is to risk bringing such power politics back into our home.

The tension may thus have produced some disquiet within the U.S. media before the Vietnam War, but presidents like John F. Kennedy were still able to dissuade the editors of the Washington Post and New York Times from running a story which might compromise the U.S. government's activities or position abroad. A basic patriotism, aroused with the novelty of major U.S. foreign policy activities in the face of major foreign threats, was still influential enough to produce such compromises--compromises that would never have been agreed to if the issues involved had been domestic.

The Vietnam War terminated a great deal of this, as Americans in the press media and the Americans who use the media discovered a shockingly large number of instances where they had been lied to, and where the lies in retrospect did not seem justified by the U.S. national interest. The Vietnam War now called into question many of the premises of the Cold War and of U.S. foreign policy in general.

Americans probably shared a consensus about foreign policy prior to the 1960s, one so gripping that it often went unarticulated, and one that viewed our purposes in the world as basically sensible and noble, offering other countries the opportunity to learn from, and duplicate, our domestic experience.[15] The press shared in this consensus, with freedom of the press being a very important part of what we were defending. The consensus is now far less strong; many Americans question the wisdom of any effort to assist liberal institutions abroad and question the sincerity of other Americans who try to enlist them in such efforts. While only a few Americans would question the desirability of liberal institutions and press freedoms for the United States, a fair number question the desirability of political democracy for the underdeveloped countries of Africa and Asia and Latin America. The press, being the press, may be the last to give up endorsing the desirability of a free press for any of these countries, but it will also now join in distrusting the sincerity or wisdom of the U.S. foreign policy leadership, and in reexamining what were once the implicit premises about any unifying consensus backing this foreign policy.

The Watergate experience at home also reinforced this dismay about the fact that so many particles of truth were withheld in Vietnam. The connection was hardly too farfetched, of course, as some of the operatives recruited to break into Democratic Party headquarters during the 1972 election were people employed earlier by the intelligence community, by the CIA.

The press thus distrusts its own government more now than at any time since the 1890s, the time when international engagements first began raising a need for giving the government some trust. Luckily for the prospects of any joint pursuit of information by the press and the intelligence community, the press also very much distrusts other governments, especially the one which the United States must regard as its most dangerous rival, the Soviet Union. However duplicitous one might find the renderings of information emanating from Washington, this is still not to be compared with the total dishonesty of that released daily in Moscow and the capitals of its satellites.

The purest form of freedom of the press (the most completely consistent with the First Amendment stipulation that the state should not be allowed to censor the media) would probably be that the media not even accept indirect governmental censorship, not respond obediently to telephone calls from the executive branch urging them to kill a story "in the national interest." Too compliant an attitude here, in response to alleged foreign threats, might kill U.S. freedoms from within, by a very gentle kind of cooption and subversion. The antidote might well be that the press just "tells it like it is," running "all the news," regardless of the possible political consequences. While such a media attitude might have looked dangerous and unpatriotic before the Vietnam War and Watergate, it might now be a very necessary reinforcement for the integrity of the press.

"Tough cases make bad law," but we might have to look at a few such tough cases, where the press might yet be so bothered by the practical consequences of a full disclosure of information that it is once again torn by a tension of choice. What if someone wishes to publish the technical details of how to design an atomic bomb or hydrogen bomb? As in the case of The Progressive, the press might have to rally behind resistance to any state-imposed censorship on such disclosures. But would not 99 percent of the editors personally feel that the national interest, and indeed the interest of all humanity, suggested that this kind of information be stifled rather than spread?[16] Common sense and an elementary awareness of the deadly technical character of this age suggest that some new canons of secrecy have to be considered.

Another, more classical variant has arisen on the disclosure of identities of secret agents, where such disclosure could not only threaten their further effectiveness at collecting information for the U.S. government, but very possibly their lives as well.

All of this is merely to indicate that the U.S. media, along with the public and Congress, have not yet settled into any permanent feelings about the pursuit of information versus the respect for secrecy. Perhaps we can expect a steadier set of attitudes and practices when the novelty of active participation in the international arena is behind us. Yet the inherent tensions of the relationships here (the dominant theme of this entire chapter) probably dictate some continuing unrest and shifting well into the future.

ELECTRONIC VERSUS PRINT MEDIA

In any discussion of the role of the U.S. media, it is important to remember and note that a tremendous shift has occurred in the physical nature of the media; Americans are reading newspapers far less than they used to and are relying on television for the bulk of their news reporting.[17]

There are several obvious ways in which the electronic media are different from the print media. Because of the presumed need for traffic management over the electromagnetic spectrum (and the moral argument that the airwaves "belong to the people"), the electronic media are subject to various kinds of state regulation (with television and radio being state-operated in many of the countries of the world which we regard as political democracies). Even if state regulation in the United States is very limited and seemingly ineffectual (limited to applications of a "fairness doctrine," with non-renewals of station licenses being extraordinarily rare), the shadow of such state regulatory authority may nonetheless psychologically inhibit the electronic media in ways amounting to an elementary compromise of press freedom. (Consider the outcry if anyone tried to apply a "fairness doctrine" to the printed press, <u>requiring</u> that the time or space accorded to one candidate for election be offered to his opponents, <u>requiring</u> that editorial comment be followed by equal time offered to spokesmen for contrary positions.)

The second major difference relates to the very nature of the medium; when watching television, we are generally less reflective, less willing to go into any issue in depth, more in the mood to be entertained or excited, more inclined to follow a story which can be illustrated with a live video image.

The press may always have had a bias toward interpreting government and the societal status quo as a series of pathologies; the "muckraking" of scandals and "uncovering" of "coverups" such as Watergate have sold newspapers in the past. If the press is the natural adversary of the executive branch or of the entire government in the U.S. political system, then this might easily be what our forefathers intended, given their initial distrust of the powers of government. Given the distrust many of us would feel for government today (in the aftermath of the world's experiences with Fascism and Communism), we might welcome some continuation of the press' inclination to look for "what's wrong" rather than "what's right" in government.

Yet the drives of the television medium toward the visual and the entertaining and exciting may exaggerate this, producing a bias even more critical of government and of incumbents, suspicious of the forms of confidentiality and secrecy with which they might want to shield themselves. The result would then be to foster even more of a conflict between this newest version of the media and the intelligence community, as the press is once again less of a partner and more of an adversary.

The more the media focus on the Soviet bloc, the more they serve as inadvertant partners to organizations like the CIA. The more they feel driven to concentrate on our country, or on the operations of our own Armed Forces, the less they are a partner and the more an adversary. Yet the television news program manager is heavily bound and guided by the territory into which he can get his cameramen. The evening news saw much more camera footage of U.S. patrols in Vietnam than of Soviet patrols in Afghanistan, in a bias which affected the electronic media far more than the printed press.

INTELLIGENCE INFILTRATION OF THE MEDIA?

Having said this much about some inherent parallels and conflicts between the news media and the U.S. intelligence community, some accusations are bound to emerge that the latter will attempt to take over parts of the former. Here the goals will be to place agents as press representatives and thus to ferret out more information when "espionage" is disguised as reporting, or to shield itself against too much scrutiny by the press, by instilling a more sympathetic attitude in the newsrooms of America.[18]

At the extreme, the Central Intelligence Agency and other U.S. intelligence agencies have actually infiltrated newspapers, bribing editors to hire one of their operatives as a "reporter." This allows more obscure U.S. newspapers to send a reporter to some far corner of the world, a reporter who could never have been justified by the normal flows of newspaper revenues and reader interests. The CIA has similarly clandestinely funded academic research and other on-campus activities and has also secretly funded some scholarly publications. Also at this extreme of what the defenders of U.S. liberalism would regard as corruption is the fact that the CIA has succeeded in getting stories printed which directly or indirectly present a sympathetic view of our intelligence community's activities, if only perhaps by presenting an alarming account of the alleged activities of the rival Soviet KGB.

A little less clearly corrupt, but also definitely dangerous (when one considers the importance of academia and the press being protective of, and secretive about, their own sources), the CIA has regularly tried to interview professors and reporters after they have travelled abroad. These people are asked about their views on what is happening (not so illegitimate, perhaps) and for the names of individuals to whom they talked (for obvious reasons, much more sensitive). Even if the intelligence community is asking only for a sharing of the very academic information that the professor or reporter is about to publish, the secretive mode of the community's approach is often regarded as aesthetically or philosophically offensive. Many professors and reporters have a standard policy, therefore, of sharing everything they publish with the U.S. intelligence agencies, but only when it is published, so that everything in effect is out in the open, since <u>publication</u> is <u>in public</u>.

There is no doubt that some of this infiltration has occurred. Happily enough for the United States, it is also clear that this has been relatively minor. The bulk of the U.S. press and academia are still quite independent, materially and financially (and even more independent now psychologically, in the wake of uncovering where it has been infiltrated and used). The press is still very much intent on unearthing facts about our intelligence community. If it today serves the purposes of organizations like the CIA by also being intent on getting information about the Soviet Union, this occurs because the press is still the press, and not because it has been taken over by the CIA. Foreign governments, not all of them Marxist dictatorships, will charge that much more infiltration has occurred, and indeed will sometimes define any press coverage of their societies by U.S. and free world reporters as "espionage," just as any criticism of their societies in print or on the air is defined as "hostile and warlike" propaganda.

The intelligence community of the United States thus gets accused of perpetrating more infiltrations than actually occur, and the media get accused of tolerating more than occur. Such false accusations persist for a number of distinct reasons. To begin, the very secrecy of intelligence, together with some necessary secrecy of a different kind in the press, preclude total and definitive rebuttals. Where the CIA will not tell everything, anything remains possible. Second, the accusations are (somewhat maliciously) often phrased in a form that cannot be disproven or rebutted, phrased almost tautologically, so that any gathering of information about the Soviet bloc which Moscow cannot control becomes "espionage." Third, to repeat, the United States remains the most open country in the world, probably with the freest and most independent printed press, and also probably with the most unregulated electronic media. Foreign observers, not just those from Marxist dictatorships, thus have a genuine difficulty in imagining and understanding how independent the media have been in the United States. Judging the United States by their own standards, they naturally assume a fair degree of state manipulation of the media, a fair amount of clandestine intelligence community activity.

Americans were appalled when the Watergate break-in was uncovered. Many West Europeans were surprised at how appalled Americans were. Judging political democracy by their own standards, they underrated the sensitivities of the U.S. tradition, and were then surprised when President Nixon had to resign his office. Just as these foreign observers would have (wrongly) concluded that wiretaps and break-ins and incumbent use of intelligence operatives for reelection purposes were normal, they would (wrongly) assume that the intelligence community has very much infiltrated, and taken control of, the U.S. news media and academic life.

As a delicious example of how not only the press, but also academic research workers (even those closest to being sophomoric academic research workers) can be accused abroad of complicity in U.S. intelligence work, we might suggest the excitement caused by some U.S. undergraduate political science majors doing their "junior year abroad" as "interns" in London assisting members of the British Parliament. Since similar students have long been spending summers or entire academic years working in Washington as interns for U.S. Congressmen, the idea of duplicating the experience in London hardly struck U.S. academic administrators as so strange. The idea was instantly popular among U.S. undergraduates intent on acquiring first-hand experience for comparing governments, while also making themselves useful, of course, as researchers for the M.P., as preparers of erudite questions for the Parliamentary question period, as correspondents responding to constituents.[19]

A danger of cultural shock arises, however, because most Members of Parliament have never had very much staff assistance. The few pioneering M.P.'s who agreed to take on such interns had some very unique (and alien) resources suddenly at their disposal, producing activity and bustle in what had been very quiet offices, utilizing libraries which previously had not gotten that much use except as places for a quiet nap, and galvanizing what had been quiet back-benchers into very active and well-informed participants in the debate.

While undergraduate students often exaggerate how much they learn in such "internships," and how usefully they are employed, there is no doubt that the freshness of the London experience let such students have access to a valuable font of information, and also let them be unusually important in their marginal product. Being something new, and something unmistakenly American, however, the student interns have also come in turn to be challenged and resented. And, almost par for the course, they have been accused of being agents of the CIA.

McCarthyism in its original form embodied a certain kind of rightwing paranoia, by which anyone of leftist sympathies might be part of a <u>secret</u> conspiracy directed by Joseph Stalin. "McCarthyism of the Left" is a reverse kind of paranoia, by which anyone gathering information abroad, as an academic of any sort, or as a representative of any of the press media, might be part of a secret conspiracy directed from within the intelligence community. The charges, in either case, have been phrased in forms which are difficult or impossible to refute. Struggles to prove one innocent then become evidence of guilt, as individuals "doth protest too much."

SOME CONCLUSIONS

Given the less abstemious attitudes of foreign governments on possible manipulations of their own press media, one should hardly sink into depression on the basis of foreign accusations. Most Europeans, in the democracies as well as the Marxist dictatorships, will have trouble comprehending how free our own press has been.

Much more a cause for concern, of course, would be the seepage by which foreign accusations and practices were viewed by our intelligence community, and government in general, as a justification for greater tampering with the media. Attitudes that "it must be all right, because everyone does it," or "it must be all right, because of the anarchy of the international system" are the most real danger to what Americans hold dear.

The afterglow of the U.S. triumph in the Cuban missile crisis led to Kennedy administration bragging about "managed news." It turns out that the British very much more managed their own news during the recovery of the Falklands, such that whatever transpired in the United States in 1962 pales by comparison. Yet this general attitude, that "the enemy is listening," so that nations have to control their own press commentary to keep the enemy from hearing too much, is part and parcel of the entry into active international politics, and this does indeed have a price in terms of the things we value so much domestically. Whether the issue be censorship, or merely disinformation, or infiltration of the press by intelligence operatives, a price gets paid, as we no longer have quite the separation of institutions that we so much cherished.

One could turn the issue around somewhat, by stressing that a greater flow of information is an important part of what we entered the active world role to achieve. If activism somewhat requires managing the flow of information by compromises between the media's role and the intelligence community's role, the same activism is more broadly intended for the goal of making information flow more generally.

We have consistently based most of our country's arguments about disarmament on the prerequisite of verification, on a need for a greater flow of information out from the closed societies confronting us. But we have many other reasons to welcome openness in places like Poland or Czechoslovakia or Southeast Asia or Japan or Western Europe because of our domestic experience with all of what comes in the wake of a more open society.

The press and the U.S. government remain the most natural of allies in this kind of interventional venture, jointly committed to beating down the information barriers of other societies, to letting information and ideas flow. The bottom line of all of what we have discussed here is that the natural competition between the intelligence community and the press media is still interlaced with a great deal of natural cooperation in our society, as the press has a vigor and life of its own, as that vigor and life are very much a part of what any of our intelligence-gathering is meant to protect in the first place.

NOTES

1. For a typical statement of the need for secrecy on method, if intelligence operatives are to succeed in breaking down the secrecy of other governments, see Senator John H. Chafee, "Why Should We Endanger Our Spies?," The Washington Post, 4 October 1981, p. C7.

2. On the trends in the guarantee of confidentiality in press sources, see Maurice Van Gerpen, Privileged Communication and the Press (Westport, CT: Greenwood Press, 1979).

3. For the tone of the debate about a "New International Information Order," see Kaarle Nordenstreng and Herbert I. Schiller (eds.), National Sovereignty and International Communication (Norwood, NJ: Ablex Publishing Company, 1979).

4. For a balanced assessment of the pendulum swings between demands for openness and scrutiny of the intelligence community and demands for a return to independence and secrecy, see Stansfield Turner and George Thibault, "Intelligence: The Right Rules," Foreign Policy 48 (Fall 1982): 122-38.

5. The difficulties in persuading Stalin of Hitler's coming attack are discussed in Barton Whaley, Codeword Barbarossa (Cambridge, MA: MIT Press, 1973).

6. On the pessimistic conclusion that it may be inherently impossible to head off surprise, see Richard K. Betts, "Surprise Despite Warning: Why Sudden Attacks Succeed," Political Science Quarterly 95 (Winter 1980-1981): 551-72.

7. See Alexander L. George, Presidential Decision-making in Foreign Policy: The Effective Use of Information and Advice (Boulder, CO: Westview, 1980), pp. 169-73.

8. See Irving Janis, Victims of Groupthink (Boston: Houghton Mifflin, 1972).

9. On the significance of the media for terrorists, see Yonah Alexander, "Terrorism, The Media, and the Police," Journal of International Affairs 32 (Spring-Summer 1978): 101-15.

10. On ways that the Freedom of Information Act (FOIA) may be contributing to industrial espionage, see Herschell Britton, "The Industrial Spy Peril," The New York Times, 30 June 1981, p. A15.

11. On the global dominance of the U.S. media, see J. Tunstall, The Media Are American (New York: Columbia University Press, 1977).

12. See Morton Halperin and Daniel Hoffman, National Security and the Right to Know (Washington: New Republic Books, 1977), pp. 107-23.

13. On the nature of Stimson's arguments about the sanctity of Japanese coded messages, see David Kahn, The Codebreakers (New York: MacMillan, 1967), p. 360.

14. On the "managed news" dispute after the Cuban missile crisis, see The New York Times, 1 November 1962, p. 17.

15. A more elaborate version of this author's argument about the erosion of American self-confidence in our foreign policy goals can be found in George H. Quester, American Foreign Policy: The Lost Consensus (New York: Praeger, 1982).

16. For a discussion of the ramifications of the case on The Progessive, see The New York Times, 11 March 1979, p. 21.

17. Some of the implications of the shift from printed newspapers to television news coverage are discussed in Edwin Diamond, The Tin Kazoo: Television, Politics and the News (Cambridge, MA: MIT Press, 1975).

18. For a discussion of CIA ventures in infiltrating the American and other media, see Victor Marchetti and John D. Marks, The CIA and the Cult of Intelligence (New York: Knopf, 1974), especially pp. 329-46.

19. For an account of U.S. students working as interns in the British Parliament, see The New York Times, 19 April 1980, p. 16.

17
Congressional Oversight: Form and Substance

Gary J. Schmitt

INTRODUCTION

 Most studies of Congress, congressional committees and the oversight process have until recently been based on "interest group" theories. According to these theories, the essential function of Congress and its parts is to facilitate the process by which various interests are aggregated and adjusted. In the view of these models, the principal activity of Congress is to bargain about and divvy up the spoils for the constituents back home.[1]
 But as one recent study has noted, "Much of what Congress and the President do cannot be described adequately by using these models." They are often "insufficient" and generally "misleading."[2] This is particularly true for the process of congressional oversight of intelligence activities. To put it simply, since the overwhelming amount of oversight takes place behind closed doors, there accrues to the congressman or senator on an intelligence committee little of the traditionally understood advantage of using his vote to serve the home district or state.
 A second model for understanding the workings of Congress takes as its basis the theory that the principal function of the legislative process is to reflect and refine the views of the community.[3] According to this understanding, congressional oversight and the committee system are used principally to ensure that executive branch decisions remain within the general consensus of a particular policy area as established by legislation or by public opinion. In contrast with the interest group model--typically defined by the narrow activities of the lobbyist--this second model takes for its point of departure an analysis of the laws, institutions, and the opinions of the community-at-large for any area of public policy. For studying congressional oversight of intelligence, these elements constitute the form and substance of oversight.

FORM

<u>Hughes-Ryan</u>

 It is often said (and it is true) that the Congress of the

United States is the most powerful legislative body of its kind in the world. Over nearly two centuries, it has maintained itself as a semi-sovereign branch of government, the growth in presidential power notwithstanding. Nonetheless, the passage of the Hughes-Ryan Amendment to the Foreign Assistance Act in 1974 was unprecedented. It was the first statute ever enacted by the Congress that explicitly provided for legislative oversight of an activity of a component of the U.S. intelligence community.

Hughes-Ryan was signed into law (P.L. 93-559) by President Ford on December 30, 1974. The amendment consisted of two key provisions: first, that no funds could be spent by the Central Intelligence Agency on activities not related to the collection of intelligence (i.e., on covert action) until the President found "that each such operation is important to the national security of the United States;" and second, that after the President had made such a finding, he was to report that fact, "in a timely fashion," to the "appropriate" committees of the Congress.[4]

Several important consequences followed from the passage of Hughes-Ryan. One was that the amendment confirmed for the first time that Congress understood the CIA's authority to include activities other than those directly related to the collection and analysis of intelligence. Under the National Security Act of 1947, the CIA was established "to correlate and evaluate intelligence relating to the national security" and to "perform such other functions and duties relating to intelligence...as the National Security Council may from time to time direct"--a rather vague formulation. These other duties, by a process of inference, could certainly include covert action.

A second consequence of Hughes-Ryan's enactment was that in the future all covert activity would clearly become the responsibility of the President. Although the executive branch claimed that internal guidelines made that the case already, the amendment gave the regulations a statutory basis. There would be under Hughes-Ryan no Thomas a Becket syndrome, or for that matter a repetition of unauthorized or ambiguously authorized attempts to assassinate Fidel Castro. There would be, neither for the President nor for the Congress, room for "plausible denial."

Hughes-Ryan also required that the "appropriate" committee of Congress be notified prior to or upon the initiation of any presidentially-approved covert action. Prior to this, Congress had monitored covert operations in a rather informal manner. Typically, a handful of senior committee chairmen were informed of major operations. The question of who should be briefed--and how extensively--was generally at the discretion of the executive branch. Under Hughes-Ryan, however, the "appropriate" committees meant the membership of the House and Senate Armed Services Committees, the Defense Subcommittees of the House and Senate Appropriations Committees, the Foreign Affairs Committee of the House, and the Foreign Relations Committee of the Senate. A few years later, the House and Senate Intelligence Committees were added to this list. In the end, eight committees were to be briefed on every covert program.

Formally, Hughes-Ryan required only that Congress be notified of covert programs. Members were to be informed of an operation, but they were not given the power to approve or disapprove. Informally, of course, Hughes-Ryan gave any member of the eight committees a virtual veto over any truly controversial covert program through this power to resort to a timely leak to the media. Since members of Congress traditionally have had strong opinions on most matters, it was hardly to be expected that unanimous consent could be achieved on each and every program. The result was inevitable. As one informed commentator put it at the time: "Most (covert actions)...which have been brought to the attention of congressional committees pursuant to Hughes-Ryan have become public knowledge." Accordingly, soon after the enactment of Hughes-Ryan, the executive branch began to propose only significant "covert" programs it was willing to see discussed in public forums. It had, in effect, "all but ruled out effective covert operations."[5]

Hughes-Ryan was generated by the critical consensus that emerged after Watergate and Vietnam. It was one of several pieces of legislation which were passed to curb the diplomatic and military powers of the so-called "imperial" presidency. Actually, several bills were introduced which would have proscribed covert action altogether. Most of these did not reach the floor of either house; when they did, they were voted down. Nevertheless, opinion about these matters was such that Senator Hughes could introduce his amendment on the floor and, without a hearing being held, have it pass the same day.

But public attitudes shift with time and, in the case of intelligence, they did. By the end of the 1970s, events in Iran and Afghanistan had altered the climate in which intelligence and national security matters in general were discussed. Congress reflected that changed consensus and amended Hughes-Ryan. The most important change to Hughes-Ryan was that the number of committees to which the President was obligated to report covert operations was reduced from eight to two: the House and Senate intelligence committees. Other provisions were added that allowed the President to act, if the circumstances warranted, with greater dispatch and secrecy. Under the new legislation the President could limit prior notification of operations to the leadership of the House and the Senate and the ranking members of the two committees; he could also act without such notice as long as he reported his actions in a "timely fashion" and provided a "statement of the reasons for not giving prior notice." The legislative vehicle for altering Hughes-Ryan was the Intelligence Oversight Act of 1980.

Intelligence Oversight Act of 1980

The Intelligence Oversight Act, or more properly Title V of the National Security Act (P.L. 96-450), became law on October 14, 1980. As noted above, the new law repealed certain portions of Hughes-Ryan. However, Title V also established a statutory basis for congressional oversight of U.S. intelligence agencies and their activities. Ironically, the Intelligence Oversight Act, while granting relief from some of the more onerous provisions of Hughes-Ryan, in fact expanded and made a matter of law the key principle of that amendment, the legitimacy of congressional oversight.

The oversight act was far different from the National Intelligence Act introduced by members of the Senate Intelligence Committee only eight months earlier. The most obvious difference was the length of the two pieces of legislation. What finally emerged as law covered all of two pages; the earlier document filled nearly 200. The latter was a comprehensive "charter"--a massive, talmudic effort at detailing the "do's" and "don'ts" for the U.S. intelligence community.

Over the spring of 1980, both the House and the Senate Intelligence Committees held hearings on charter legislation. Those hearings made it clear that a comprehensive charter, no matter how wisely crafted, was unlikely to make its way into law. In May, the Senate committee reported out instead the Intelligence Oversight Act of 1980. In June, it passed the Senate by an overwhelming margin, 89-1. To ensure action by the House, the Act was attached to the Intelligence Authorization Act for FY 1981.

The Act established four basic obligations for intelligence officials. The first and most important is that they keep the two intelligence committees "fully and currently informed of all intelligence activities." The second concerns the revised notification procedures regarding covert action. The act also prescribes that the intelligence agencies "furnish any information...requested by either of the intelligence committees" needed to carry out their oversight responsibilities. The fourth and final obligation concerns illegal or failed intelligence activity; both are to be reported to the committees in a "timely fashion."

It is worth noting, however, that the obligations laid down by the Act are themselves bound by provisions that seem to recognize the legal and constitutional duties of executive branch officials. For example, after detailing the various reporting requirements mandated by the legislation, the Act directs the House and the Senate to establish procedures, "in consultation with the Director of Central Intelligence," to protect the classified information it has been given. Even more important is the preambular language, which introduces the various mandates establishing congressional oversight:

> To the extent consistent with all applicable authorities and duties, including those conferred by the Constitution upon the executive and legislative branches of the Government, and to the extent consistent with due regard for the protection...of classified information and information relating to intelligence sources and methods, the Director of Central Intelligence et al. shall...

The language of the act is quite moderate, especially when compared with the proposed intelligence charters. With passage of the Intelligence Oversight Act of 1980, congressional oversight became a matter of comity, rather than one of extended legality.

The Intelligence Committees

To a large extent, the relationship between the intelligence community and the Congress had always been a matter of comity. What was new was the existence of permanent, standing committees dedicated uniquely to overseeing intelligence activities. Indeed, this arrangement appeared revolutionary; no other legislature of a democratic nation has ever created such an entity.

While the establishment of the committees was novel, the idea was not. As early as April 1948, a motion was made in the Congress to establish a Joint Committee on Intelligence. Over the next quarter century, almost 150 bills were introduced to provide close congressional oversight of U.S. intelligence agencies. Of these, however, only two proposals ever made it to the floor. In January 1955, Senator Mike Mansfield threw into the legislative hopper a resolution to create a joint committee on intelligence. He modeled his proposal on the successful Joint Committee on Atomic Energy. The resolution reached the Senate floor on the 11th of February and was rejected by a vote of fifty-nine to twenty-seven. A decade later, in 1966, the Foreign Relations Committee, under the chairmanship of Senator J. William Fulbright, reported out a resolution to establish a separate Senate committee. Fulbright's proposal came to the floor on the 14th of July. When the debate began, Senator Richard Russell, chairman of the Armed Services Committee, raised a point of order. (Historically, the Armed Services Committee had exercised jurisdiction over intelligence.) The Senate sustained Russell's point of order by a vote of sixty-one to twenty-eight and referred the matter to his committee, where it died.

The idea that there should be an intelligence committee was not unique to the corridors of Congress. One of several recommendations put forward in 1955 by the Second Hoover Commission, the U.S. Commission on the Organization of the Executive Branch of the Government, was the establishment of a joint committee on foreign intelligence. Twenty years later, the Rockefeller Commission (the Presidential Commission on CIA Activities within the United States) made the same proposal. A little over a half a year later, in February 1976, President Ford advanced the Commission's recommendation of a joint committee in a message sent to Congress.

Ford's recommendation, however, was not much in advance of the Congress' own. By the beginning of 1976, it was clear that the tide of opinion in the Congress was such that the creation of a committee or committees tasked specifically with oversight of intelligence was a foregone conclusion. The previous year had seen the establishment, in both chambers of Congress, of temporary select committees tasked with investigating abuses by the intelligence agencies. In their final reports, both committees urged the creation of permanent intelligence committees.

The Senate committee's final report (S.Rept. 94-755) was issued in April 1976. Less than a month later, on May 19, by a vote of seventy-two to twenty-two, the Senate created the Senate Select Committee on Intelligence (SSCI). There was little debate over the wisdom of the precedent. With one exception, there was overwhelming agreement that a committee with consolidated jurisdiction over all intelligence activities was required. That exception was a Tower-Stennis proposal to delete from the jurisdiction of the new committee the intelligence activities of the Department of Defense. Even here, however, the motion was defeated by a margin of more than two to one, sixty-three to thirty-one.

The House did not act as rapidly. The lower chamber's hesitancy was caused by the turmoil surrounding the House Committee's final report. The report contained information that the executive branch thought should remain secret. While the committee rejected those pleas, the House as a whole voted not to make the report public. Subsequently, large portions of it were leaked to and published by the Village Voice. Chastened by the experience, the House took a wait-and-see attitude toward the establishment of a separate intelligence committee. Essentially, the leadership delayed putting forward a proposal until they had seen how the Senate committee fared during its first year. Satisfied with the committee's performance, the Rules Committee of the House reported out a resolution establishing an intelligence committee in July 1977. On July 14, by a vote of 247 to 171, the House Permanent Select Committee on Intelligence (HPSCI) was born.

The resolution (H.Res. 658) establishing the HPSCI followed the resolution (S.Res. 400) establishing the SSCI not only in time but in substance as well. H.Res 658 is very much an echo of S.Res. 400. The House Committee does differ from its counterpart in the Senate in certain key respects. However, those differences are overshadowed by the fundamental fact that both are given legislative, investigative, and authorizational authority for the whole intelligence community. Under their respective founding charters, each committee is given exclusive jurisdiction over the CIA and the Director of Central Intelligence and shares jurisdiction over the remainder of the intelligence community (NSA or the National Security Agency, DIA or the Defense Intelligence Agency, and the intelligence components of the Departments of Defense, State, Treasury, Justice, and Energy) with the Armed Services, Foreign Relations/Affairs, and Judiciary Committees. With these broad mandates in hand, the SSCI and the HPSCI gave Congress, according to one participant, "a position for the first time, to exercise its own independent judgment with respect to intelligence operations."[6]

The resolutions are the same in other respects as well. The most important feature is that both intelligence committees are "select" committees (that is, members are chosen by the majority and minority leaders of the respective chambers). The majority and minority leaders also serve as ex officio, although non-voting, members of the committees. Provisions in the two resolutions are also the same with regard to the professional staff. All employees are required to sign secrecy agreements and to receive "an appropriate security clearance as determined...in consultation with the Director of Central Intelligence."

The two resolutions also establish elaborate procedures for declassifying information. With slight variations of detail, the resolutions require a vote of the committee and presidential approval before either committee is allowed to proceed with declassification. In any instance where the President has not given his consent, the committee must refer the matter to the whole chamber, where behind closed doors a final determination may be made.

H.Res. 658 and S.Res. 400 are similar in other respects. Both the SSCI and the HPSCI are required under the resolutions to maintain "crossover" members from the Armed Forces, Foreign Relations/Affairs, Judiciary, and Appropriations Committees. The difference between the two committees is that S.Res. 400 mandates that from each of those committees two Senators (one from each of the two major parties) be named to the SSCI, while H.Res. 658 requires only that one Representative from those committees be designated to the HPSCI.

The resolutions also speak of rotating, "to the greatest extent practicable," a substantial portion of the committee's membership each new Congress (that is, every two years). For the House, the suggested number of new members for the committee of fourteen is four; for the Senate, the amount is one-third of the committee's total membership of fifteen.

Finally, both H.Res. 658 and S.Res. 400 establish proscriptions concerning the length of time a Senator or Representative may remain on the intelligence committee. For members of the HPSCI, there is a six-year rule; for members of the SSCI, the limit is eight years.

There are, of course, important differences between the two resolutions. A very important difference concerns jurisdiction. Under S.Res. 400, the SSCI's authority extends to the realm of intelligence, strictly construed. It does not, according to the terms of the resolution, "include tactical foreign military intelligence serving no national policymaking function." H.Res. 658 provides the HPSCI with a broader mandate. Under its provisions, the House committee is to exercise jurisdiction not only over the "intelligence" activities of the Pentagon, but "intelligence-related" activities as well. This language is understood to include tactical military intelligence.

The most important distinction between the two resolutions is that S.Res. 400, in contrast to H.Res. 658, creates a bipartisan committee. Unlike a normal Senate committee, the ratio of majority to minority members on the SSCI is not distinctly disadvantageous to the minority party. Of its fifteen members, seven are from the minority side of the aisle. Moreover, the next ranking member on the SSCI is not, as is usually the case for congressional committees, from the majority. The next ranking member is from the minority and is titled Vice Chairman. In the absence of the Chairman, he is acting Chairman of the SSCI. It was by such means that the authors of S.Res. 400 hoped to create an institution which would, in their words, "reflect the composition and philosophy of the entire Senate."[7]

H.Res. 658 makes no mention of, nor any attempt to establish, bipartisanship. Of the HPSCI's fourteen members, nine come from the majority. There is also no mandate, as there is in S.Res. 400, that a percentage of the "crossover" members be from the minority. Finally, there exists nowhere in the House resolution language to establish a position comparable to that of the Vice Chairman on the SSCI. The fact that these provisions were not incorporated into H.Res. 658 was a matter of considerable dispute when the resolution reached the floor of the House. The Minority Leader at the time, Representative John Rhodes, strongly objected to "the absence of any provision establishing bipartisan membership for this committee." His complaint did not go unchallenged. Representative Richard Bolling, chairman of the Rules Committee (which had reported out H.Res. 658), parried the objection by appealing to the democratic ethic: "The gentleman ...knows that matters of intelligence...involve policy...it is only reasonable for us to follow the mandate of the American people in our election to the House of Representatives on policy matters."[8]

The Senate's decision to establish an intelligence committee on a bipartisan basis was primarily a product of its judgement that, because of the turmoil of the mid-1970s, the once favorable consensus regarding the intelligence community had largely disappeared. If the institutions of U.S. intelligence were ever to regain their vigor, prudence dictated that policy in the future be set on the firmest base possible, a policy about which there existed virtual unanimity. The bipartisan makeup of the SSCI was designed to ensure that by guaranteeing that all intelligence activities would be passed on by the broadest consensus possible.

The problem with this arrangement is that it seems to presume that a bipartisan consensus actually exists or can be created. The fact is that while the debate in the 1970s had produced a shared sentiment about what it was that we did *not* want the intelligence community to do, there was no corresponding agreement about what it was to do and how. The danger with the "bipartisan" framework of the SSCI is that it is susceptible to deadlock on the most contentious and critical decisions.

In contrast, the HPSCI, by adopting a more traditional framework for the composition of its membership, has a working majority already largely in place. Stalemate within the committee is not a problem. What is a problem, however, is that the committee could be used for partisan political purposes. If the SSCI is susceptible to a fruitless search for a nonexistent consensus, then the HPSCI is likely to employ its powers at times to disrupt the opposition's policies--producing, in turn, its own kind of deadlock.

SUBSTANCE

A Matter of Deference

For more than a quarter of a century, deadlock in the legislative process was not a worry of the U.S. intelligence community. In fact, the legislative process was hardly a matter of concern to the intelligence community at all. By all accounts, the exercise of oversight by the Congress was nominal at best.
Reviewing, for example, the committee reports for the National Security Act of 1947, one is hard pressed to find more than a phrase or two pertaining to the creation of the CIA. The role of Congress did not grow larger in the years that followed. In 1951, Truman merged, by executive fiat, the Office of Policy Coordination (OPC) with the Office of Special Operations, centralizing all clandestine activities within the CIA. It was also by executive order that the National Security Agency was established (as well as the Defense Intelligence Agency). In short, while Congress authorized millions of dollars for these agencies, their creation and operations were viewed for nearly three decades as lying within the realm of executive prerogative. As a former chairman of the Senate Appropriations Committee noted at the time, "Legislative interference with intelligence would tend to impinge upon the constitutional authority and responsibility of the President in the conduct of foreign affairs."[9] For Congress, oversight of the intelligence community was very much a matter of deference.
To a large extent, this attitude toward oversight of intelligence reflected the post-World War II consensus about foreign affairs. By 1947, there was almost unanimous agreement that active war had come to an end only to be replaced by a situation in which the United States and its allies inhabited a world of undeclared hostilities. The hot war had become cold, but it was a war nevertheless. For most members of Congress, it was only proper that the restraint they had shown toward the executive branch during the war would carry over to this novel--but no less dangerous--age. This restraint held particularly with respect to U.S. intelligence. The Soviets were, as Dean Rusk was later to say, a lot like hotel burglars--they trudge up and down the corridors trying the locks on each door. If given a chance, in they will go. To counter this behavior and contain the Soviets, Washington needed the means to roam the halls and find those unlocked doors first. This capacity was as necessary then as tanks had been in North Africa only a few years before. As Harry Howe Ransom put it: "Congress' World War II motto was said to be 'Trust in God and General Marshall.' In the Cold War atmosphere...the attitude seems to have been: 'Trust in God and Allen Dulles.'"[10]
Formally, congressional oversight did in fact exist. In each house of Congress, both the Armed Services and the Defense Subcommittee of the Appropriations Committees were charged with monitoring the intelligence community. The process of review was

actually handled by special subcommittees in each of those four committees. The chairman of the full committee was also the chairman of the intelligence subcommittee.

Substantively, however, oversight was minimal. The number of Senators and Representatives involved in oversight of intelligence was never more than a handful. In fact, because Senate rules on committee membership are less restrictive than those in the House, there were Senators who held seats on both Senate intelligence subcommittees. During the 1960s, when Senator Richard Russell of Georgia was chairman of both the Armed Services and Appropriations' Defense Subcommittees, membership on the two intelligence subcommittees overlapped so much that, for most of the period, they met as a single unit.[11]

It goes without saying that there was little staff assistance. As for subcommittee hearings, their number varied markedly from year to year. Some years, the "joint" committee of the Senate would assemble only once or twice. In other years, a committee might meet as many as a dozen times. On the whole, subcommittee hearings were few and far between.[12] According to the CIA, from 1967 to 1972 it averaged twenty-three annual appearances before congressional committees. Ironically, most of those hearings were before committees other than the four charged with overseeing the intelligence community.[13]

In general, there appears to have been no hesitation on the part of the CIA or the rest of the intelligence community to keep the oversight committees informed.[14] The subcommittees were routinely told of covert programs and were offered briefings on the intelligence community's budget. In fact, there is some evidence that during the 1960s the community sought to appear before its oversight committees more frequently than those committees themselves wanted.

The mechanism for oversight clearly existed; what was missing was an interest in using it. As one member of the Senate Armed Services Subcommittee on Intelligence admitted: "It is not a question of reluctance on the part of CIA officials to speak to us. Instead, it is a question of our reluctance, if you will, to seek information and knowledge on subjects which I personally, as a member of Congress and as a citizen, would rather not have."[15]

In hindsight, such a statement appears irresponsible. One of the duties of being a member of Congress is to see that the executive branch, including its intelligence arm, carries out the government's policies and laws in a responsible fashion. However, it is also a congressman's duty to represent his constituent's views. To the degree that such statements about intelligence oversight accurately reflected and were a product of the dominant foreign affairs consensus that existed for a quarter of a century following the end of World War II, that latter duty stood largely fulfilled.

A Matter of Restraint

From the late 1940s to the mid 1960s, there was an overwhelming consensus in the United States about the challenge posed by the Soviet threat. By the late 1960s, that consensus--under the pressure of the war in Vietnam--began to dissolve. As it disappeared, so did the confidence in the institutions that had implemented the nation's foreign policy. Deference to presidential leadership gave way to challenging the "imperial" presidency. The "arrogance of power" (to borrow a phrase from Senator Fulbright) was supplanted by an intolerance of its use.

The reaction against an active U.S. role in the world implied a diminished role for the President and that part of the executive branch concerned with foreign affairs. To curtail presidential discretion in foreign affairs, Congress passed legislation designed to make the executive more accountable to Congress.[16] The reforms were intended to reduce the resources and autonomy of key elements in the executive branch concerned with overseas operations: the military and intelligence agencies.

The animus in favor of restraining the executive branch in general and the intelligence community in particular was further heightened by a rather constant stream of disquieting headlines. In 1971, the Pentagon Papers appeared; in 1972, the Watergate break-in occurred; in 1973 Spiro Agnew resigned; in August 1974 Richard Nixon resigned. In September of 1974, the press disclosed a controversial CIA covert action program in Chile. Three months later, during Christmas week, the New York Times broke a banner story detailing what it called a "massive" domestic intelligence operation run by the CIA. Within weeks, the Senate and the House had established special committees to investigate the nation's intelligence agencies.

The two committees, known by the names of their respective chairmen (Senator Church and Representative Pike)--in conjunction with the President's own investigating body, the Rockefeller Commission--in the next eighteen months exposed, in a deluge of revelations, the past failures and abuses of the intelligence establishment. Congress was, in the words of Senator Church, after the "rogue elephant." What they found were: questionable domestic surveillance activities; assassination plans; interception of mail and cable traffic; infiltration of domestic dissident groups; drug experiments on unwitting recipients; use of missionaries and journalists as agents; and efforts to overthrow foreign governments.

Upon completing their investigations, both the Church and Pike Committees recommended to their respective chambers that there be established permanent committees charged with overseeing the intelligence community. In May 1976, the Senate established the Select Committee on Intelligence and, one year later, the House created its own Permanent Select Committee on Intelligence. Their origins were, both in fact and in spirit, the legacy of the Church and Pike Committees' exposures of past wrongdoings.

It was no surprise, then, that the permanent intelligence committees established by the Congress focused initially on setting down new rules and creating new restraints. Because the debate about intelligence during the mid 1970s had been concerned almost exclusively with instances in which the intelligence agencies had stepped beyond the bounds of legality and propriety, it was natural for the new committees to take as their principal aim the imposition of new restrictions on the intelligence community.

Three pieces of legislation, two of which became law, dominated the first three years of the new oversight process. The most prominent of these was an amendment to the 1974 Foreign Assistance Act, known as Hughes-Ryan. As previously noted, the effect of the act was to rule out the possibility that significant, disputed "covert" activities could be undertaken.

The second piece of intelligence legislation was the Foreign Intelligence Surveillance Act of 1978, commonly referred to as FISA (P.L. 95-511). FISA governs electronic surveillance (wiretaps, etc.) of persons or groups (foreign or American) believed to be involved in espionage or terrorism in the United States. Under the act, before any U.S. citizen's home or office can be wiretapped, the intelligence community must document before a special secret court the reasons justifying such surveillance. The judge, if convinced by the government's presentation, issues a warrant allowing the tap. The standard the judge uses to rule on each case is specified by the statute and is essentially a criminal standard: i.e., there must be probable cause to believe that the U.S. citizen in question is knowingly involved in clandestine intelligence activities or terrorism. In short, the government, under FISA, cannot tap someone's phone just to gather sensitive intelligence which is otherwise unavailable.

The third piece of legislation, one proposed by the Senate committee but never enacted, was a comprehensive charter for governing the whole of the intelligence community. The first charter drafted by the committee was an unwieldy 300 pages in length. It attempted to establish, with as much finality as possible, a complex set of prohibitions and regulations to rule and restrain the U.S. intelligence establishment. Ironically, its very length bespoke the fundamental problem with charter legislation--it was an attempt to codify the un-codifiable.

From 1976 to 1979, the proposed intelligence charter was the dominant topic of discussion between the intelligence community and the oversight committees, especially the Senate committee. As one scholar has correctly noted: "Charters had in effect become the Senate committee's raison d'etre. From 1976 to 1979 its institutional identity was inseparable from the charter issue."[17]

This congressional effort to restrain the intelligence community reflected the prevailing public distrust and cynicism regarding the institutions of government. The immediate legacy of Vietnam, Watergate, Agnew, etc. was to produce a population both indignant about and distrustful of its government. Congressional oversight of intelligence mirrored both. Yet what was not reflected in the early years of the oversight process was an equally pressing concern about the competence of the intelligence agencies themselves. As Samuel Huntington has bitingly noted:

> In a different atmosphere...congressional committees investigating the CIA might have been curious as to why the agency failed so miserably in its efforts to assassinate Lumumba and Castro. But in 1975, no one was interested in the ability of the agency to do what it was told to do, but only in the immorality of what it was told to do.[18]

A Matter of Relief

Failure to enact a prescriptive charter signalled a change in the perspective of the oversight process in general, a change confirmed institutionally by the nearly simultaneous decision of the SSCI to drop its Subcommittee on Investigations. After three years, it appeared that the oversight process was moving away from the confrontational style that had marked the Church and Pike Committees and their successors, the permanent select committees of the House and the Senate.

To some extent, this change was produced simply by the passage of time and the fact that the intelligence community and committees got to know each other a little better. Familiarity bred not contempt but confidence. The committees recognized that the abuses of the past were not the norm and that new, internal community guidelines and executive orders made future abuses of the kind that had been investigated much more unlikely. The key, however, to the change in the perspective of the two committees was the growing recognition on the part of the U.S. public that a decade of detente had not, as expected, nurtured a stable and relatively peaceful coexistence between the United States and the Soviet Union. Angola, Ethiopia, and Afghanistan all supplied ample evidence that Moscow's aggressive behavior had not been modified by the process of "normalization." As former Secretary of Defense Harold Brown, speaking of the strategic arms race, noted: "When we build, they build. When we stop, they build." Faced with these incontrovertible facts, the public changed its attitude about the issue of national security in general and the intelligence community in particular. Not surprisingly, so did their representatives--including those charged with overseeing the intelligence community.

As was to be expected, this change in perspective helped establish a new legislative agenda, granting relief to the intelligence agencies. This program has more or less, with one important exception, dominated the two committees' calendars the last four or so years. 1980 was a particularly important year.

It was in FY 1980 that the intelligence budget began to grow in real terms, reversing the long-standing decline in the resources made available to the intelligence community. The second important development that year was the modification of

Hughes-Ryan. The reporting requirement for new covert programs was reduced from eight to two committees by passage of the Intelligence Oversight Act of 1980. While the Act itself was unprecedented in its codification of intelligence oversight, it nevertheless was understood to be a measure of relief when compared to what might have been if the charter proposals had made their way into law.

1980 also saw the enactment of the Classified Information Procedures Act (P.L. 96-456). This piece of legislation, known as the "Graymail Act," established new procedures for the introduction and protection of classified information at trials. In the past, the government and the intelligence agencies had been frustrated in going forward with prosecution of security-related cases because of threats by defendants to subpoena volumes of classified information and expose that information in the trial proceedings. With this statute on the books, blackmailing the government into dropping its case became less of an option.

The final event that marked 1980 as a turning point in the oversight process was the introduction of the Intelligence Identities Protection Act. This legislation made it a crime, even for journalists, to seek out and publicize the names of U.S. intelligence agents. Enacted into law (P.L. 97-200) two years later by large majorities in both the Senate and the House, the Intelligence Identities Act confirmed the existence of a newly emerging consensus about intelligence. The latest piece of evidence that this new consensus was taking hold was the passage in 1983 by the Senate of a bill (S.1324) to grant relief to the CIA from the Freedom of Information Act (FOIA) by exempting the CIA's operational files from FOIA's normal search and review process.

In brief, where once the general thrust of congressional oversight had been to restrict and bind the activities of U.S. intelligence, it currently is to loosen and free those same capacities. The kind of confrontational style that implied that intelligence was, at best, a necessary evil no longer rules in either committee.

OF POLITICS AND INSTITUTIONS

One could easily challenge the previous sanguine assessment by raising the topic of covert action in Nicaragua. Events in Central America seem to have shattered the calm that followed the storm of the intelligence committee's first years. Headlines, leaks, congressional investigations, and new efforts to curb the CIA have all reappeared. Consequently, it is tempting to conclude that the committees have not moved very far from the spirit that animated their earliest days.

Yet there are crucial differences between today's crisis and that of six and seven years ago. The largest difference is that the debate today centers on a relatively isolated program in a particular policy area. This was not the case with the controversies of the 1970s. Congressional investigators then were concerned with nothing less than the very legitimacy of intelligence per se. Today's debate is essentially a policy dispute--little different in nature from that surrounding any other controversial foreign policy issue.

Evidence about the nature of the current dispute is found, I believe, in the relative calm that has greeted published reports detailing purported covert U.S. aid to the Mujahidin of Afghanistan. No major figure in either the media or Congress has challenged this reported program.

If the current debate about U.S. support to those fighting the Sandinistas were really founded on the question of the legitimacy of covert action per se, then one would expect to hear similar objections in response to reports of covert aid to Afghan rebels. None exists. The critical fact is that there exists no coherent public consensus about what to do in Central America, while one does exist--both here and in Europe--with regard to the Soviet invasion of Afghanistan.

It should be no surprise that the new oversight committees reflect rather accurately U.S. public opinion with regard to Central America. Just as a new consensus regarding national security affairs in general began to evolve in the late 1970s and found itself expressed by the intelligence committees' turn from their prior confrontational agenda, so a lack of a consensus on Central America finds itself expressed in a stalemated and fragmented authorization process.

The current debate between Congress and the President over what should or should not be done--covertly or not--in Central America seems to be an example of the U.S. constitutional system of separation of powers in action. According to the orthodox view of these matters, only programs and policies that are based on a broad and relatively deeply held consensus are strong enough to overcome the institutional breaches and barriers established by the framers. Looking at the character of the current debate over Central America and the role of the intelligence committees in it, one is led to conclude that, rather than returning to the earlier era of confrontation, the oversight process has merely begun to subject the intelligence community to what most people understand to be the traditional patterns and practices of the U.S. political system. Today, with the establishment in both houses of Congress of committees specifically enjoined to oversee American intelligence, the intelligence community finds itself in a situation not dissimilar to that of other executive branch agencies. Putting aside the select composition of both committees, the fundamental institutional fact is that intelligence policy, to the extent it becomes public, will be treated much like any other public policy.

The most interesting question is what effect this development in the oversight process will have on intelligence itself. What will be the consequence of bringing the activities of the U.S. intelligence community into the traditional framework of congressional oversight?

The long term effect at this point is of course not known. However, to highlight what it might be, it seems useful to examine a particularly sensitive area of intelligence, covert action, to see what benefits and drawbacks there are to the new oversight process.

Covert Action

Covert action, euphemistically called "special activities," is defined in statute (Hughes-Ryan) as "operations in foreign countries, other than activities intended solely for obtaining necessary intelligence." This negative definition (i.e., "A" is everything "not B") suggests the wide range of possible activities that may be undertaken under the rubric of covert action. Covert programs may range from the mundane--equipping and training the bodyguards of a foreign head of state--to the more exotic--planting stories in a foreign nation's press--to the most dramatic: training, arming, and conducting a paramilitary operation. Covert action may be used to change a government's behavior or to change a government altogether.

On the face of it, the law grants the president a great deal of discretion in implementing covert programs. The only prohibition is a self-imposed one against assassination. As previously discussed, the Congress and its committees have, formally at least, a decidedly small role to play. After the president signs a "finding" which outlines a proposed covert action, the committees are informed and briefed on the program. The oversight committees have no statutory basis on which to veto any particular program.

In practice, of course, the committees have exercised and potentially exercise a good deal of control over these programs. They do so in at least two significant ways. The first form of control is direct. While neither the House nor the Senate has, under the law, a programmatic veto, both intelligence committees exercise budgetary authority; this allows them to decide whether or not to authorize funds for each program.

The second form of control is much less direct--but significant nonetheless. The very fact that the committees are informed acts to inhibit the options even considered by officials of the Executive Branch. As control over, and information about, covert programs has gone beyond the White House and the operations directorate of the CIA, the ability to keep "covert" programs covert has diminished dramatically. Hence, while a president, in theory, may have at his disposal a wide range of options to consider in any covert program, he has in practice only a limited number of options, that is, the ones non-controversial enough to make it through the process without being leaked.

The intelligence committee's tendency to be a brake on proposed covert programs is reinforced by the fact that, from a Senator's or Congressman's point of view, the political benefit of being a member of an intelligence committee is small. Since the overwhelming percentage of their work is done behind closed doors, their constituents are not likely to appreciate what their representatives are doing for them--with the one exception of covert action. The major political problem for a member of either committee is the exposure of a sensitive, perhaps embarrassing, and often misrepresented covert program. Not free under the self-imposed rules of secrecy established by each committee adequately to defend himself or the reasonableness of a particular program, a member is bound to feel politically exposed. His nervousness is without question transmitted back to those in charge of designing and approving "special activities." In general, congressional oversight of covert action does and will continue to have a tendency to push programs toward means and areas where a general consensus already exists.

On the whole, this may not be such a bad thing. Perhaps an extra measure of prudence and circumspection should guide the intelligence community, one buffetted in the recent past by damaging exposures. There is little evidence that the new consensus toward the CIA and its sister agencies is deeply held. While events in the late 1970s led to a new appreciation of the threat posed by the Soviets, there still exists an underlying skepticism about intelligence institutions. In short, events, not principle, have produced this new view--and events could undermine it just as quickly.

A second reason why it is generally good for covert programs to be founded on a solidly held consensus is that, not infrequently, presidents have recommended them from a desire to achieve a foreign policy goal "on the cheap." Presidents can be "more alarmed...by the possibility of a noisy success than the prospect of a quiet failure."[19] Instead of articulating foreign policy goals and persuading the U.S. public of their value, presidents often choose covert action. This is no reason to abandon covert activities altogether. It is an argument, however, in favor of the view that, in the long run, the nation's foreign policy is better served by presidents who attempt to educate first and act second.[20]

Moreover, thinking about foreign policy and covert action in this manner tends to make covert action a more useful tool. An attempt to influence either governments or events abroad, whether done secretly or not, is to make foreign policy. Common sense suggests that covert action programs are more likely to succeed when the other tools of the foreign policy establishment are brought to bear on the particular problem as well. Covert action, like any tool, has its limits. It should be used to support a policy, not to carry one. Keeping covert activities within the bounds of an established consensus is conducive to maintaining that perspective.

The problem is, however, that in foreign affairs events often outrun policy. Recall the relation of Athens to Sparta after their joint victory over the Persians; or, similarly, the relation of the United States to the U.S.S.R. after the Allied defeat of Nazi Germany. A nation's foreign environment may be largely outside of its control. Friends in battle may overnight become one's enemies.

As a result, the necessities of foreign affairs may easily outrun the consensus that ordinarily must exist if a democracy is to pursue a policy. Most of the time, this does not pose a great problem. At other times, however, the very existence of a nation may be at stake. Witness Britain's situation after the fall of France in the early days of World War II. In spite of the obvious seriousness of the situation, opinion both in Congress and within the U.S. public was opposed to Washington's giving any aid to London. However, no prudent person would argue that Roosevelt should have foregone a covert program to alleviate Britain's plight because no consensus existed at the time to establish one.[21]

The central question, however, then, that must be raised in view of the effect the current system of congressional oversight has on covert action is this: in inhibiting imprudent risk-taking, does it not also inhibit necessary risk-taking?

CONCLUSION

The system of separation of powers that shapes the U.S. governmental process is a complex one that attempts to mix the moderating, deliberative capacities of legislative bodies with the "energy, dispatch and secrecy" of a unitary executive. It is, as a recent essay on the subject notes, an "uneasy blending of effectiveness and safety."[22] It is not, as is often claimed, a system designed simply to facilitate stalemate.

If deadlock had been the goal of the Constitution's framers, almost any division of power among any number of arbitrarily chosen branches of government would have sufficed. (Indeed, if stalemate had been their desire, retaining the Articles of Confederation would have sufficed.) Of course, this is not what happened. Powers were defined and then distributed to the branches that had been specifically built to house them. As one scholar correctly states, "Implicit here is the belief that kinds of power are best exercised by particular kinds of bodies."[23]

During the decade of the 1970s, the prevalent mix of "effectiveness and safety" was increasingly criticized. As these criticisms grew, Congress passed a number of reforms designed to curb presidential discretion in foreign affairs by involving Congress more directly in the process. No exception was made for intelligence.

The reforms that became law were meant to ensure--for safety's sake--that the American intelligence community in the future would operate within an existing consensus of public opinion about foreign affairs. Today, two questions remain to be asked about the effect of these reforms. First, can a system designed for achieving and maintaining a long term political consensus also make and carry out decisions inevitably marked by urgency, secrecy, and often contention? Second, can any U.S. institution long survive which lies outside the consensus?

NOTES

1. For a discussion and defense of these models, see David B. Truman, "Introduction to the Second Edition," *The Governmental Process: Political Interests and Public Opinion*, 2d ed. (New York: Knopf, 1971).

2. Arthur Maas, *Congress and the Common Good* (New York: Basic Books, 1983), pp. 4-5.

3. Ibid., pp. 7-12.

4. Under Hughes-Ryan, the President could ignore these provisions either in time of war or when acting under the War Powers Resolution.

5. Roy Godson, "Congress and Foreign Intelligence," in Ernest W. Lefever and Roy Godson, eds., *The CIA and the American Ethic* (Washington, DC: Ethics and Public Policy Center, Georgetown University, 1979), p. 27.

6. *Congressional Record*, May 12, 1976, p. S7094 (Senator Robert Morgan).

7. *Congressional Record*, May 13, 1976, p. S7275 (Senator Abraham Ribicoff).

8. *Congressional Record*, July 14, 1977, p. H22942.

9. Statement of Senator Carl Hayden, cited in Harry Howe Ransom, *The Intelligence Establishment* (Cambridge, MA: Harvard University Press, 1970), p. 161. Concerning the issue of presidential power, its nature, and its extent in the area of foreign affairs, see Glen E. Thurow, "Presidential Discretion in Foreign Affairs," *Vanderbilt Journal of Transnational Law* (1973).

10. *The Intelligence Establishment*, p. 172. Representative of this opinion was the following statement made by Senator Richard Russell, chairman of the Senate Armed Services Committee: "If there is one agency of Government in which we must take some matters on faith without a constant examination of its methods and sources, I believe that agency is the Central Intelligence Agency." Ibid., pp. 166-67.

11. In 1967, the chairman of the Senate Armed Services Committee invited three members of the Foreign Relations Committee to attend subcommittee meetings. This practice continued into the 1970s.

12. "At their most active, the House 'subcommittees' reportedly met with agency officials a half-dozen times a year, spending as much (or as little) as fifteen to twenty hours in oversight. There was little, if any, record of keeping formal reporting or staffing with the exception of budget review....The pattern in the Senate was similar." Godson, "Congress and Foreign Intelligence," p. 33.

13. The most thorough examinations of intelligence activities during this period were actually conducted on an ad hoc basis by the Senate Foreign Relations Committee. The first such review was generated when Gary Powers' U-2 was shot down over the U.S.S.R. in 1960--on the eve of a summit between Eisenhower and Khrushchev. The second investigation followed the failed, covertly-planned invasion of Cuba at the Bay of Pigs. In both cases, extensive closed hearings were held by the Foreign Relations Committee. In neither instance, however, did the final report result in an effort by the committee to review in a more systematic fashion the foreign operations of the intelligence community.

14. "There has never been a staff request to the Agency made that hasn't been fully complied with." Statement of Guy C. McConnell, clerk of Senate Appropriations Defense Subcommittee. Cited in Michael D. McNamee, Norman D. Sandler, and David N. Tenenbaum, Congressional Oversight of the CIA (Cambridge, MA: MIT Center for International Studies, 1974), unpublished manuscript, p. 38.

15. The Intelligence Establishment, p. 169.

16. See Allen Schick, "Politics through Law: Congressional Limitations on Executive Discretion," in Anthony King, ed., Both Ends of the Avenue (Washington, DC: American Enterprise Institute, 1983).

17. Anne Karalekas, "Intelligence Oversight: Has Anything Changed?," The Washington Quarterly (Summer 1983): 24.

18. Samuel P. Huntington, American Politics: The Promise of Disharmony (Cambridge, MA: Harvard University Press, 1981), p. 191.

19. Thomas Powers, The Man Who Kept the Secrets (New York: Knopf, Pocket Books, 1981), p. 142.

20. "Anticipation of losses creates an obvious temptation to proceed covertly and thereby avoid damage to U.S. prestige, a temptation that should be resisted for several reasons. One reason is that to acquire and sustain support within the United States...prior debate, including recognition of costs as well as benefits, is necessary. Without the former the credibility of the latter will be diminished. Another reason is simply the difficulty of assuring covertness, and the high likelihood in the

U.S. context that efforts to do so will backfire." Charles Wolf, Jr., "Extended Containment," in Aaron Wildavsky, ed., <u>Beyond Containment</u> (San Francisco, CA: W.H. Freeman, 1983), p. 157.

21. See in general Joseph Lash, <u>Roosevelt and Churchill</u> (New York: W.W. Norton, 1976).

22. Joseph M. Bessette and Jeffrey Tulis, "The Constitution, Politics and the Presidency," in <u>The Presidency in the Constitutional Order</u> (Baton Rouge, LA: Louisiana State University Press, 1981), p. 29.

23. Ann Stuart Diamond, "The Zenith of Separation of Powers Theory," <u>Publius</u> (Summer 1978): 59.

Part 5
Summary

18
The Future of the Intelligence Community

Bruce W. Watson

The organization, accomplishments, problems, and major controversies of military intelligence have been presented in the preceding chapters of this book. It remains for us to look to the future and to estimate whether any of the problems and controversies can be resolved.

ORGANIZATION

In his analysis of the British Admiralty, Parkinson observed that in peacetime, the Navy's operational forces were curtailed, while its staff grew enormously. The U.S. military intelligence community certainly conforms to this bureaucratic trend. The modest service intelligence outfits of World War II have grown into the national behemoths of today. And yet this is as it should be since, as the United States allowed its impressive military superiority over the Soviet Union to be reduced to a position of roughly equal parity, it was necessary to increase its intelligence capability so that the U.S. leadership had the most accurate and timely information on any event which might upset this precarious balance.

Concerning the cohesiveness of the U.S military intelligence community, both General Thomas and Captain Strong are certainly correct in their observations that the intelligence organization of today is a more cohesive community than it was thirty years ago. This trend is expected to continue as further efforts are made to streamline the military intelligence process. An excellent example of this phenomenon is the Defense Intelligence Agency's opening of its Defense Intelligence Analysis Center on Bolling Air Force Base in Washington, D.C., in 1984. In doing so, it colocated its major estimative, scientific and technical, and basic intelligence branches in one facility, which has affected most positively the quality of intelligence the agency produces. Similar efforts in the future will insure an even higher quality of U.S. intelligence.

COLLECTION

Concerning intelligence collection, the future seems to

promise greater emphasis on automated systems. The field of signals intelligence will continue to enjoy a significant share of U.S. military intelligence funds as advances in electronics dictate that more advanced collection systems be developed to insure adequate access to intelligence information.

Likewise, further advances in the collection of imagery intelligence will be costly, but will be financed, since the field has proven to be such a lucrative source of information.

America's emphasis on technology in the development of intelligence systems has certainly paid off handsomely. No other nation has an intelligence organization that even approaches the U.S. capability. And yet, this emphasis has not been without its liabilities. Here, the lack of appreciation for human source intelligence (HUMINT) is the greatest problem. In recent years, military intelligence has invested far less in HUMINT than it has in its technical systems. Additionally, the emphasis on technology has produced an empirically oriented attitude which views HUMINT as "soft intelligence," less worthy of consideration than technologically originated intelligence. It appears that this has created two significant liabilities. First, it has caused what seems to be an undue reliance on technical systems, and when these systems malfunction, they cause major disruptions in the collection and processing of information. Secondly, it has prompted us to neglect alternative sources of information. Here HUMINT has suffered most from the trend. Perhaps the best example of these points is to contrast the British performance in the Falklands War with U.S. performance in Grenada. In the Falklands case, the British certainly took advantage of all their technological systems in prosecuting the war. But in doing so, they did not neglect other intelligence sources. Rather, they interviewed scientists, school teachers, retired ladies--anyone who had recent, accurate information of the Falklands, and in doing so they had a most accurate picture of the situation. By contrast, America relied heavily on its technical systems for information. It did not interview students and others who had recent knowledge of the island, thereby neglecting an important source of information. And the technical systems failed to compensate for this oversight because they simply could not collect the essential elements of information available from HUMINT. Secondly, the systems failed because they did not provide the U.S. fighting forces with the information they needed. Hence, U.S. personnel did not know of the mental hospital, which was attacked. The message appears to be that too great a reliance on technical systems results not only in neglecting other valuable intelligence sources, but also inhibits that human creativity so evident in the British forces' prosecution of the Falklands War. Fortunately, such immobility did not affect the rank and file of U.S. forces, who performed innovatively and impressively in Grenada. Nonetheless, the lesson is there and, hopefully, it will be heeded in the future.

ANALYSIS

Likewise, in analysis, although great progress has been made, problems still exist. Here, the greatest advances have appeared in processing scientific and technical information, current intelligence information, and maintaining a basic intelligence data base. In these fields, U.S. military intelligence is extremely accurate, timely, and complete, and no major deficiencies exist. In other fields, however, problems are evident. Here, the greatest problems are found in management, estimative intelligence, indications and warning, terrorism, and communications.

Concerning management, the problem centers on passing intelligence to those who need it. In the Grenadian case, cited above, and other instances, those who needed the information in order to act were not always given the data. The cause was that the intelligence community is so large and there is normally such a glut of information (often referred to as information pollution) that it can be difficult to extract those essential elements of information that are vital to a given problem. Fortunately, the community has recognized this problem and has taken measures to ease its severity. Continued emphasis on dissemination should futher resolve the issue.

More persistent problems exist in the estimative intelligence and indications and warning (I&W) fields. These are due to the fact that in both, intelligence analysis is attempting to forecast human behavior. Certainly secondary systems which report on preparatory actions help us to more accurately predict the intentions of our adversaries. Nonetheless, such intentions are the products of the human mind, and intelligence analysis is no better than the current state of psychology and behavioral sciences in predicting behavior. Likewise, improvements in these fields are not likely to be dramatic, which means that the dependent intelligence disciplines are also likely to improve only gradually. The results will be mixed--accurate predictions in some cases, and "intelligence failures" in others.

Terrorism is a phenomenon that has enjoyed a recent resurgence, and military intelligence has responded to the problem. Again the record has been mixed--dramatic successes such as rescuing General Dozier from the Red Guard against a background of terrorism against U.S. forces and officials in the Middle East, Puerto Rico, and elsewhere in the world. The U.S. military intelligence capability to combat terrorism is likely to improve steadily in the coming years, as our systems become more sophisticated and our understanding of terrorist motives becomes more precise. However, there is one problem that deserves immediate attention. This is the current tendency to divide terrorist and insurgent activity into several disciplines. Today, vast amounts of funds are spent by both the government and the private sectors to study insurgency, low level conflict, terrorism, indigenous wars, counter-terrorism, and the like, when it appears that much of this falls under the rubric of terrorism. It may be far more productive to treat terrorism as a single entity. The terrorist is indeed a weapon system to the extent that he has mobility, guidance, and a destructive capability which can be directed against an enemy. From here, it would be logical to analyze the system, so that it can be combatted effectively when it threatens U.S. interests. At any rate, the current examination of terrorism is still a very young field, and significant advances should be expected in the future.

Finally, the issue of communication, discussed so expertly by Gerald Hopple, is a problem deserving greater attention. It is not enough to collect and analyze information--it is also necessary to communicate the resulting intelligence effectively. We are well aware of the list of intelligence failures--the Mayaguez, the October 1973 War, Iran, and Beirut, to name but a few. What we do not know is how many of these failures were the result of leaders either misinterpreting or simply not heeding the intelligence they had been provided. Indeed, great emphasis is placed on the written word in intelligence in an attempt to convey events and information as accurately as possible. And yet there is much to be done in order to convey information more effectively.

THE ISSUES

The issues discussed in Part IV of this book are the most important controversies concerning intelligence in the 1980s, and are likely to remain prominent for decades to come.

The chapters by Senator Wallop and Mr. Halperin state admirably the alternative sides concerning the issue of the ethics and legality of intelligence. Additionally, the questions they raise are persistent and are perhaps insolvable, for when a democratic system such as ours creates a large, secret organization such as the military intelligence community, it creates a potential threat and friction will result. And such friction is a healthy phenomenon, for it creates public interest which contributes to the assurance that the privileges afforded the community are not abused.

Likewise, the conflict between intelligence and the news media is an enduring one because of their conflict of purposes-- the media seeks free access to information, while the community seeks to safeguard its secrets. In the aftermath of Watergate and Vietnam, neither side can claim total innocence. More importantly, the existence of the two independent entities generally benefits the public, even in the context of past intelligence abuses on the one hand and biased reporting, replete with the divulgence of intelligence secrets on the other, for it is in these contrasting institutions that both our national security and our democratic system of government are preserved.

Similarly, the system of Congressional oversight must be maintained, for it is through this system that the nation is assured that the intelligence community is fulfilling its function and that abuses do not occur.

CONCLUSIONS

Thus, in the final analysis, the military intelligence community is a vital, if controversial, entity, that, while it is essential to the national security, is also one that, with its essential secrecy, has spawned suspicion. This, in turn, has created controversies--adversary relationships which will endure and will certainly affect the community's actions in the future. These controversies are both beneficial and somewhat predictable, and will insure the community's proper functioning as we move into the twenty-first century.

About the Editors and Contributors

Editors

GERALD W. HOPPLE is Senior Analyst at Defense Systems, Inc. Previously, he was a faculty member at the Defense Intelligence College, where he designed courses and taught in the areas of advanced methods for intelligence production, the intelligence research process, and the psychology of intelligence analysis. He has also been affiliated with several private research organizations and has taught at George Mason University and the University of Maryland. In addition to a recent article in World Politics on intelligence and the Falklands conflict, he is the author or coauthor of eight books (including National Security Crisis Forecasting and Management, Westview Press, 1984, and Revolution and Political Instability: Applied Research Methods, St. Martin's Press and Frances Pinter Publications, 1984).

Commander BRUCE W. WATSON, U.S. Navy, is the Director of Publications at the Defense Intelligence College and is an Adjunct Professor in the School of Foreign Service, Georgetown University. Dr. Watson is the author of Red Navy at Sea: Soviet Naval Operations on the High Seas, 1956-1980. He has also edited several books, including The Military Lessons of the Falkland Islands War (coedited with Peter M. Dunn), and Military Intelligence and the Universities: A Study of an Ambivalent Relationship (also coedited with Peter M. Dunn). A contributor to the U.S. Naval Institute Proceedings, the U.S. Naval War College Review, and the Air University Review, Dr. Watson is currently coediting three books, two on the Soviet Navy and one on the U.S. invasion of Grenada; all will be published by Westview Press in 1985. In addition, he is coauthoring a study on Soviet, Cuban, and U.S. interests in the Caribbean Sea with Dr. James L. George, which will be published by the Hoover Institute in 1985. Dr. Watson currently serves as the Vice Chairman, Comparative Foreign Policy Section, International Studies Association.

Contributors

STEPHEN J. ANDRIOLE, President of International Information Systems in Marshall, Virginia, is formerly the Director of the Defense Department's Advanced Research Projects Agency's Cybernetics Technology Office (DARPA/CTO), where he was also a Program Manager. He has taught international relations, national security analysis, and applied methodology at the University of Maryland, the Johns Hopkins School of Advanced International Studies, and the George Washington University; he was also a Research Analyst and Project Manager at Decisions and Designs, Incorporated. Dr. Andriole is the author, coauthor, editor, or coeditor of sixteen books and over seventy-five articles.

Captain STEPHEN S. BEITLER, U.S. Army, is currently assigned to the CJCS/SECDEF Presentations Division of the Directorate for Current Intelligence of the Defense Intelligence Agency. He attended graduate school at both the University of Chicago and the Defense Intelligence College and has served in various special forces, intelligence, and advisory positions in the United States and abroad.

Commander DAVID L. CHRISTIANSON, U.S. Navy, has been a military intelligence officer since 1969. CDR Christianson has held a variety of posts in the Navy and defense intelligence areas, including estimative intelligence (the Persian Gulf region) and the Middle East. He received a B.A. from Morningside College and an M.P.A. from The American University.

ALAN R. GOLDMAN has been with the U.S. Army Intelligence and Threat Analysis Center since 1978. He was formerly with the Office of Current Intelligence, Central Intelligence Agency. Dr. Goldman, who holds a Ph.D. in Political Science from Brown University, is a Captain in the U.S. Army Reserve.

BERNARD J. GRUNDY is the chief of the Production Control and Resources Branch in the Directorate of Scientific and Technical Intelligence of the Defense Intelligence Agency.

MORTON H. HALPERIN is Director of the Center for National Security Studies, which is jointly sponsored by the Fund for Peace and the American Civil Liberties Union Foundation. He also directs the ACLU National Security Project and is an Adjunct Professor of Political Science at Columbia University. Previously, Dr. Halperin was a Senior Fellow associated with the Foreign Policy Division of the Brookings Institution and served for more than three years in the federal government (as a Senior Staff member of the National Security Council Staff and as Deputy Assistant Secretary of Defense, in the Office of the Assistant Secretary of Defense for International Security Affairs). Prior to that time, he was an Assistant Professor of Government at Harvard University and a Research Associate of the Harvard Center for International Affairs. He has authored, coauthored, and edited more than a dozen books, including Bureaucratic Politics and Foreign Policy (Brookings, 1974) and Freedom vs. National Security (Chelsea House, 1977). Dr. Halperin has also contributed articles to a number of newspapers, magazines, and journals, including the New York Times, the New Republic, Foreign Affairs, Foreign Policy, and World Politics.

G. PAUL HOLMAN, JR. is a career intelligence officer who has served in operational, analytical, and estimative positions with several agencies. He was graduated from Harvard in 1963, Magna cum Laude, and received his Ph.D. from Georgetown in Russian

History in 1973. He is now a professor at the Naval War College, Newport, Rhode Island.

Captain E. LUTHER JOHNSON, U.S. Navy (Retired), is the President of Courtland International, Ltd. in McLean, Virginia. He is a foreign affairs consultant and translator. Dr. Johnson is also a lecturer in Swedish at the Swedish Adult School in Potomac, Maryland. His naval career involved a number of naval and defense intelligence assignments, including Director of Estimates, Office of Naval Intelligence and Head, Eastern European Section of the Military Attaches, Defense Intelligence Agency. Dr. Johnson, who received a Ph.D. in International Relations from The American University, specializes in indications and warning and European, Middle East, and African area studies.

Lieutenant Colonel TIMOTHY M. LAUR, U.S. Air Force (Retired), served as a member of the Defense Intelligence College faculty. Prior to this, he was Chief, Indications and Warning Center, Military Airlift Command. His current research involves crisis management and international terrorism warning problems. He is currently an instructor at the University of Maryland, and holds an M.S. in Climatology/Geography and an M.A. in International Relations.

GEORGE H. QUESTER is chairman of the Department of Government and Politics at the University of Maryland, where he teaches courses in International Politics and Defense Policy. Prior to coming to Maryland, he taught at Cornell University, Harvard University, U.C.L.A., and the National War College. He is the author of The Politics of Nuclear Proliferation, Offense and Defense in the International System, and American Foreign Policy: The Lost Consensus.

GARY J. SCHMITT, currently with the President's Foreign Intelligence Advisory Board, was formerly Minority Staff Director, Senate Select Committee on Intelligence. Dr. Schmitt, who was awarded a Ph.D. in Political Science from the University of Chicago in 1980, is the author of a number of articles on executive-legislative relations and other aspects of American government.

Captain J. Thompson Strong, U.S. Air Force, is a member of the faculty, Defense Intelligence College, where he lectures on U. S. foreign policy and the National Foreign Intelligence Community. He holds an M.S. in Strategic Intelligence from the Defense Intelligence College, and is a prolific writer, contributing frequently to the Air University Review and other professional journals.

Dr. JACK E. THOMAS (Major General, USAF, Retired), is currently a consultant to the Under Secretary of Defense for Policy, and is an Adjunct Professor at the Defense Intelligence College. Previously, he served as a member of the staff of the Director of Central Intelligence, and as Special Assistant to the Deputy DCI for Resource Management. While on active duty, Dr. Thomas served as The Assistant Chief of Staff for Intelligence at Headquarters U.S. Air Force.

The Honorable MALCOLM WALLOP (United States Senate, Republican, Wyoming) was first elected to the Senate in 1976. He serves on the Energy and Natural Resources and Finance Committees and is also a member of the Select Committee on Intelligence. Senator Wallop previously served in the Wyoming Senate (1973-1977) and House of Representatives (1969-1973). He received a B.A. from Yale University in 1954.